Celtic Magic—Make Changes in Your Life . . . Today!

Celtic Magic. These words conjure up pictures of Druids and mystical oak groves, daring Irish warriors existing cheek to cheek with fairies, elves and ancient deities who took an active part in the lives of their worshippers.

In its practical, easy-to-understand format, *Celtic Magic* offers important features that distinguish it from other books written about the Celts:

- In-depth discussion of the Celtic pantheon, the Celtic way of life and worship
- Complete listings of Celtic myths and deities
- Step-by-step instructions (including required tools and materials) for the immediate performance of spellwork and the practical application of magic in everyday life

Celtic Magic is an informative guide for both beginners and intermediates in the field of magic—or for those who simply have a great interest in Celtic culture, myth and history.

Celtic Magic makes it easy for a practitioner to go from following concise, step-by-step "guided" spells to writing his or her own spells. The spells and rituals included in this book cover almost all aspects of life that a person may want to influence or change. Rather than floating helplessly on the tides of these ever-changing times, some people are seeking ways to improve their physical, mental and spiritual selves. This is what *Celtic Magic* is all about.

About the Author

D.J. Conway was born in Hood River, Oregon to a family of Irish-North Germanic-American Indian descent. She began her quest for knowledge of the occult more than twenty-five years ago, and has been involved in many aspects of New Age religion from the teachings of Yogananda to study of the Qabala, healing, herbs, ancient pantheons and Wicca. Although an ordained minister in two New Age churches and holder of a Doctor of Divinity degree, Conway claims that her heart lies within the pagan cultures. No longer actively lecturing and teaching as she did for years, Conway has centered her energies on writing.

To Write to the Author

If you wish to contact the author or would like more information about this book, please write to the author in care of Llewellyn Worldwide, and we will forward your request. Both the author and publisher appreciate hearing from you and learning of your enjoyment of this book and how it has helped you. Llewellyn Worldwide cannot guarantee that every letter written to the author can be answered, but all will be forwarded. Please write to:

D.J. Conway
c/o Llewellyn Worldwide
2143 Wooddale Drive, Dept. L136-9,
Woodbury, MN 55125-2989, U.S.A.
Please enclose a self-addressed, stamped envelope for reply,
or $1.00 to cover costs.
If outside the U.S.A., enclose international postal reply coupon.

Llewellyn's World Magic Series

Celtic Magic

D. J. Conway

Llewellyn Publications
Woodbury, Minnesota

FIRST EDITION
Seventeenth Printing, 2006

Cover art by Lissanne Lake   FR

Library of Congress Cataloging-in-Publication Data
Conway, D.J. (Deanna J.)
    Celtic magic / by D.J. Conway.
        p.   cm. — (Llewellyn's world magic series)
    Includes bibliographical references.
    ISBN 13: 978-0-87542-136-0
    ISBN 10: 0-87542-136-9
    1. Magic, Celtic. I. Title. II. Series.
BF1622.C45C66 1990
133.4'3'089916—dc20
                                                    90-3213
                                                        CIP

Llewellyn Worldwide does not participate in, endorse, or have any authority or responsibility concerning private business transactions between our authors and the public.
    All mail addressed to the author is forwarded but the publisher cannot, unless specifically instructed by the author, give out an address or phone number.

Llewellyn Publications
A Division of Llewellyn Worldwide, Ltd.
2143 Wooddale Drive, Woodbury, MN 55125-2989
www.llewellyn.com
Llewellyn is a registered trademark of Llewellyn Worldwide, Ltd.

Printed in the United States of America

LLEWELLYN'S WORLD MAGIC SERIES

At the core of every religion, at the foundation of every culture, there is MAGIC.

Magic sees the World as *alive*, as the home which humanity shares with beings and powers both visible and invisible with whom and which we can *interface* to either our advantage or disadvantage—depending upon our awareness and intention.

Religious worship and communion is one kind of magic, and just as there are many religions in the world so are there many magical systems.

Religion, and magic, are ways of seeing and relating to the *creative* powers, the *living* energies, the *all-pervading* spirit, the *under-lying* intelligence that is the universe within which we and all else exist.

Neither Religion nor Magic conflict with Science. All share the same goals and the same limitations: always seeking Truth, forever haunted by human limitations in perceiving that truth. Magic is "technology" based upon experience and *extrasensory insight*, providing its practitioners with methods of greater influence and control over the world of the invisible before it impinges on the world of the visible.

The study of world magic not only enhances your understanding of the world in which you live, and hence your ability to *live better*, but brings you into touch with the *inner essence* of your long evolutionary heritage and most particularly—as in the case of the magical system identified most closely with your genetic inheritance—with *the archetypal images and forces most alive in your whole consciousness*.

Other Books by D.J. Conway

Norse Magic
Maiden, Mother, Crone
Dancing with Dragons
By Oak, Ash, and Thorn
Animal Magick
Flying Without a Broom
Moon Magick
Falcon Feather & Valkyrie Sword
Magick of the Gods & Goddesses
Magickal, Mystical Creatures
Perfect Love
The Dream Warrior (fiction)
Lord of Light & Shadow
Shapeshifter Tarot (with Sirona Knight)
Soothslayer (fiction)
Warrior of Shadows (fiction)
The Mysterious Magickal Cat
Celtic Dragon Tarot (with Lisa Hunt)

*To Charles, my magic partner
and balance in life.*

CONTENTS

Ogham Alphabet
Deity Chants for Rituals
Sample Spell

ELVES
by D. J. Conway

By the fern brake, deep and shady,
There I met an elfin lady.
Dressed in cobweb silk and flowers,
There she whiled away the hours,
    Waiting until dark.

On the soft green moss beside her,
Lay a baby wrapped in eider.
Skin so fair and hair like midnight,
The lady watched the coming twilight,
    Waiting till 'twas dark.

Silently, I sat beside her,
Hoping for some words to gather
In my numb and startled mind.
Said the lady, "You're most kind
    to wait with me till dark."

"Are you lost?" I asked lady.
"Is this your home, this fern brake shady?
Will others come by star and Moon?"
She only smiled, began to croon
    To the elfin child.

The baby slept. The lady told me
Deep magic of the Earth and Sea.
Spells she whispered, strong and old.
"Use them well," she said. "Be bold
    When spelling in the night."

"Can I work these?" The lady smiled,
Gathered up her sleeping child.
"Oh yes," she answered, " 'Tis a boon
For waiting with me till the Moon
    Slips up the sky."

Thinking deep, I sat beside her,
Keeping watch. I heard the rider
Coming through the fern brake shady.
"Are you there, my lovely lady?"
    Called an elfin voice.

An elfin lord, his clothes all viney,
Armed with sword and dagger shiny,
Rode his horse into the fern brake.
Then my heart began to quake
    On seeing his dark eyes.

Twilight gathered; birds were still.
The Moon came up above the hill.
Suddenly I felt alone.
"Have no fear, for you have sown
    Good friendship."

The lady smiled and raised her hand.
Upon her brow a shining band
Glistened by the light of Moon.
"Would you too give forth a boon?"
    She asked her lord.

"For here is friend, a watcher bold."
"But they are enemies of old,"
The elf lord answered.
    "No," she said,

"But guarded us in this fern bed."
   He smiled.

"So there are some who wish us well."
His voice was like a distant bell.
A ring he took from off his hand.
"This will tune you to the land
   and magic."

Its stone was pale, just like the Moon.
The air was filled with eldritch tune,
As they mounted, lord and lady,
Rode off through the fern brake shady.
   I stood alone.

People say elves are not there.
But I have heard their voices fair,
When I sit down in the brake.
Magic spells I've learned to make
   All from the lady.

Elf lord's ring is on my hand
To help with magic from the land.
Sometimes I talk with lord and lady
In the fern brake, deep and shady,
   Secretly.

Is there magic? For me 'tis so.
For when the sun is sinking low,
I feel Earth's power within my heart
And know that I shall never part
   From the lord and lady.

1 Celtic Magic and Its Uses Today

For several decades there has been a growing interest in the old pagan beliefs. People are seeking a more practical, personal system of belief, some way to be spiritual yet improve their lives. This includes pagan religion and magic, which is both practical and spiritual.

The Celtic and/or Druidic systems are generally thought of as being Irish, British and Welsh. In fact, the Celts at one time inhabited much of western Europe. Remains of their civilizations range from southern France and areas of Spain north into lowland Germany, the British Isles and Ireland.

It is not necessary to be of those racial backgrounds to practice Celtic magic. All that is needed is an interest in Celtic mythologies and magic itself, a deep sympathetic feeling for Nature and her powers.

Celtic magical beliefs are firmly rooted in the Earth herself and in the elemental spirits that are the very essence of all Nature. This includes the four basic Elements which make up Nature: Earth, Air, Fire and Water.

The ancient Celts had a vast knowledge of, and respect for, the healing and magical qualities of plants and stones. They knew and used the power flows of the Earth, trees and special outcroppings of rock. They called upon the elemental spirits, the "little people" of the Irish, the gnomes and fairies of the British.

But perhaps the strongest belief, almost unique among ancient peoples, was their devotion to the Great Mother, the mother and warrior goddesses. In fact the Celtic peoples, before Roman and Christian intervention, were one of the few races to give their goddesses equal footing with their gods.

This is not to say that other pagan religions did not honor the Great Mother. But upon close inspection you will find that the male deities of most other pantheons were considered more important, more powerful. The goddesses were allowed their place in worship so long as their followers did not try to usurp the prime position of power which was always held by a male deity.

The goddesses of the Celts did not hold a secondary position in their worship or their legends. This respect bled over into Celtic society. As a result Celtic women were highly respected, having many rights of property, person and status. Priestesses were held in honor. Women were warriors as well as mothers, and had equal rights with men.

Did this harm or weaken the society or lessen the men? According to history, decidedly not. The Celts were one of the fiercest, most spiritually advanced races of the Old World, weakening only when they accepted and bowed to the inroads of Christianity.

The life of a Celt was filled with magic and its

uses. Their intertwining artwork on jewelry, clothing, utensils and their houses was a form of magic
meant to avert the evil eye and send back curses.
They believed that their deities could appear in any
place and at any time, that it was the duty of humans
to call upon them for aid. They also believed that it
was the responsibility of each person to do whatever
he or she could to better his or her own life, and that
decidedly meant the use of magic, both small and
large. To accomplish this, a person had to be continually willing to learn and grow.

To practice effective Celtic magic today, you
must be willing to learn about and use plant and herb
magic. Certain stones must be sought, enticed into
your service, and cherished as reservoirs of energy.
The powers of the elementals and Elements must be
respected, petitioned for help, and befriended. You
must seek the ancient reservoirs of god-power that
were built and fed by Celtic worship, and which still
exist today.

But most of all, you must suspend all the narrow
definitions of reality you have learned. You must
rethink what is possible or impossible, realizing that
when certain actions are taken, nothing is impossible.
The practice of these particular actions is the practice
of what is known as magic.

Magic is a suspension of what we see, and a
belief in and use of what we cannot see, but know
instinctively is there. Celtic magic is simply applying
that invisible ingredient in certain ways, using natural
or Nature's powers, to improve life.

Magic cannot be tested in a laboratory, dissected
and placed under a microscope. Magic lives in the
mind of the user, manifesting itself in practical living.

Pagan magic is both practical necessity and part of a religious experience. Pagans are people who live very much in reality. Long ago they realized that when you no longer have to struggle for everyday necessities, spirituality can be freely sought and more easily attained. They also know that when you can do for yourself, it is seldom that another person will be able to manipulate or control you against your will.

The time is right for Celtic magic to come back into its own place in the world. More and more people are dissatisfied with what they see as socially accepted religions. They are seeking along old pathways, clouded by disuse and overgrown by falsehoods. But the very search of these people is creating a fresh wind that will scour those ancient tracks. The way will become clear; the old wisdoms will once again be found and put into practice. To those who seek, success and growth will come. Success will be visible in the improvement of life itself.

Pagan-thinking people do not tend to be followers of the accepted social norm. They are innovators, thinkers, pursuers of wisdom and spiritual growth. They know that improving you, the person, and your immediate life is as important as perfecting the spiritual you, or the soul. A well-balanced personality and a successful life, by whatever terms you define success, is the true guidepost along the ancient paths. Striving for these worthy goals and getting there are what really matter, not the opinions of others.

May you find your way down the ancient pathways to the Groves of Wisdom.

2 Understanding Celtic Magic

To the Celtic peoples, magic was as common as breathing. It was not something set aside for special occasions anymore than was their beautiful twisting artwork. Like their intricate designs that decorated even ordinary utensils, magic was a part of everyday life.

The Celts had no difficulty reconciling materialism and spiritual insight because they clearly understood that each is present in the other, that matter is only solidified spirit. Today we have trouble accepting that magical law. Our minds have been bombarded by prejudiced opinions until we have become programmed to believe a blend of the material and spiritual is impossible. We have been taught an error: that to be spiritual one cannot be materialistic. In defining materialistic I mean concerned with material well-being, not controlled by material things. By continuing to believe this lie, we place ourselves within a tightly-bound area that prohibits us from manifesting, by magic, what we need in our lives.

Ritual magic removes this programming, sometimes with drastic effect in an unprepared person. The practice of magic will quickly bring out the hidden side of any magician. That is why it is so important for a magician to really, truthfully, know him or herself and exercise self discipline.

Ritual magic is merely the taking of energy from another plane of existence and weaving that energy, by specific thoughts, words, and practices, into a desired physical form or result in this plane of existence. The whole idea of magic is to contact various energy pools that exist in a dimension other than our own. Magicians do this deliberately because these energies add a vast amount of power to the energy for manifestation that we hold within ourselves. The prime purpose of ritual is to create a change, and we cannot do that without the combination of these energies. We need the assistance of those energy pools, which can be called gods, deities and elementals.

Everything used during ritual is a symbol of an energy that exists on another plane. Whether or not the magician properly connects with that specific energy and believes he or she can work magic depends upon how well he or she understands its representative symbol which is used on this plane or world. Study of, and meditation on, ritual symbols is an important part of training.

In order to bring through the energy of the gods or energy pools, the magician must set up a circuit of communication along which that power can flow. This is done by ritual use of symbols, ritual itself, visualization and meditation. To keep the incoming power from dissipating before being directed toward a particular goal, rituals are performed within a cast and consecrated circle. This provides a neutral energy area which will not siphon off or dissipate the incoming energy.

To correctly contact the appropriate energy pool, the magician uses as many symbols as possible that represent a specific deity power. For example, he or she will choose a color, incense, plant, stones, and statue or picture to help his or her visualization.

The ability to visualize is extremely important, as the magician must invoke, or call into him or herself, a godform (also called an archetypal energy pool). However, you must realize that you can never invoke the entire power of such an archetypal being into your physical body. Trying to do that would destroy your physical form. That much potent energy simply can never be contained within such a limited mundane structure as the human body. You would not try to use a 440 volt line when 110 volts is called for. It is rare that total inflow of energy is ever achieved. The gods and magical laws prohibit this from ordinarily happening.

Also be aware that if you consistently call upon one particular deity power to the exclusion of all others, you will eventually begin to manifest characteristics of that energy pool within your personality. If this is done correctly in order to gain positive results, these changes will become an important part of your magical personality. If not, they can cause changes of a negative kind.

At the end of each ritual, the godform or power is dismissed so that it can manifest the desire formed during the ritual. This enables the magician to gain the manifestation for which the ritual was done and also to be able to function in the physical world again. To continue holding the power after the ritual is completed would make it impossible for you to live a normal life.

Ritual magic helps to open the doors to your creative mind and the subconscious. To effectively do magic one must get the creative side of the mind, or right brain, to operate uninhibited by the analytical left brain. This is accomplished by a consistent routine of visualization and meditation.

The dominant left brain generally maintains control. It is closely connected with the conscious mind and deals totally with what it calls reality, or this world. It is the side of the brain that makes us feel guilty and criticizes us for things we do or do not do.

The creative right brain pertains entirely to what we call imagination, or other worlds. It is artistic, visualizing. It is the powerful belief formed in this area of the mind that contacts the deity energy pools and creates manifestations.

One of the first things a magician must do is reprogram his or her subconscious mind to eliminate all the old messages of failure and dissatisfaction that are recorded there. From infancy we are programmed by everyone around us with words and actions that express displeasure or approval. Unfortunately, this programming continues throughout life. Therefore, it is important to choose friends carefully at all ages so that the ideas for limitations and failures are kept to a minimum. This programming can be changed into positive actions by the use of certain techniques during meditation (explained further in the chapter on Preparing for Magic).

The right brain and the subconscious mind perform best when presented with symbols, since symbology is the language of the creative mind. During ritual, the left brain is lulled into a sense of control by the chants, tools, candles, and movements; all tangible, logical things. The left brain becomes so involved that it forgets to monitor the right brain. At the same time these tools and activities become symbols to the right brain for use in its creative work.

Emotion is important in ritual magic. Not fluctuating emotions, but controlled emotions. The more emotionally involved you are during spellwork, the more effective the manifestation. There must be a strong desire in order for a manifestation to take place.

Repetition also plays an important part in manifestation and ritual work. Certain numbers hold mystical power; these numbers are 3, 5, 7 and 9. The ancient Celts were well aware of the significance of repetition and numbers. By repeating rituals or spellwork 3, 5, 7 or 9 times consecutively, the creative activity of the right brain and subconscious mind is reinforced. Repetition becomes the pleasure-pain motivator that influences the creative mind to bring forth the desired manifestation.

The number thirteen is very ancient, and is the prime number of importance among the Wiccan religion. Traditionally, the seventh son of a seventh son, or the seventh daughter of a seventh daughter, was said to be a born witch or magician. There is also an old belief that certain years in a person's life are years of great importance or destiny. These were considered to be the seventh and ninth years, and their multiples by the odd numbers of 3, 5, 7 and 9.

Among the Celts and Druids, the number three was of great significance. It was considered the balance between two extremes. The Druids even expressed their lore in triads. The Druidic symbol was the Tribann, or the Three Rays of Light. The shamrock symbolized this belief, long before St. Patrick used it to explain the Christian doctrine.

The importance of numbers is also shown in the relationship between certain numbers and the planets: Sun, 1 and 4; Moon, 2 and 7; Jupiter, 3; Mercury, 5; Venus, 6; Saturn, 8; and Mars, 9.

To effectively work magic, you must believe you can cause things to happen, that you have the power within you to change your life. Until you can re-program your subconscious mind to believe this, manifestations will take longer to come into being.

To begin the changes needed to really believe you can do magic, you must begin by working on your hidden or inner self. You must change bad habits: negative thoughts of yourself, lying, cheating, stealing, broken promises, addictive habits. As you start to create changes in the inner self, you will find that magical results flow more freely. Your life will manifest health, happiness and prosperity.

Some schools of magical thought will tell you that doing magic for yourself is selfish and wrong. This is an erroneous idea held over from Judeo Christian beliefs and has nothing whatsoever to do with ritual magic and spellworking. The truth is, if you cannot manifest for yourself, you have little chance of manifesting for others.

This brings us to one great rule of morality in magic: Do what you will if you harm no being. You never really benefit by deliberately harming another creature through magic. The eventual backlash of karma is not worth the risk. However, one must also look at the opposite side, what happens if evil is left to flourish? In Wicca it is believed that allowing a wrong or evil to exist unhampered is harmful to everybody.

There are many ways to solve a problem with troublesome people through the use of positive magic. By no means should you be a doormat when it comes to protecting yourself and your loved ones. Be creative in doing protective spellwork. Brainstorm on paper, if necessary, until you are certain you are aware of all the options, have not limited yourself or destructively harmed others. It is essential to think through your reasons for doing magic.

The "Four Powers of the Magus (Magician)" is a very old teaching in magic. It is: to know, to dare, to will, to be silent. *To know* means to gain the knowledge to do ritual magic; *to dare* to practice it; *to will* the manifestation; and *to keep silent* about what you are doing. The last part is especially important. Talking about magic diffuses the energy flow. Silence also keeps unsympathetic people from directing negative thoughts toward your efforts. People who talk about their magical operations never achieve real magic. I firmly believe that a copy of the Four Powers and the Wiccan law of morality should be in every ritual room.

The ancient Latin names for the Four Powers of the Magus were: *noscere, audere, velle* and *tacere*. It was believed that to be balanced, all these powers had to be present in the magician. There is also a correspondence between the Four Powers and the Four Elements. *Noscere* (know) corresponds to Air; *audere* (dare) to Water; *velle* (will) to Fire; and *tacere* (silence) to Earth. A fifth power *ire* (to progress or evolve) corresponds to Spirit.

The Celts knew the powers of the Moon phases and used them. In fact, their calendar was based on the lunar year. It is traditional that spellworking for the decrease or removal of problems takes place from after the Full Moon until the New Moon, with the day or night of the New Moon being strongest. Spellworking for increase, growth and gain takes place from after the New Moon until the Full Moon, with the day or night of the Full Moon being the most powerful.

It is logical that the Moon should affect your body and emotions just as it affects the tides of the Earth. After all, most of the human body is made up of water or liquids. The type of energy from the phases of the Moon conceivably will be reflected in our bodies. It is better for magic to work with the flow of Moon energy than against it.

Celtic magic basically works with and employs the powers of planetary and natural energies. It is a magic that is in harmony with our planet, indeed with our very being. It is a magic that can change your life.

3 *Preparing for Magic*

Preparation for ritual magic of any kind requires the self-discipline and techniques learned from concentration, focusing, visualization and meditation. If you desire to obtain physical manifestation from your efforts, it is essential that you actually do and practice these exercises.

Concentration is holding an image or idea in your mind without interruption. It is of great importance during rituals when you must exclude everything not directly related to what you are doing. No thoughts of the day's happenings, no extraneous noise, must be allowed to dominate your attention for any length of time. If such things do intrude, they must be immediately dismissed as unimportant at the moment.

To strengthen your powers of concentration, you will need to practice two exercises. The first exercise is done with a minimum of supplies. Light a candle and set it on a table before you. Sit comfortably and look at the flame. It is easiest on the eyes to look at the blue around the lower part of the wick instead of the bright upper flame. Do not stare; blink your eyes whenever you need to. After a few minutes, close your eyes and look for the flame. You will see it against your closed eyelids. Keep your thoughts on that flame image, and see how long you can maintain the mental picture before your conscious mind begins to intrude.

The second exercise is much the same, but uses a picture instead of a candle. Choose a picture that pleases you. Tarot cards are especially good for this. Stand or hang the picture at a comfortable level and look at it for some time. Close your eyes and see if you can discern a mental image against your eyelids. Hold that image as long as you can.

Focusing is important to ritual magic as it is the process of adjusting your "inner eye" or attention on a particular object or goal. You must have a clear idea or picture of what you wish to produce while doing magic. This is very similar to concentration but more refined. An idea is harder to hold in the mental realms than a reflected picture.

It is not necessary to visualize a goal in absolute detail. Too much detail tends to limit the manifestation, especially if you could have had something better. Know what you want, but never restrict yourself. The gods may be more generous to you than you are to yourself.

Focusing and concentrating on performance during ritual will channel your mental powers, thereby clarifying and strengthening the function. The act of casting and consecrating a magical circle (explained later) must have focus and concentration if it is to be done properly. If you fail to do this, the circle will not provide you with the neutral area in which to perform magic, and most certainly will not give you protection.

Again, using the picture or card, this time elicit all associated images. See if you can create movement within the picture.

Go through the same exercise with the candle flame, this time changing the size, height and color of the flame. Summon up associated images and follow them through. Some startling ideas have come out of such exercises.

Meditation is a great aid in centering yourself, controlling destructive emotions and gaining insight. But it should also bring a greater sense of awareness and increase your ability to visualize. All of these skills are necessary in the practice of magic, especially if you want feasible results.

Meditation is really not a complicated exercise, unless you lack self-control. If you do, you need meditation more than ever. Relaxing, smooth music is an excellent background to help mask minor noises and help you relax. Turn off the telephone, hang a "do not disturb" sign on the door, and choose a comfortable chair.

Listen to the music while taking a few deep breaths. Relax and let yourself unwind. Next mentally surround yourself with white light for protection. Imagine yourself standing on a wooden bridge over a calm pond. Drop all your problems into the water, and watch it close over them. This is a symbolic release that tells your subconscious mind that you need an answer to solve these troubles. Then visualize yourself walking on across the bridge, leaving everything behind.

To continue the meditation, project yourself into

a meadow on the other side of the bridge. A small stream runs through the grass and flowers. Shady trees surround it. Wander through this meadow, soaking up the peacefulness and healing. You may see people or nature spirits. Talk with them if you like.

As long as you remain objective and do not push to hear what you want to hear, you can receive very accurate guidance while in meditation. If you strain to hear what you want, you will get only messages from your conscious mind, which does not believe in what you are doing.

When in meditation, you are in an astral state. Therefore, it is always possible that at some time you will meet a being that makes you fearful or uncomfortable. If this should happen, recall the white light and leave.

You will be able to escape the meditation any time you choose. Simply become aware of your body and open your eyes. As during ritual, time in meditation is non-existent. Time is a limited idea belonging to the left brain and conscious mind. When working with the right brain and subconscious mind, time has no meaning at all.

The symbolism of dropping your problems into the pond is essential. It is never a good idea to go into meditation without doing this, just as it is imprudent not to use the white light. Both are protective measures to eliminate taking negative vibrations into an otherwise productive exercise.

4 Magical Elements

To a magician, all magic is based on four Elements:
Air, Fire, Water and Earth. Ancient occult philosophers
and the Druids stated that all life is made of these
four Elements; without them life could not exist. *Tan*
or *Teine* (Fire in the old Celtic language) was considered the most sacred as it is the closest to pure
energy.

These four Elements correspond to the four
directions of our physical world, the four quarters of
the universe, the four winds, and most importantly to
the four quarters of the magical circle. Water and
Earth are considered female energies; Fire and Air
are male.

The Old Gaelic term for the four points of the
compass was the Four Airts or Airs. The general
definitions of these Elements were originally based
on the prevailing winds in Britain. In Scotland, the
Gaelic words for the cardinal points were *aiet*, east;
deas, south; *iar*, west; and *tuath*, north.

The four Elements are forces and energies that

make up the universe and everything in it. They influence our personalities and magic. They also possess form as well as force. Each Element is known for having certain qualities, natures, moods and magical purposes; each has positive and negative traits. Magical ritual calls to each Elemental kingdom and its ruler to protect its quarter of the circle. Because of this, it is very important to completely understand what each Element is and does.

In Wiccan and ceremonial magic, each Element is associated with a color: east, yellow; south, red; west, blue; north, green. Although the ancient Celts correctly knew the forces and energies of the Elements, the colors for them were different: east, red; south, white; west, grey; north, black. To the Celts, red symbolized the rising Sun; white, noonday; grey, twilight; black, midnight.

The Element of Air governs the eastern quarter of the circle. Its ruler is Paralda who oversees the Sylphs, Zephyrs, and Nature spirits or fairies. Its color is pure yellow; it is considered warm and moist. The positive associations of Air are: sunrise, Spring, incense, the wand, clouds, breezes, breath, optimism, joy, intelligence, mental quickness, any kind of helpful air. Negative associations are: frivolity, gossip, fickleness, inattention, bragging, forgetfulness, wind storms, tornadoes, hurricanes, destructive air in any form.

The Element of Fire governs the southern quarter of the circle. Its ruler is Djin (dee-yin) who oversees the Salamanders, Firedrakes, and the little ones of the sunbeams. Its color is pure red; it is considered warm and dry. The positive associations of Fire are: noon, Summer, the dagger and sword, candles, any kind of helpful fire, the Sun, the stars, the blood, enthusiasm, activity, courage, daring, willpower, leadership. Negative associations are: hate, jealousy, fear, anger, war, ego, conflicts, lightning, volcanoes, harmful fire of any kind.

The Element of Water governs the western quarter of the circle. Its ruler is Niksa who oversees the Nymphs, Undines, Mer-people, and the little ones of the springs, lakes, ponds, and rivers. Its color is pure blue; it is cold and moist. The positive associations of Water are: sunset, Fall, the chalice and cauldron, any form of helpful water, compassion, peacefulness, forgiveness, love, intuition. Negative associations are: floods, rain storms, whirlpools, any kind of harmful water, laziness, indifference, instability, lack of emotional control, insecurity.

The Element of Earth rules the northern quarter of the circle. Its ruler is Ghob, sometimes called Ghom, who oversees the gnomes and dwarfs and the little ones of the moonbeams. Its color is clear dark green; it is cold and dry. Positive associations are: midnight, Winter, the pentacle, ritual salt, gemstones, mountains, caves, soil, respect, endurance, responsibility, stability, thoroughness, purpose in life. Negative associations are: rigidity, unwillingness to change or see another side to a problem, stubbornness, lack of conscience, vacillation, earthquakes, slides.

The fifth Element, Spirit (or *nyu* to the Druids), dominates the center of the circle, thus balancing all the other Elements. Through invocation of the gods, or Spirit, we are able to blend Elements bringing forth the desired manifestation.

The spirits or beings of the Elements have been known to many cultures, particularly the Greeks and

Romans from whom we get our names for them. In Greek *gnoma* (gnomes) meant knowledge or the knowing ones. *Unda* (undine) in Latin meant wave, creatures of the waves. The Greek word *silphe* (sylph) was a butterfly or being with gauzy wings. *Salambe* (salamander) in Greek described a fireplace; however, the actual being was more like a very small dragon.

The Elemental kingdoms and their rulers are represented in their appropriate quarter of the magical circle by a symbol and/or candle of the correct color. The magician always draws the magical circle sunwise, beginning and ending in the east. When welcoming the Elements, he or she begins with Air in the east. When he or she ends the ritual and dismisses the kingdoms, he or she again begins with the eastern position. Before opening the circle, the magician returns to the center and dismisses the Element of Spirit.

Become familiar with the traits of the Elemental kingdoms and their rulers for they will play a very important part in all your magical activities.

5 Casting The Magic Circle

To almost all cultures, the circle is a symbol of infinity and eternity. It has no beginning and no end. When properly drawn, with the candles of the Elements at the cardinal directions and the altar in the center, the circle becomes a mandala, or sacred drawing, upon which the magician stands.

In magic and spellworking, the circle is drawn by the dagger or sword as protection against potentially dangerous forces or spirits. It also concentrates the cone of power that is raised within its boundaries. The cone of power raised within the circle, and seen by outsiders, is likely what brought about the idea of witches or magicians wearing pointed hats.

The Celtic wheel-cross, a pre-Christian symbol, is a representation of the magic circle mandala. The equal-armed cross surrounded by a circle symbolizes the balance of male and female forces and the four Elements, the four winds, and the four cardinal directions. In the center where the lines cross is the hidden fifth Element of Spirit. The surrounding circle is the

manifested universe contained within a circle of infinity.

In magic a properly drawn circle becomes an invisible boundary, having power in this and other realms. The energy of that boundary keeps out negative influences and contains the power you raise until you are ready to release it. The circle is a neutral working area, capable of regenerating and amplifying the kind of power the magician is creating.

A traditional circle has a nine-foot circumference. Sometimes a ten-foot circle is drawn outside of this and the Element candles and certain symbols are placed between the two boundaries. However, it is not absolutely essential that the circle be a certain size. The concentration and visualization used during the casting determines the value of the circle.

Before you draw the circle, be certain that all the supplies you need are inside the ritual area. Once cast and sealed, it is unwise to cross the boundary until the ritual is finished and the Elements dismissed. For some unexplainable reason, cats and small children are able to cross the circle without disturbing the power flow. However, I do not consider it a good idea to have small children in the room while performing magic. You need total concentration without any unnecessary distractions. Cats generally enter the circle, watch quietly until the ritual is finished, or leave. Some cats actually amplify energy and love ritual.

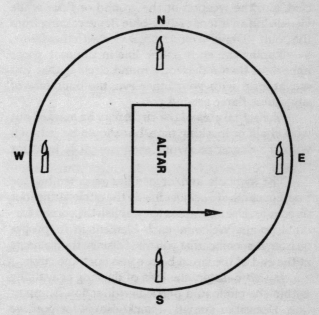

In Wiccan rites, the wand directs magical power and is used to persuade. The black-hilted athame (dagger) or the sword, with steel or iron blade and sharp point, is used for defense and banishing.

You must have concentrated visualization and focusing of inner energy to cast a proper magical circle. The dagger or sword must be consecrated (see later chapter on Magical Tools). All major gestures should be done with your power hand. This is the dominant hand, usually the one you write with and use daily.

Holding the ritual tool in your power hand and beginning at the eastern quarter of the area to be circled, aim the weapon at the ground or floor while visualizing an intense silver-blue flame coming from the point. "Draw" a circle clockwise with that flame, overlapping the ends of the line in the east. More important than a perfectly round circle is that you see, at least with your inner eye, the boundary of silver-blue flame around you.

The actual area of the circle may be marked out with chalk or masking tape, but should be redrawn with the dagger or sword each time it is used for ritual.

The symbols and/or candles representing the four Elements are set just inside the circle at the four directions. Use a compass to establish the correct cardinal points. Welcome each Element in its proper quarter. Remember that you must dismiss the Elements at the end of the ritual before you open the circle.

In Celtic magic, the idea of dancing or walking within the circle in a particular direction is important. Deaseil or sunwise (clockwise) is for positive magic; tuathal or widdershins (counterclockwise) is for cursing or diminishing magic. After the circle has been cast and sealed, it is important to the power flow that you turn or walk within the cast circle according

W   E

to the type of magic you are using. In other words, you would not walk against the Sun (tuathal) in a ritual for positive or increasing magic.

When the magical procedures are finished, "cut" the circle by a backward or reverse movement of the sword or dagger across a section of the circle. The silver-blue flames will wink out of existence.

SAMPLE RITUAL

Put everything you will need for your altar and spellworking inside the ritual area. Place on or near your altar the following items: everything needed for specific spells; a chalice with a little fresh water in it; a dish of salt; pentacle disk (see chapter on Magical Tools); sword and/or dagger; wand; incense burner (preferably with attached chains for carrying) with lighted charcoal; incense; one or two altar candles for light; four Element candles. After the circle is cast, unless it is an emergency, do not cross the boundary until the Elements are dismissed.

The burning of incense is one of the oldest religious and magical rites. In fact, the word "perfume" comes from the Latin *profumum* (by smoke). Scents of all kinds have a fast, subtle effect upon the human mind and subconscious. It appeals to past memories. In my opinion, the best type of incense is the kind burned on charcoal. Please do NOT use barbecue charcoal! It is dangerous when burned within an enclosed area. Use the little self-lighting tablets especially made for incense.

The candles of the four Elements in Celtic magic are red, east; white, south; grey, west; black, north. In the Wiccan and magical tradition, the colors are yellow, east; red, south; blue, west; dark green, north. In the following ritual, the Celtic colors are listed first, with the Wiccan colors in parentheses.

You are striving to create an atmosphere in which magic can work. The candle-lit room, the wearing of robes and scented incense smoke can transform any ritual area into a shrine of power.

Set the altar in the center, facing east. The Celtic

peoples honored the east as a place of renewing power because of the daily rising Sun in that area. Play soft instrumental music to help create atmosphere. Relax, and take several deep breaths to center yourself.

Taking your magical dagger in your power hand and starting in the east, visualize that powerful, protective silver-blue flame shooting from the tip of the ritual blade. Aim it at the floor. Move clockwise from the east, drawing the magical boundary. Remember to overlap the ends in the east when you finish. Note that in casting the circle it is acceptable to use a dagger (as demonstrated), a sword, or the forefinger of your power hand. While you are drawing the circle, say:

> I consecrate this circle of power to the Ancient Gods.
> Here may they manifest and bless their child.

Move back to the altar, facing east. Raise your dagger or wand in greeting, say:

> This is a time that is not a time, in a place that is not a place, on a day that is not a day.
> I stand at the threshold between the worlds, before the veil of the Mysteries.
> May the Ancient Ones help and protect me on my magical journey.

Set the water chalice on the pentacle disk. Hold your dagger over it and say:

> Great Mother, bless this creature of Water to your service.
> May I always remember the cauldron

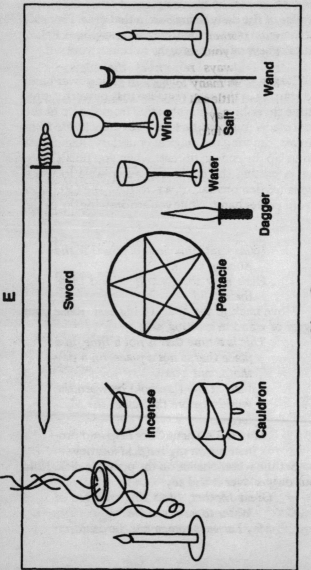

E

Sword

Wand

Wine

Salt

Water

Dagger

Pentacle

Incense

Cauldron

Altar Setup

waters of rebirth.

Hold your dagger over the salt, say:

*Great Mother, bless this creature of
Earth to your service.*

*May I always remember the blessed
Earth, its many forms and beings.*

Sprinkle a little salt into the water, then hold the chalice up high. Say:

Great Mother, I give you honor!

Beginning in the east and moving clockwise, sprinkle the water-salt mixture lightly around the edges of the circle. Replace the chalice on the altar.

Hold your dagger over the lighted incense burner, saying:

*Great Father, bless this creature of
Fire to your service.*

*May I always remember the sacred
Fire that dances within the form of
every creation.*

Hold your dagger over the incense, saying:

*Great Father, bless this creature of
Air to your service.*

*May I always listen to the spirit winds
that bring me the voices of the
Ancient Ones.*

Put a little incense on the lighted charcoal. Do not put too much incense in the burner, as a little goes a long way in an enclosed room! Using the attached chains, touch the burner briefly to the pentacle disk, then raise the burner high, saying:

Great Father, I give you honor!

Carry the burner around the circle clockwise, beginning in the east. Return it to the altar.

Go to the eastern quarter of the circle. Light the red (yellow) candle and hold your hand up in greeting. You may also salute the Element with your dagger, sword or wand instead of your hand:

> *I call upon you, Powers of Air, to witness this rite and to guard this circle.*

In the southern quarter, light the white (red) candle and greet the Element:

> *I call upon you, Powers of Fire, to witness this rite and to guard this circle.*

Move to the west; light the grey (blue) candle and hold up your hand in greeting:

> *I call upon you, Powers of Water, to witness this rite and to guard this circle.*

End by going to the north; light the black (green) candle and greet the Element:

> *I call upon you, Powers of Earth, to witness this rite and to guard this circle.*

Move back to the central altar, and stand facing east. Raise your arms in greeting:

> *This circle is bound,*
> *With power all around.*
> *Between the worlds, I stand*
> *With protection at hand.*

Proceed with your planned spellworking or ceremony. When everything is completed, hold your hand or dagger over the altar and say:

> *By the powers of the ancient Gods,*
> *I bind all power within this circle*
> *Into this spell. So mote it be.*

When you are ready to end the ritual, go to the east and extinguish the red (yellow) candle. Say:

> *Depart in peace, O Powers of Air.*
> *My thanks and blessings.*

Go to the south, extinguish the white (red) candle. Say:

> *Depart in peace, O Powers of Fire.*
> *My thanks and blessings.*

Go to the west and put out the grey (blue) candle. Say:

> *Depart in peace, O Powers of Water.*
> *My thanks and blessings.*

Finish by going to the north and extinguishing the black (green) candle. Say:

> *Depart in peace, O Powers of Earth.*
> *My thanks and blessings.*

Return to the altar in the center and say:

> *To all beings and powers of the visible and invisible, depart in peace.*
> *May there always be harmony between us.*
> *My thanks and blessings.*

Cut the circle with a backwards movement of your dagger or sword to release all remaining traces of power for manifestation. Say:

> *The circle is open, yet ever it remains*
> *a circle.*
> *Around and through me always flows*
> *its magical power.*

Put away all magical tools and clear the altar. Leave any candles or objects which must remain either to burn out or be empowered for a stated period of time.

You have completed a ritual. Practice will make the power flow easier and more freely. You will become more self-confident. Soon you will be looking forward to the time you spend between the worlds with the Ancient Ones.

6 Tools of Magic

Magic is a very difficult subject to explain, yet we know it works. The results of spellworking speak for themselves. Generally, magic is performed with the use of certain movements, words and objects which signal to the subconscious mind that something extraordinary needs to be done. The success of magic is determined, not by elaborate or expensive tools, but by the belief, emotion and discipline you bring to the rituals. Half-hearted playing at magic will not produce results.

The tools or objects used in making magic are essential, although they are just tools. They hold no inherent power within themselves, but focus and refine the power within you. They are visual and manual aids or symbols to help in contacting the subconscious mind and persuading it to work the magic you desire. Any magical implement is an expression of a magician's will and the ability to carry out that will.

For each spellworking, it is best to gather as

many symbols as you can of the deity who represents the manifestation you wish to see. This includes the use of specific colors and incenses, statues or pictures, plants or herbs, even stones and/or minerals. To help you in this selection, I have included a chapter called Table of Correspondences (Chapter 11), which covers all the major Celtic deities mentioned.

Basic tools of Celtic magic-work are: altar; cauldron; pentacle; wand; staff; headband; armband; goblets; incense burner; knife; sword; robes; candles; herbs; stones.

The first thing you will need is an altar or working place. Ideally, you should have a special room for this, but few of us live in ideal situations. The altar can be as simple as a coffee table or chest that does double-duty as regular furniture, or as elaborate as a specific table that is used only for spellwork.

A small chest with rollers is a good investment. The drawers can be used to hold your supplies, and the rollers enable you to move it into place in a room where you plan to work. It should be wide and long enough to accommodate the equipment you might need for any particular spellworking, and be a comfortable height, whether you choose to stand, kneel or sit.

Narrow scarves of various colors can be draped across the altar, the colors coordinated to the spellworking at hand. The altar is the Earth connected with Spirit, and is a grounding station to bring your spells into reality on this plane of existence.

The cauldron or small kettle with bail handle is an essential in Celtic magic. It represents the element of Water. The cauldron is mentioned in many Celtic myths and always in connection with magical happenings. Black cast iron is the best and most traditional material for the cauldron, although it can be of other metals. Filled with water, the cauldron can be used as a scrying apparatus, similar to a black mirror or crystal ball. During certain spells, candles are set in it and allowed to burn out. It is an all-purpose tool; a vital part of your Celtic spellworkings.

The pentagram, a five-point star with one upward point, is a Spirit symbol used in Wiccan and other pagan rituals. The earliest examples of the pentagram were found among ancient Babylonian relics. Christians, who have since denounced its application, used it for centuries to represent the Five Wounds of Christ. Also known as the Druids' Foot, Wizards' Foot, Witches' Foot, and Goblins' Cross, the pentagram can be inscribed, even invisibly, on doors and windows to stave off evil. This symbol was painted on Sir Gawaine's shield. A potent form of the pentagram is the fossilized stem of the sea lily.

A pentagram is often engraved or painted on a wooden or metal disk (sometimes set with semiprecious gemstones). Referred to as a pentacle, this disk is used as a power-point for consecrating ritual objects, such as water or wine in a chalice, amulets and tools. It can also be used to control wayward Elementals.

Satanists in the U.S. have corrupted this sacred symbol by using it with one point in the downward position. Proper use of the upright pentacle has absolutely no correlation to Satanism. In fact, you cannot be a Satanist and Wiccan at the same time. Witches do not believe in the Devil. In order to be a Satanist you have to believe in Christianity and God's powerful alter ego, the Devil.

Traditionally, both a wand and staff should be of wood and made by the person who will use them. If you purchase these or have them made, fill them with your own vibrations before using them. This is easily done by handling them often and deliberately sending your own positive thoughts into the object. The wand and staff can be naturally-formed tree branches or made of dowels ornamented with crystals and wooden beads.

The length of the wand depends upon what feels comfortable to you, but should be no longer than your forearm; the staff should be at least shoulder-high. Sometimes men fasten a small cone to the tip of their wand. For women, I have seen Celtic wands with either a crystal or a crescent Moon on the end. The wand is a charming tool; the staff a symbol of both magical knowledge and the right to petition deities or archetypal powers. They are both of the Element of Air.

The headband and armband represent the per-

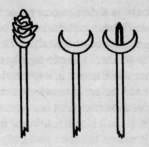

sonal male or female energies with which you work; in other words, the very personal you. Women most commonly wear silver or silver-tone bands. The headband for women is often set with a crescent Moon, horns turned upwards. Men use gold or gold-tone metal; their headbands are set with a symbol of the Sun. The Sun may be represented by a simple circle or a circle with radiating flares around it. The headband, armband and all personal talismans are of the Element of Spirit.

The goblets can be of any shape, size or composition. They hold water or wine, but occasionally are used empty. If you plan to use a goblet to hold wine, please do not use one of brass or pewter unless lined with silver. There is a dangerous poisonous reaction between wine and these metals. Wood, ceramic, stone, glass or silver are quite acceptable. The goblet, like the cauldron, is of the Element of Water.

A good incense burner is essential, especially if you plan to use the better incenses that are burned on charcoal. Choose a burner that has some sort of a foot or stand under it. Fill it with a layer of fresh sand, which makes it easier to clean and cuts down on the heat that will pass into the altar. If you plan to move it at all while hot, chains are a necessity.

If your burner does not have chains, an easy addition can be made. A metal ring, just smaller than the bowl of the burner, can be attached to four lengths of small chain, which are then fastened to a smaller ring for carrying or hanging. The burner is set into the larger metal ring and can be picked up or transported by the chains. Representative of the Element of Fire, the incense burner can also be used in spells that require the burning of paper.

The dagger preferably should be new, the shape and size depending upon what appeals to you. In the Wiccan tradition, the hilt is usually black and the blade sharp on both sides. However, the blade is usually not longer than the palm and fingers of your hand. The blade should also be of a metal that can be sharpened, as you will use this knife to cut herbs and incise candles.

If you do purchase a used knife, be very certain that there are no negative vibrations on it. This can be ascertained by the feelings you get when holding the knife. If such vibrations are present and you still feel that you want the knife, cleanse it within your circle by sprinkling it with consecrated water and passing it through incense smoke. Both the knife and sword are of the Element of Fire.

The sword, like the staff, is a tool of command. It is not used often, but is necessary for certain spell-workings. Its size, style and length are a personal choice; just be careful that you can easily handle the sword you choose. The weight and length of a Scottish claymore, for instance, becomes a real test of endurance after several minutes. For a woman, a sword length of 17-25 inches is a good choice.

Candles, another representation of both the Elements of Air and Fire, are used for everything from lighting the altar to specifics in spells. Wax composition does not matter as much as the colors. Colors needed are: white, black, red, pink, orange, yellow, green, blue, purple, brown, magenta, indigo, gold, silver. The meanings of these colors are given in the Table of Correspondence.

Herbs are best gathered by the magician using his or her own ritual dagger. However, this is not always possible, especially when you live in a city or certain herbs are required which do not grow in your area. If you buy a larger quantity of an herb than you plan to use at one time, store it in a sealed glass or ceramic container, away from heat and sunlight. Herbs are of the Element of Earth. A listing of their uses is also found in the Table of Correspondence.

Colorful stones of various shapes and sizes are used in some Celtic spellworks. Whether you purchase them or find them yourself, be certain that their vibrations feel comfortable to you. There is no set number of stones, yet never more than thirteen will be used at any one time. An Earth element, they play an important part in Celtic spellworkings. Crystals and other stones are good conductors of magical energy in their natural state and need not be polished to be of use.

Stones of the following colors are useful. The stones listed are only a representation of the color: pink (rose quartz), red (red jasper, carnelian), yellow (amber, topaz, citrine), orange (carnelian, jacinth), blue (lapis lazuli, labradorite), green (jade, malachite, amazonite), white (moonstone, quartz, rock crystal), brown (tigereye, smoky quartz), black (onyx, obsidian), purple or lavender (amethyst, quartz, beryl).

In fact, your collection of stones need be none of these. They can be as simple as rocks you have picked up while walking; you need not even know what they are. The fact that they are the right color and feel good to you is what really matters.

There are four additions to your stones that are essential for certain spellwork. These are moonstone, pyrite (fool's gold), rock crystal, and lodestone.

An amulet or piece of pagan jewelry can be helpful to the magician, both as protection and as a stimulus for the magical transformation which takes place when performing rituals. Chanting over this jewelry will "charm" it, thus making it also a luck-bringer. Acquiring an amulet (which should be concealed if worn everyday) can restore a person's self-confidence. And by restoring that confidence the luck is changed. There were several ancient symbols known for their protection and luck powers: the pentagram, the ankh cross, and the 6-point star or Solomon's Seal. Although an amulet is not a ritual tool, most magicians consider it a valuable asset.

When you become more adept at the spellworkings, you may wish to include other divinatory aids, such as tarot cards. We do know that the ancient Celts cast marked stones and pieces of wood. We can assume that these were marked with the Ogham alphabet or pictures of some sort.

A robe that is saved only for spellworking is the last fundamental part of your magical paraphernalia. It can be plain, decorated and of any color that appeals to you as long as it makes you feel "magical." It is nice to have more than one robe, each in a different color. The colors can be matched to the candle colors listed in the Tables of Correspondence.

Something you should choose for yourself, but which is not really a "tool" in the physical sense, is a magical name. This name should be personal and private, never revealed to anyone, unless you are working with another respected magician. By assuming the magical name when you enter the circle, you are presenting yourself to the god-powers as a different person, one who is qualified to approach them and work magic.

Place your altar or table so you can face the east. When you become more acquainted with magic, you can turn the altar to face a different direction, if you choose. Until you become a more accomplished magician, however, it is best to face the east. To determine the appropriate direction for more advanced work, use the category of Ritual Work in the Table of Elementals found in the chapter Tables of Correspondence.

The best way to assemble your magical tools is by a slow, steady process. The Wiccan say one must never haggle over the price of any ritual object. Everything does not have to be found or purchased at once. There is a special joy in discovering the right stone or tool, sometimes quite unexpectedly in the most unusual place.

7 Celtic Wicca and the Lady

Witchcraft or Wicca is both a religion and a magical system. But it is also a way of life, of looking at everything around you. The word Wicca or witch comes from the Anglo-Saxon language and means wise one. Originally, the word for a male witch was *Wicca* and a female *Wicce*, with the plural being *Wiccan*. Today, however, the common word for both sexes is Wicca. The word "warlock" is actually a Scottish term and is not used in Wicca.

Witches are practical people who seek hidden powers and knowledge, and usually do not conform to society's so-called "acceptable" molds. Many a person who has made the mistake of harassing a real witch has eventually suffered a very long run of bad luck.

The male and female aspects of Nature were personified by the Celts as the White Moon Goddess and the Horned God. The White Moon Goddess and her consort the Horned God are the oldest known deities. This is the basic idea still held by witches, although they also petition various aspects of each of these main deities, just as the Celts did. The Wiccan believe that all gods are one god, all goddesses are one goddess, and both are united.

Both Wicca and Celtic pagans believe in another world which is made up of spirits, both human and Elemental. The Wiccan believe that powerful witches of the past are still able to help those practicing the craft today. The Celts believed that dead ancestors could do the same. Most pagan groups believe in reincarnation and the destiny of karma.

Both the ceremonial magician and the Wiccan share a belief in the astral plane. This other-world plane is made up of a different type of energy which vibrates at a higher rate than this physical world. At the same time, the astral plane and this world surround and interpenetrate each other. The astral plane is very responsive to thoughts and emotions. The souls of Nature spirits, animals and beings created by many strongly projected human thoughts dwell on certain areas of this plane.

The human astral body, which survives after death, is how we function in the astral world. While still in this world, humans can travel on the astral during sleep or by deliberate out-of-body methods. This is the reality behind the old stories of witches flying.

Higher levels of the astral plane contain the beautiful Emania of departed higher souls, while the lower levels are inhabited by spiritual darkness and lower souls.

The Wiccan and many magicians choose a secret name for themselves that is used only during rituals. The use of this magical name helps them to separate their minds from the everyday world and prepare for supernormal workings. This is part of convincing yourself that you are a totally different person, capable of accomplishing paranormal actions within the cast circle.

Monthly Wiccan meetings are held at or near the Full Moon. The Full Moon is the high point of psychic power. Eight festivals called Sabbats round out their year. The four Greater Sabbats are: Imbolc, Beltane, Lunasa and Samhain. The four Lesser Sabbats are the equinoxes and solstices.

At the equinoxes the flow of power is strong, especially good for spelling on a thought or idea for growth. The tides of the solstices are quieter, a time for regrouping energy and praising. The remaining festivals, or the four Greater Sabbats, release energy currents at each quarter of the year.

Magicians and the Wiccan know that what appear to be opposites of matter, form, energy and force are not really opposing at all. They are simply different manifestations of each other. Even the Celts understood this.

The Wiccan and Celtic pagans believe that this world is only part of reality, that divinity is both male and female. They say humans have more than five senses and that they can be trained to be aware of the Other Worlds. The concept of the Ultimate Creative Force, or God behind the gods, is the inexplicable life-force of the universe. Their pantheon of gods and goddesses who rule over different parts of Nature and help in the evolution of the universe are merely different aspects of this life-force.

They say it is logical to believe in reincarnation rather than obliteration at death, because, as modern science tells us, nothing in this universe can be destroyed; it only changes its form. Karma, which is deeply involved in reincarnation, means simply that every action brings about an equal reaction; it is not necessarily punishment.

The Wiccan and Celtic religions teach that between reincarnations the soul rests in the Land of Faery, a pagan paradise, called by the Celtics *Tir-Nan-Og* or Land of the Young. The Celtic explanation that this afterlife land co-exists with our own identifies it with the astral plane.

A natural and powerful form of magic circle is the fairy ring of darker grass or mushrooms, provided, of course, that you are on good terms with the little people. If you are not, it is a good idea to leave their sacred place alone.

Certain gestures and postures in a Wiccan circle have definite hidden meanings. For example, when a priestess stands with her feet together and her arms crossed over her breast, she is representing the God of Death and the Beyond. When she stands with her feet apart and her arms outstretched, she symbolizes the Goddess of Life and Rebirth.

The Wiccan Book of Shadows, or "cookbook" as a friend calls it, is a book in which witches write rituals, invocations and spells. Its name comes from the fact that everything in it is only a shadow of reality of the Other World.

Dancing around the circle is an excellent way to raise power. The leader must be aware of the rising power and direct it into a specific purpose at the proper time. Light hypnosis and a state of ecstasy can be self-induced by magical forms of dancing. Dancing in a spiral pattern into the center of the magic circle and out again symbolizes entering into the mysteries of the Other World. The old Bards called it the place of the Cauldron of Inspiration and Celtic heroes the Spiral Castle. Spiritually entering this castle is symbolized by the spiral dance.

The Triple Goddess, or triple aspects of the Goddess, was well known to the Celts and is still used today in Wicca. To the Celtic peoples, the Triple Goddess was represented by Anu or Danu as the Maiden, Badb as the Mother, and Macha as the Crone. To the Celts of Wales, the Maiden was Blodeuwedd, the Mother Arianrhod, and the Crone Cerridwen. Even in Arthurian times, we find the same triplicity: Elaine as Maiden, Margawse as Mother, Morgan as Crone.

The Maiden is essential to the continuation of all life; her color is white, denoting innocence and newness. She is the springtime, the dawn, eternal youth and vigor, enchantment and seduction, the waxing Moon.

The Mother is the ripeness of womanhood, the boiling pot of Badb which is the richness of life. Her color is red, the color of blood and the life force. The Mother is Summer, the day, lustiness, teacher, the Full Moon.

The Crone, or Dark Mother, sometimes called the Hag, has black as her color, the color of darkness where all life rests before rebirth. This aspect of the Goddess is Winter, night, wisdom, counsel, the gateway to death and reincarnation, the waning Moon.

The Celtic pagan year was based on thirteen lunar months which were named after trees and plants. According to the Brehon Law of Ireland, these trees corresponded to the Ogam alphabet and had three categories: chieftains, peasants and shrubs. The rankings were based on the symbolic importance of each to the Druids. The tree alphabet will be discussed fully in the chapter on the Ogam Alphabet.

The Celtic new year began on November 1, after Samhain. This month was called *Beith* or Birch. Following this were: *Luis* or Rowan for December; *Fearn* or Alder for January; *Saille* or Willow for February; *Nuin* or Ash for March; *Huathe* or Hawthorn for April; *Duir* or Oak for May; *Tinne* or Holly for June; *Coll* or Hazel for July; *Muin* or Vine for August; *Gort* or Ivy for September; and *Ngetal* or Reed for October. The thirteenth month was *Ruis* or Elder. This was a very short period to wrap up the year.

Celebration of the solstices and equinoxes is done on a particular day when the Sun changes into particular signs. These are listed on astrological calendars and vary from year to year. The remaining six pagan holy days are honored by many on specific days also. However, there are two ways to determine these remaining holy days: one, on a definite date; two, on the closest Full Moon. I will list both options at the beginning of each festival ritual.

The ancient pagan world counted nights rather than days. All their festivals were celebrated on the Eve, or night before. Their day began at sundown.

Samhain, pronounced sow-en and called Halloween today, was the ending of the Celtic year. The new year actually began with sunset on October 31. The ritual was known as Ancestor Night or Feast of the Dead. Because the veil between the worlds is thinnest on this night, it was and is considered an excellent time for divinations. Feasts are made in remembrance of dead ancestors and as an affirmation of continuing life. A time for settling problems, throwing out old ideas and influences. This is either celebrated   October 31, or the first Full Moon in Scorpio.

Winter Solstice occurs about December 21. This is the time of death and rebirth of the Sun God. The days are shortest, the Sun at its lowest point. The Full Moon after Yule is considered the most powerful of the whole year. This ritual is a light festival, with as many candles as possible on or near the altar in welcome of the Sun Child.

Imbolc, February 1 or the first Full Moon in Aquarius, is a time of cleansing and newborn lambs. The name Imbolc comes from the word 'oimelc' or sheep's milk. It is a festival of the Maiden in preparation for growth and renewal.

Spring Equinox, about March 21, is when light and darkness are in balance but the light is growing stronger.

Beltane is May 1 or the first Full Moon in Taurus. Other names for it are May Day or Lady Day. It is primarily a fertility festival with nature enchantments and offerings to wildlings and Elementals. The powers of elves and fairies are growing and will reach their height at Summer Solstice. A time of great magic, it is good for all divinations and for establishing a woodland or garden shrine. The house guardians should be honored at this time.

Summer Solstice, about June 21, is when the hours of daylight are longest. The Sun is at the highest before beginning its slide into darkness. Traditionally, herbs gathered on this day are extremely powerful. On this   night elves and fairies abound in great numbers.

Lughnassadh is August 1 or the first Full Moon in Leo. It is a preharvest festival, the turning point in Mother Earth's year. The last herbs are gathered. It is a celebration in honor of the god Lugh's wedding to Mother Earth.

Autumn Equinox, about September 21, was a time of rest after labor, completion of the harvest. Again the hours of day and night are in balance, with the darkness increasing. All preparations for the dark of the year and the year's ending were made, thus bringing us back to Samhain.

Self-Initiation

Special Notes: Best done on a Full Moon. Prepare yourself with at least one hour of silence before beginning this ritual of dedication to the pagan way. Either wear a magical robe or go nude. Have a magical name chosen.

Altar Supplies: dagger; chalice of water; chalice of wine; salt; burner; incense; white taper candle in cauldron; piece of magical jewelry; pentacle; 4 Element candles.

With casting the circle as your basic starting point, perform the same ritual illustrated in the section of chapter 5 titled 'Sample Ritual,' inserting the following steps where the Sample states "proceed with your planned spellwork or ceremony":

Put a pinch of salt on your tongue and say:

> *I am a mortal, loved and cared for by the Triple Goddess and the Great God. Through the Great Mother, all things are born; to her, all things, in their season, return. Through her sacred cauldron, I enter and leave this physical world, until by my actions I no longer must return to learn.*

Set the perfumed oil on the pentacle. Kneel before the altar and say:

> *I, (magical name), come into this sacred place willingly. I come to dedicate my life to the pagan way, to the Old Celtic Gods, whose power is still strong and vital. Here I give my word-bond to follow the ancient*

> paths that lead to true wisdom and know-
> ledge. I will serve the Great Goddess and
> give reverence to the Great God. I am a
> pagan, a stone of the ancient circle, stand-
> ing firmly balanced upon the Earth, yet
> open to the winds of the heavens, and
> enduring through time. May the Old Celtic
> Gods witness my words!

Rise and go the the eastern quarter. Say:

> Behold, O Powers of Air! I, (magical name),
> am a follower of the Lord and Lady.

Go to the south, say:

> Behold, O Powers of Fire! I, (magical name),
> am a follower of the Lord and Lady.

Go to the west, say:

> Behold, O Powers of Water! I, (magical
> name), am a follower of the Lord and
> Lady.

Go to the north, say:

> Behold, O Powers of Earth! I, (magical
> name), am a follower of the Lord and
> Lady.

Return to the altar. Take the perfumed oil and, with a
drop on the forefinger of your power hand, anoint
your forehead. Say:

> Let my mind be open to your truth.

Anoint your upper lip, say:

> Let my mouth be silent among the un-
> believers.

Anoint your heart, say:

> *Let my heart seek you always.*

Anoint the center of the palms of your hands, say:

> *Let my hands lift in praise of you.*

Anoint the tops of your feet, say:

> *Let my feet always walk your secret paths.*

Stand in silence to receive a blessing. Lay your piece of jewelry on the pentacle, saying:

> *This emblem shall I wear for all things magical.*
>
> *Bless this (name of jewelry), O Great Ones, that I may be blessed and protected in all ways.*

Place the wine chalice on the pentacle for a few moments, then lift it high, saying:

> *To the Old Gods! Merry meet and merry part and merry meet again.*

Drink the wine, saving some to be put outside for the little people.

> Now is a time for meditation.

Refer to the Sample Ritual in chapter 5 at this time for the standard closing or departure ritual, commencing where the Sample states "when everything is completed . . ."

SEASONAL RITUALS

Ancestor Night or Feast of the Dead

(October 31, or the first Full Moon of Scorpio. Also called Samhain and Halloween.)

Special Notes: This is the Time of the Thin Veil or communion with the dead, the ruling time of the Crone aspect of the Goddess.

Altar Supplies: incense; burner; chalice of water; salt; pentacle; dagger or sword; wand; 4 Element candles; cauldron; chalice of wine; plate of bread and salt. You will need extra candles (one white, one red, two black, one yellow, and one green) and holders for them. Arrange the white, red and black candles on the left side of the altar and the green, black and yellow candles on the right side.

With casting the circle as your basic starting point, perform the same ritual illustrated in the section of chapter 5 titled 'Sample Ritual,' inserting the following steps where the Sample states "proceed with your planned spellwork or ceremony":

Turn to the three candles on the left side of the altar, saying:

> *I light three candles for the Triple Goddess . . . the Great Lady of Three Aspects.* (Light the white.) *Glorious Maiden, Goddess of youth and new beginnings, dawn and the planted seed.* (Light the red.) *Great Mother, Goddess of magic and plenty, love and knowledge.* (Light the black.) *Dark*

> Crone, wise Goddess of the night, death
> and rebirth. I welcome the Goddess in all
> her forms.

Turn to the three candles on the right side of the
altar, saying:

> I light three candles for the Triple God
> . . . Great Lord of many faces. (Light the
> yellow.) Bright Sun King, God of success
> and plenty. (Light the green.) Horned God
> of the Woodlands, God of fertility and
> growth. (Light the black.) Dark Lord of the
> Underworld, God of protection and rest. I
> welcome the God in all his forms.

Raise your arms over the altar and say:

> This night is the Feast of the Dead, the
> night of the wheel-turning year that brings
> us to the Thin Veil. The gates between the
> worlds stand open this night. I honor my
> ancestors whose voices come to me on the
> whispering wind. All those who wish me
> well are welcomed within this circle.

Place the plate of bread and salt on the pentacle.
Say:

> This is Ancestor Night, the night strongest
> for communication with those gone into
> Emania, those who now dwell in the pres-
> ence of the Old Gods. The Veil has been lif-
> ted that I may know I am not forgotten. All
> those who wish me well are welcomed
> within this circle.

Lift the plate of bread and salt up over the altar. Say:

> I ask all who have gathered here to join me in this feast.

Dip a piece of the bread into the salt and eat it.

> May I always have good health, prosperity and happiness.

Set the plate aside and put the wine chalice on the pentacle for a moment. Take up the cup of wine and say:

> May I always be strong in body, mind and spirit. To the Old Gods! Merry meet and merry part and merry meet again.

Drink some of the wine. Save some of the wine, bread and salt to be placed outside later for the "little people" (see the chapter on Deities for more information on the fairies and this offering). Replace the wine chalice on the altar.

Turn back to the Goddess candles. Say:

> The year wheel has turned, the harvest has come again. I have sown many thought-seeds since last Samhain. Let the good be harvested; let those that would hinder or harm me be cast aside. The Triple Goddess has covered me with her gentle hands, guided my steps, heard my desires. For this I give her honor and love.

Turn to the God candles. Say:

> The year wheel has turned, the harvest has come again. Once more I stand before

> *the Thin Veil, before the gates that divide the worlds. The Triple God has protected me with his sword, guided my steps, heard my desires. For this I give him honor and love.*

Tap the pentacle gently with your wand, saying:

> *Give me clear knowledge of the path I must follow. Hear my desires, O Great Ones! Guide and protect me. Lead me to greater knowledge and fulfillment.*

Stand in silence while you ask what you need of the Gods. Also listen for spirit guidance that may come from those in Emania. When finished, say:

> *All love and honor to the Great Lady and her Lord. Blessed be!*

Now is a time for divination, meditation, or spellwork. The spellwork should be to begin new projects and end old attachments or projects.

Refer to the Sample Ritual in chapter 5 at this time for the standard closing or departure ritual, commencing where the Sample states "when everything is completed . . ."

Winter Solstice

(About December 21. Called Alban Arthuan by the Druids. Also called Yule.)

Special Notes: Time of the Goddess of the Cold Darkness and the birth of the Divine Child, the reborn Sun god. A time of rebirth and the turning of the earth force tides.

Altar Supplies: incense; burner; chalice of water; salt; pentacle; dagger or sword; 4 Element candles; cauldron; chalice of wine; bell. Green candle in the cauldron with a red, a white, and a black candle arranged around it.

With casting the circle as your basic starting point, perform the same ritual illustrated in the section of chapter 5 titled 'Sample Ritual,' inserting the following steps where the Sample states "proceed with your planned spellwork or ceremony":

Ring the bell three times. Say:

> *This is Winter Solstice, the longest night of the year. Darkness reigns triumphant, yet gives way and changes into light. The Sun King has gone into Emania. Yet, within the sacred cauldron of rebirth he is once more transformed into the newborn Divine Child of Light.*

Put a little more incense on the coals.

> *All is cold, and I await the coming of dawn. As the Sun rises, the Triple Goddess once more gives birth to the Divine Child.*

In silence and wonder I stand before the sacred cauldron of rebirth, knowing that one day I too must pass through the cauldron and be reborn. For this I now give honor to the Triple Goddess.

Light the white candle near the cauldron.

White is for the Maiden. May you plant your seeds of joy and new beginnings within my life.

Light the red candle near the cauldron.

Red is for the Mother. May you grant me gifts of creative ideas and the strength to bring them to completion.

Light the black candle near the cauldron.

Black is for the Crone, the Wise One. May you give me wisdom to understand the magical mysteries.

Light the green candle inside the cauldron.

Green is for the newborn Lord of the Forests, the Divine Sun Child who comes once more into the world. I welcome you, child and consort of the Goddess.

Take the bell and go to the east. Ring the bell once.

Rejoice, O Powers of Air! Welcome the Divine Child.

Go to the south and ring the bell once.

Rejoice, O Powers of Fire! Welcome the Divine Child.

Go to the west and ring the bell once.

> *Rejoice, O Powers of Water! Welcome the*
> *Divine Child.*

Go to the north and ring the bell once.

> *Rejoice, O Powers of Earth! Welcome the*
> *Divine Child.*

Go back to the altar and stand facing east. Ring the bell three times.

> *Hail, O God of the woodlands and new*
> *life! I give you honor and ask your blessing.*

Stand in silence to receive the blessing. Ring the bell again three times.

> *Hail, Triple Goddess, bringer of light out*
> *of darkness and new life out of the cauldron*
> *of rebirth. I give you honor and ask your*
> *blessing.*

Again stand in silence to receive the blessing. Place the wine chalice on the pentacle for a few moments, then lift it high, saying:

> *To the Old Gods! Merry meet and merry*
> *part and merry meet again.*

Drink the wine, saving some to be put outside for the little people.

Refer to the Sample Ritual in chapter 5 at this time for the standard closing or departure ritual, commencing where the Sample states "when everything is completed . . . "

Imbolc

(February 1, or the first Full Moon of Aquarius.
Also called Brigantia, Imbolg and Candlemas.)

Special Notes: First stirrings of Mother Earth;
spring cleaning; time of cleansing and purification;
preparation for growth and renewal. A festival of the
Triple Goddess Brigit, whose breath gave life to the
dead.

Altar Supplies: incense; burner; chalice of water;
salt; pentacle; dagger or sword; 4 Element candles;
cauldron; chalice of wine; wand. White candle on left
of cauldron, green candle on right.

With casting the circle as your basic starting
point, perform the same ritual illustrated in the section of chapter 5 titled 'Sample Ritual,' inserting the
following steps where the Sample states "proceed
with your planned spellwork or ceremony":

Add a little more incense to the burner, then say:

*Mother Earth stirs from her long slumber.
The fields and forests hear her whisper to
awake. The creatures of her realms answer
her summons. Everything waits in antici-
pation for spring.*

Tap the altar three times gently with the wand.

*This is the festival of the Maiden who
gives to all the breath of life. This is a time
of waxing light and receding darkness.
This is the season of purification, a renewing of life. At this time and in this*

> place between the worlds, I come into the
> presence of the Lord and Lady that I may
> gain wise and truthful counsel.

(Time of silence while you ask the God and Goddess
for inspiration and guidance for the future.)

Tap the altar again gently three times with the wand.

> O Ancient Ones, I know my life-path is
> within your keeping. Only with your help
> and guidance can I hope to avoid any pit-
> falls and reach my destination safely.

Light the white candle on the left of the cauldron.

> I salute the glorious Maiden, preparer of
> new life out of darkness. This is her season
> of the year-wheel when she spreads her
> blessings over the land.

Light the green candle on the right of the cauldron.

> Behold, the Lord of the Forests caresses
> the dreaming Earth. As there is a renewal
> within the plants and animals, so should
> there be renewal in my life also.

Place the wine chalice on the pentacle for a few moments, then lift it high, saying:

> Make my life fertile with insight, good
> health, prosperity and magical power.
> Honor to the Old Gods! Merry meet and
> merry part and merry meet again.

Drink the wine, saving some to be put outside for the
little people.

Refer to the Sample Ritual in chapter 5 at this

time for the standard closing or departure ritual, commencing where the Sample states "when everything is completed . . ."

Spring Equinox

(About March 21. Called Alban Eiler by the Druids. Roughly corresponds to the Christian Easter.)

Special Notes: Balance of light and dark. Sowing time in the north; earth cycle of plant and animal fertility, spell producing, new beginnings.

Altar Supplies: incense; burner; chalice of water; salt; pentacle; dagger or sword; 4 Element candles; cauldron with red candle; chalice of wine; wand; dish for burning; paper and pen; bell. Colored eggs and spring flowers for decorations.

With casting the circle as your basic starting point, perform the same ritual illustrated in the section of chapter 5 titled 'Sample Ritual,' inserting the following steps where the Sample states "proceed with your planned spellwork or ceremony":

Take up your wand and raise your arms in greeting again and say:

> Behold, the Lord and Lady of life and the giver of life. Without her Lord, the Goddess is barren. Without his Lady, the God has no life. Each is needful of the other for completion and power, as Sun to Earth, the spear to the cauldron, spirit to flesh, man to woman.

Light the candle in the cauldron. Rap the cauldron lightly with the wand, say:

> O Great Goddess, be with me now in your aspect of the Maiden, the fair one

who brings joy and new life.

Ring the bell once and say:

> *O Great God of renewal, be with me now in your aspect of the Lord of the Forests, the Horned God who brings warmth and love.*

Rap the cauldron once more with the wand.

> *May the strength of the old enter into the new. Great Lord and Lady, make all things strong and giving of new life. Blessed be.*

Put a little incense on the coals and carry the burner again around the circle clockwise. Put the burner back on the alter and raise your arms, saying:

> *Awake! All creatures in the realm of Earth, awake! Greet the Maiden and her Lover, who herald the coming of spring.*

Touch the parchment paper with the dagger, saying:

> *Now I cast behind me the darkness of Winter and the past. I look only to that which lies ahead. This is the time for me to plant seeds in the physical, mental and spiritual.*

Write on the paper your desires for the coming year. Write only one desire on each paper. Fold the papers and hold them up over the altar in offering to the Old Gods.

> *This is a joyous time, a time for planting. With joy and trust, I place these requests in the hands of the Goddess and her Lord.*

Light the papers one by one from the candle in the cauldron and drop them into the dish for burning.

> *These thought-seeds do I willingly place into the hands of the Lady and her Lord, that these desires and dreams may manifest and become reality. Blessed be the Old Gods!*

Place the wine chalice on the pentacle for a few moments, then lift it high, saying:

> *Honor to the Old Gods! Merry meet and merry part and merry meet again.*

Drink the wine, saving some to be put outside for the little people.

Refer to the Sample Ritual in chapter 5 at this time for the standard closing or departure ritual, commencing where the Sample states "when everything is completed . . ."

Beltane

(May 1, or the first Full Moon of Taurus. Also called Lady Day and May Day.)

Special Notes: Time of the Horned God and the Lady of the Greenwood; honor of the house guardian.

Altar Supplies: incense; burner; chalice of water; salt; pentacle; dagger or sword; 4 Element candles; chalice of wine; wand. Somewhere within the circle area, the house guardian or his symbol, in whatever form you have chosen; perfumed oil.

With casting the circle as your basic starting point, perform the same ritual illustrated in the section of chapter 5 titled 'Sample Ritual,' inserting the following steps where the Sample states "proceed with your planned spellwork or ceremony":

Raise your wand in greeting, saying:

> *I give greetings to the Goddess of things wild, of trees, of skies and of waters. I do call upon you, lovely Lady, to be here with me.*

Dance or at least march around the altar, beginning in the east, and moving clockwise. Pause to salute each Elemental quarter with raised arms. Move back to the altar when finished.

> *Blessed be the words of the Lady of May and the laughing Lord of the Greenwood. Let now thy great light come into me. I am a cup to be filled, that I may do what is needful. Blessed ever be the Lord and Lady!*

Stand before the house guardian or symbol.

> *Lovely Lady, great Lord, I present to you*
> *the guardian of this house, the special spirit*
> *I have invited into my home as protector*
> *and helper. I honor this spirit in this sym-*
> *bol of its being. Great Ones, bless this*
> *guardian of this house. And to your blessings,*
> *I add my thanks. Blessed be.*

The guardian symbol or statue is lightly anointed with perfumed oil. If the symbol is such that it cannot be oiled, at least swing the smoking incense burner around it.

Place the wine chalice on the pentacle for a few moments, then lift it high, saying:

> *Honor to the Old Gods! Merry meet and*
> *merry part and merry meet again.*

Drink the wine, saving some to be put outside for the little people.

Refer to the Sample Ritual in chapter 5 at this time for the standard closing or departure ritual, commencing where the Sample states "when everything is completed . . ."

Summer Solstice

(About June 22. Called Alban Heruin by the Druids.)

Special Notes: Rededication to the Great Goddess and Great God. The time when the Sun casts three rays to light the world.

Altar Supplies: incense; burner; chalice of water; salt; pentacle; dagger or sword; 4 Element candles; chalice of wine; wand. A red candle (set to the right of the cauldron); a cup of fresh water set in the cauldron with a green or blue candle on the left.

With casting the circle as your basic starting point, perform the same ritual illustrated in the section of chapter 5 titled 'Sample Ritual,' inserting the following steps where the Sample states "proceed with your planned spellwork or ceremony":

Light the green candle to the left of the cauldron, say:

> *Green forest Mother, bless this water, I do ask. Great One of the stars, spinner of fates, I give honor to you, and call upon you in your ancient names, known and unknown.*

Light the red candle to the right of the cauldron, say:

> *Mighty Sun God, god of fertility and plenty, be here with me now, I do ask. I give honor to you, and call upon you in your ancient names, known and unknown.*

Raise your arms over the cauldron, say:

> This is the sacred cauldron of the Triple
> Goddess. The touch of its consecrated water
> blesses and renews, even as the rays of the
> Sun nourish and bless all life.

Pass your hands and arms between the two candles,
making wishes as you do so. Or set the candles on the
floor and carefully, slowly walk between them.

Dip the forefinger of your power hand into the cauldron
water and trace a pentagram on your forehead. Kneel
before the altar to rededicate your life to the Old
Gods. Say:

> I will serve the Great Goddess and give
> reverence to the Great God. I am a pagan,
> a stone of the ancient circle, standing firmly
> balanced upon the Earth, yet open to the
> winds of the heavens, and enduring through
> time. May the Old Gods witness my words!

Place the wine chalice on the pentacle for a few
moments then lift it high, saying:

> Honor to the Old Gods! Merry meet and
> merry part and merry meet again.

Drink the wine, saving some to be put outside for the
little people.

Refer to the Sample Ritual in chapter 5 at this time for
the standard closing or departure ritual, commencing
where the Sample states "when everything is completed . . . "

Lughnassadh

(August 1, or the first Full Moon of Leo. Also called Lunasa.)

Special Notes: The turning point in Mother Earth's year; a harvest festival in the northern lands. The waning God and the waxing Goddess. Spellwork for good fortune and abundance is especially appropriate.

Altar Supplies: incense; burner; chalice of water; salt; pentacle; dagger or sword; 4 Element candles; chalice of wine; wand; plate of bread. Cauldron with an orange or yellow candle in it. Fall flowers, ivy and leaves for decoration.

With casting the circle as your basic starting point, perform the same ritual illustrated in the section of chapter 5 titled 'Sample Ritual,' inserting the following steps where the Sample states "proceed with your planned spellwork or ceremony":

Light the cauldron candle, say:

> O Ancient Gods of the Celts, I do ask your
> presence here. For this is a time that is not
> a time, in a place that is not a place, on a
> day that is not a day, and I await you.

Set the plate of bread on the pentacle. Stand still and breathe deeply for a few moments. Concentrate upon the cleansing power of the breath and air. When you feel ready, say:

> I have purified myself by breathing in

> the life force of the universe and expelling
> all evil from me.

Lift the plate of bread high, then set it back on the altar. Say:

> I know that every seed, every grain is a
> record of ancient times, and a promise to
> all of what shall be. This bread represents
> life eternal through the cauldron of the
> Triple Goddess.

Eat a piece of bread. Put the chalice of wine on the pentacle. Hold high the wine chalice, then set it back on the altar. Say:

> As the grape undergoes change to become
> wine, so by the sacred cauldron of life
> shall I undergo change. And as this wine
> can give man enchantment of the divine
> or sink him into the lower realms, so I do
> realize that all humans rise or fall accord-
> ing to their strength and will.

Drink some of the wine. Say:

> As in the bread and wine, so it is with me.
> Within all forms is locked a record of the
> past and a promise of the future. I ask that
> you lay your blessings upon me, Ancient
> Ones, that this season of waning light and
> increasing darkness may not be heavy. So
> mote it be.

Refer to the Sample Ritual in chapter 5 at this time for the standard closing or departure ritual, commencing where the Sample states "when everything is completed . . ."

Autumn Equinox

(About September 21. Called Alban Elved by the Druids.)

Special Notes: Balance of light and dark. Time of rest after labor, completion of the harvest, thanksgiving. A good time for meditations on reincarnations in preparation for Ancestor Night or Halloween.

Altar Supplies: incense; burner; chalice of water; salt; pentacle; dagger or sword; 4 Element candles; chalice of wine; wand; autumn-colored ribbons tied on the dagger. Autumn leaves for decoration. Three candles (white, red, black) set around the cauldron. Ivy in the cauldron.

With casting the circle as your basic starting point, perform the same ritual illustrated in the section of chapter 5 titled 'Sample Ritual,' inserting the following steps where the Sample states "proceed with your planned spellwork or ceremony.

Light the three candles around the cauldron. Say:

> *I call upon the blessed Lady, queen of the harvest, giver of life and plenty since before time began. Bestow upon me your joy and beauty, power and prosperity, I do ask.*

Salute the ivy-filled cauldron with your dagger or sword. Say:

> *I call upon the Lord of the harvest, sacred King, giver of riches and protection since before time began. Bestow upon me your strength and laughter, power and prosperity, I do ask.*

Take the ribbon-tied dagger in your power hand, the wine chalice in the other. Say:

> *Always has life fulfilled its cycle and led to life anew in the eternal chain of the living. In honor of the Old Gods, I mark the fullness of my life and the harvest of this year's lessons.*

Walk three times clockwise around the circle, beginning in the east. Chant:

> *The year-wheel turns, and bounty comes.*

Move back to the altar and lay aside the dagger. Set the wine chalice briefly on the pentacle. As you make the following toasts, raise the chalice high each time before taking a sip.

> *To the good seasons that have gone and the good ones yet to come. Blessed be.*
>
> *To the Goddess! May she bring peace and fulfillment to all her children. Blessed be.*
>
> *To the God! May he protect his followers and bring me prosperity and happiness. Merry meet and merry part and merry meet again! Blessed be.*

Refer to the Sample Ritual in chapter 5 at this time for the standard closing or departure ritual, commencing where the Sample states "when everything is completed . . ."

8 Introduction to the Celts

History

The Celts are commonly thought of as the ancient Irish. In fact, their civilization covered a much larger area than Ireland. The Celts first appeared in history as they came out of the East in waves of migrants in the 9th century BC. They spread into Gaul, the Iberian Peninsula, north Italy, the Balkans, Asia Minor, Britain, Scotland, Wales and Ireland. By the 5th century BC, they were sacking towns in Italy, France, Germany and Switzerland, areas where they settled for a time. At their height of power their territory stretched from the British Isles to Turkey, but they finally fell to the Romans and Germanic tribes.

Although they were not all of the same ethnic stock, they spoke dialects of the same language. They were among the greatest technologists of the ancient world: skilled metalworkers, builders of roads and chariots, experts in agriculture and animal husbandry. They were also warriors of unparalleled courage and ferocity, feared even by the tough Roman legions.

They laid the foundation of western European civilization.

The Celts were brilliant, flamboyant, fearless and dynamic people, but also given to drunkenness and boasting. Although they were poorly organized as tribes, they were first and foremost warriors, often hiring themselves out as mercenaries to any who could afford their high price.

The women, who were held in high regard, were as good warriors as their men. Any Celtic woman with her temper aroused was a dangerous force to be reckoned with. In early Celtic history, it was not unusual for women to fight alongside their men.

By the 1st century BC, the Romans began encroaching on Celtic territory, finally conquering most of their land, with the exception of Scotland and Ireland. Even after this, there were sporadic uprisings; the one led by Queen Boadicia in Britain around 61 AD nearly wiped out the Roman legions in that country. The Celtic beliefs were not destroyed until the Christians began to make inroads.

From about 600 B.C. the Celtic peoples had an alphabet, called the Ogham (pronounced owam). The Ogham alphabet was sacred and probably used only for special recordings. The Druids knew and used the Greek alphabet for ordinary messages, although the later Bards of Wales continued to use Ogham to write down what they remembered of Druidic tradition. Eventually the Christian church forcibly replaced Ogham with the Latin alphabet. With the knowledge of three alphabets it is likely that at some point, at least in Ireland, the Celts began to record their history and legends.

Although it is said that the Celts kept no written

records, St. Patrick personally burned almost 180 Irish books written in the Celtic language. This set an example for Christian zealots who destroyed every piece of Druidic literature they could find. Christian monk-scribes, for some unknown reason, felt compelled to record the Celtic myths, even while the missionaries determinedly stamped out belief in the ancient gods and goddesses.

Religion

The Celts were religious to a high degree. The ethical teaching of the Druids can be summed up as: worship the gods, do no evil, be strong and courageous. They believed in reincarnation and transmigration (the transfer of a human soul into an animal or plant form). Their pantheon held a great number of female deities of primary importance—mother goddesses, war goddesses, tutelary goddesses. They also had the concept of the triune god, three aspects of a single deity. They did not believe in punishment by the gods after death.

The Druids were the Celtic priesthood. In the beginning, until the Romans and other patrilineal religions forced change, the Celts had similar organizations of women. There are some clues in historical writings to suggest that these women were called Dryads and lived in sacred groves. It is very probable that they were in existence before the Druids, being part of the very old goddess religions.

In *The Underside of History*, Elise Boulding states that some Druidesses, such as one group who served the goddess Brigit, were secluded orders, never having contact with men. Other priestesses were married and periodically left their duties for time with their families. A third group, more like Grove servants, lived normal lives with families. It is also possible that witchcraft or the Wiccan may have evolved when the Druids were driven underground.

The Druids and priestesses were the healers, judges, astronomers, teachers, oracles and religious leaders of the Celtic clans.

The head Druid was the Arch Druid, and his female counterpart likely called the High Priestess of the Grove. Special schools were available for would-be initiates of either sex. It was no easy matter to become part of this elite religious community. According to Julius Caesar's *Gallic War*, about 20 years of study were required, slowly working through the exacting levels of the orders. All formal education consisted of teacher recitation and pupil memorization.

The Druids had three divisions within their order: the Bards (poets), who wore blue robes; the Ovates (prophets, philosophers), who wore green; and the Druid priests, who wore white. Their tonsure was later copied by Christian monks.

In Ireland, the Ovates and Bards were known collectively as the *Filid*. The Druids were the philosophers, judges and advisors to tribal leaders. The Ovates compiled knowledge of all kinds. The Bards praised, ridiculed, and taught through the use of music and poetry.

This entire teaching survived in Ireland as the Brehon Law. They sang Veda-like hymns, sacrificed with special plants and occasionally animals or humans, and used sacred fires. However, the practice of human sacrifice does not appear to have been very common in Ireland and Britain.

The higher priests sometimes wore masks or crowns with horns during certain fertility ceremonies. The horns were in honor of the Celtic god Cernunnos (in Britain) or the Horned One, and symbolized the male virility needed for fertility. The Horned God was the opener of the Gates of Life and Death, the masculine, active side of Nature, god of the Underworld. This is the oldest form of the god that this world has.

The female counterpart of Cernunnos was the naked White Moon Goddess. This oldest Earth goddess is the Primal Mother, who creates everything; the passive, feminine side of Nature.

The Druids as a whole were extremely powerful. They could easily pass from one warring tribe to another, or go into any region they chose. In fact, they were so powerful and well trained that in later periods they were prohibited from carrying or using any physical weapons. It is said that by words alone they could conquer enemies and cause all kinds of hardship. They taught a very special relationship with Nature.

The Ogham alphabet of the Celts, in use until about 700 A.D., was primarily a sacred teaching. Each letter represented a wealth of ideas and thoughts. Druidic initiates could also use it as a secret sign language by stroking the nose, legs or any straight object. By this means, a silent message could be passed to another initiate while talking to a third person about something quite ordinary and innocent. This ability made the Druids so formidable that eventually use of this sign language was outlawed.

In Celtic belief, the areas of being or existence were represented by three concentric circles. Abred, the innermost, is where life springs from Annwn; it is the arena where the human soul must perfect itself. The next circle out is Gwynedd (purity) where the life spark finally triumphs over evil and can rest forever from reincarnation. The outermost is called Ceugant (infinity); it is the dwelling place of the ultimate power of creation. This idea of a triune universe is represented by the three-pointed knot in Celtic artwork.

Druidic lore taught that a human soul had to pass through many incarnations in Abred, the Circle of Necessity, before it could reach Gwynedd, the Circle of Blessedness. Abred is earthly life; once the lessons are learned, the soul does not return. The Druids taught that three things could hinder progress: ego or pride, lies, and unnecessary cruelty.

The priestesses, or Druidesses, were highly revered among the Celts, as they knew the power of words, stones and herbs. Priestesses sang the dying to sleep, did enchantments, prophecies, charms, birthing and healing. A cauldron, bowl, spring or pool was one of the central features of a Grove and was probably used for scrying. Red-haired women were sacred to the war goddesses, as red was the color of life blood and menstrual blood.

Blacksmiths ranked high in the social order because they were trained in special magic. They trained for a year and a day on Scath's Island (possibly Skye), learning metal magic and the martial arts. They could also heal, prophesy and make weapons filled with magical powers. Blacksmiths were dedicated to the goddess Scathach or Scota. Most pagan cultures held blacksmiths in awe because of their ability to create using the four Elements of Earth, Air, Fire, and Water. My grandmother told me that as a young girl she and others had to take leave of the smithy at a certain point in the operation. Curious, she sneaked back to watch the smith whisper certain "things" over the metal, but she could not hear what he was saying.

Certain hills, lakes, caves, springs, wells, monoliths, clearings within groves, and ancient stone circles were sacred worship places because of their connection with ley lines and significant happenings in the past. Wells, springs, fountains and ponds were considered female symbols, water-passages to the underground womb of the Great Mother. But the Druids preferred oak groves and forests. They even built some large rectangular or horseshoe-shaped wooden buildings as temples. The horseshoe shape symbolized the womb of the Great Mother, the Great Gate of the Goddess, or knowledge gained through ritualistic rebirth. Roughly carved tree trunk images or stones ornamented with metal plates occasionally represented devotion to the deity. Each Celtic temple had its sacred cauldron, a symbol of the Great Mother's cosmic womb of reincarnation.

Most celebrations were held at night as the Celtic day began at midnight; they reckoned time by nights rather than days. Their calendar was based on the

Moon and had thirteen months. The bright half of each month was made up of the fifteen days of the waxing Moon, while the dark half was the fifteen days of the waning Moon. During the waxing Moon, the priests/priestesses did positive magic; during the waning Moon, binding or dark magic.

The months of a Celtic year were named after trees, which corresponded to letters of the Ogham alphabet. They also knew and used the solar year, based on the time it takes the Sun to circle the Earth and return to the same place. They adjusted their lunar year to the solar year by inserting an extra 30-day month alternately at two-and-a-half and three-year intervals.

The Druids understood and used the Greek Meton cycle. This consists of 235 lunar months, the time it takes the Sun and Moon to travel back to the same positions of a previous 19-year cycle.

A Druidic Cycle was completed in six Lustres or thirty years, based on a solar year. A Lustre was a cycle of five years. A period of 630 years was called a Druidic Era. All eras were dated from the Second Battle of Mag Tuireadh in Ireland, when the Tuatha De Danann defeated the Fomorians.

In the Celtic areas of Britain and Ireland, a new year began after Samhain (Halloween). Each year was divided into a dark and a light half, with Samhain beginning the dark half and Beltane (May Day) beginning the light.

The Celts always performed certain movements in the direction of the Sun (clockwise) during rituals. They considered it very unlucky to go widdershins (counterclockwise), except for specific rituals. This moving in the Sun's direction extended to the passing around of drinking horns at feasts.

Religious holidays centered on the solstices, equinoxes and Moon phases. Four Fire Festivals (the solstices and the equinoxes) were the highlights of a Celtic farming year. They represented plowing, sowing, growing and harvest.

There is also evidence that they observed Imbolc (February), Beltane (May), Lughnassadh (August), and Samhain (November). Special ceremonies were held at Samhain (Halloween) when, they believed, the veil between the worlds was thinnest and the dead could be contacted for help and knowledge.

Mai or Maj (May) was a month of sexual freedom in honor of the Great Mother and the Horned God of the woodlands. Trial marriages of a year and a day could be contracted at this time; if this proved unworkable, partners simply went their separate ways at the end of that time. Virginity was not prized among the Celts since a family was important to them. Sexual activity was encouraged, especially at Beltane; children conceived at this time were considered very lucky. Green, worn at this time to honor the Earth Mother, was later called unlucky by the Christians in hopes that the people, especially women, would discontinue following the old sexually promiscuous ways.

Green was and is also the color of the fairies or little people. It was considered an unlucky color to wear unless you were on good terms with the fairies in their *sidhs* (shees). The *sidhs* were the ancient burial mounds seen around the countryside. In Scotland the fairy host was called the *Sluagh Sidhe*. The fairy world later was considered the world of souls of the pagan dead, of Nature spirits and the Celtic gods. Fairy rings of dark grass or mushrooms are still considered places full of magic and power.

The terrifying Celtic gods were only personifications of the destroying natural forces in this world. It is known to all psychics that certain Nature spirits haunt lonely places; these are neither good nor evil, simply different. The Celtic peoples knew this and took an open attitude towards the fairies or little people, calling them the Good Neighbors or the People of Peace, with the idea that it is better to be on friendly terms with unpredictable elements than to court trouble.

In Britain, Glastonbury Tor is supposed to be the haunt of Gwynn ap Nudd, king of the fairies and the ancient Celtic god of the dead. Local tradition at Glastonbury says that there is a secret cave shrine inside the Tor. A maze-like processional path can clearly be seen up the sides of the hill, and the Chalice Well at its foot is credited with supernormal healing powers.

Avalon is often identified with the present Glastonbury. The name Avalon means 'Place of Apples'. Apples have been grown in Britain for a very long time. The tree itself was sacred to the Celts because of its fruit. When an apple is cut crosswise, a pentagram or 5-point star is visible. The pentagram was a symbol of the Welsh Sow Goddess Cerridwen, otherwise known as the Morrigu, the underworld goddess of death and regeneration. The star was a reminder that everyone journeyed to the land of death. In view of this, it is thought that the custom of bobbing for apples at Halloween may have begun as a symbolic cheating of the Death Goddess. In an attempt to attract new pagan converts however, the Christians adopted both the pentagram, as a symbol of Christ's five wounds, and Cerridwen's sacred cauldron, as the Holy Grail.

Feasting and games, particularly warrior skills, were part of the four seasonal holidays: Imbolc, Beltane, Lughnassadh, and Samhain. Pork, because it was the chief food of the Tuatha De Danann, was served at these festivals, especially at Samhain. Mead, special breads and other foods were also served.

Oak and mistletoe were two of the most sacred plants. Sexual rites were part of the ancient ceremonies of the oak and mistletoe gods. Although no details have been preserved, we can assume, by comparison to similar ancient rites, that a priest and priestess physically and symbolically copulated. This sexual combining represented the power of the Sky God (lightning which strikes the oak) fertilizing the Mother Goddess. Such a sexual religious act is known as sympathetic magic. The same sexual sympathetic magic was practiced in the newly plowed fields to entice crop fertility.

Holly was sacred to the Morrigu. Its red berries were symbolic of menstrual blood, while the white berries of the mistletoe signified semen.

Among the birds, wrens were thought to be the most prophetic, possibly because it was believed that the Celtic "fays" or fairies could change themselves into birds.

Dress & Ornamentation

The Celts actually were a very clean people, using soap long before the Romans did. The Celtic men and women of Britain sometimes wore swirling blue tattoos or paintings on their bodies. All Celts played lyres and harps, loved song, music and recitation of legends and epic adventures. They used metal or ornamented natural horns for drinking.

Children took the mother's name, and daughters inherited her possessions. Virginity was not valued; twice the dowry was given for a woman previously married or with children. Abortion and choice or change of mate was a woman's right.

Both sexes loved jewelry: brooches decorated with gold filigree, cuttlefish shell, garnets, lapis, and other stones; buckles of gold filigree and stones; pins and linked pins with animal-style decoration; necklaces of amber, granulation and chip carving. They wore torques, pendants, bracelets, pins and necklaces. The women sometimes sewed little bells on the fringed ends of their tunics. The elaborate intertwinings of their artwork was a guard against the evil eye or curses.

Celtic women painted their fingernails, reddened their cheeks with roan, darkened their eyebrows with berry juice. They wore their hair long and braided or piled up on the head. Their usual dress was a sleeved tunic tucked into a large, gathered, belted skirt or simply an ankle-length tunic with a belt.

Celtic men on the continental mainland wore trousers with a tunic, but in Britain and Ireland the men wore a thigh-length tunic and a cloak, the ever-present dagger or sword, and leather or fur footgear tied around the legs. Mustaches were common, and the hair shoulder-length. A horned helmet indicated a powerful warrior.

Clothing was usually wool dyed in bright colors of clear red, green, blue or yellow. Some of the natural plant dyes used were woad (Old Irish, glastum; Welsh, lliwur glas) for blue; acorns for brown shades; Queen

Anne's lace for a yellow-green. Various parts of the alder produced many shades: red from the bark, green from the flowers, brown from the twigs.

In the early cultures, both men and women had huge rectangular cloaks pinned at the right shoulder. These cloaks were generally woven in bright plaids, checks or stripes. Later, they wore large hooded capes reaching to the knees.

The Celts were an energetic people with a zest for life. They were strong psychics, in tune with the forces of Nature and the power of the human mind. Ordinary objects were decorated with highly spiritual, symbolic designs, a visual reminder that their beliefs went beyond lip-service. What we now call magic was an integral part of their belief system. And the basics of that system are still as usable today as they were then.

9 Myths and Deities

Religion and reverence of the gods was a firm part of everyday Celtic life, as was the belief in magic. Study of Celtic mythologies is the best way to understand the basic powers behind each deity. It would be impossible to include here every myth of Ireland, Scotland, Wales and Britain. There are several good books listed in the bibliography for those who wish to study the mythologies in depth. I have chosen interesting stories, stories that explain powers and magic. The recurring theme in most of the stories is that it was possible for humankind to gain the knowledge and power needed to reproduce the magic exhibited by the deities.

These tales are contained in the only manuscripts known to exist today. The Irish myths come from the Books of Leinster, the Dun Cow, Ballymate, and the Yellow Book of Lecan. The oldest of the Welsh documents is the Black Book of Caermarthen (12th century). This, along with the Book of Aneurin (late 13th century) and the Book of Taliesin (14th century), is known as the Four Ancient Books of Wales. Welsh legends are readily accessible today in the Mabinogion, compiled from tales in the White Book of Rhydderch (transcribed 1300-25), the Red Book of Hergest (1375-1425) and the Hanes of Taliesin (16th century).

There are a variety of spellings for the names of the Celtic gods and goddesses. In the lists that follow, I have given the many different spellings, but to avoid confusion, have used the most common ones in the adventure myths. The pronunciations that follow some of the names are approximations only, as it is very difficult to translate the Celt and Welsh tongues.

Major Celtic Myths

The tribe of the Fomorians was on the scene long before any other races came to Ireland. However, the Fomors lived mainly in the sea. The first outside race to invade Ireland was the race of Partholon; very little is known of them. After 300 years of struggle against the Fomors, the race of Partholon died of an epidemic.

Next came the race of Nemed who also suffered from an epidemic. This time, however, some of them survived, only to be oppressed by the cruel Fomors. The Fomorian kings Morc, son of Dela, and Conann, son of Febar, built a glass tower on their stronghold of Tory Island. From there they taxed the Nemedians with a terrible price. Two-thirds of the children born each year had to be delivered on Samhain to the Fomors. During the ensuing war over this tax, all of the race of Nemed was slain.

Later came colonizers from Spain or Greece called the Fir Bolgs. They were actually three tribes: men of Domnu, men of Gaillion, and men of Bolg.

They intermarried with the Fomors and became their allies. The new settlers divided Ireland into five provinces which met at Balor's Hill, later called the Hill of Uisnech in West Meath. These people practiced strange magical rites in their hillforts and continued to hold the country until the arrival of the Tuatha De Danann.

The Tuatha De Danann (children of the Goddess Danu) ensued in the invasion of Ireland. Some legends say they came from the sky, others say from far away islands. The four cities from which they originated were: Findias, Gorias, Murias, and Falias. They were skilled in poetry and magic. With them they brought four great treasures: Nuada's sword from Findias, Lugh's terrible spear from Gorias, the Dagda's cauldron from Murias, and the Stone of Fal (Lia Fail or Stone of Destiny) from Falias.

The Tuatha De Danann landed on Beltane (May 1), hidden by magic used by the Morrigu, Badb, and Macha. They met the armies of the Fir Bolg and the Fomors on the Plain of the Sea near Leinster where they bargained for peace and the division of Ireland. But the Fir Bolg king Eochaid refused.

On Summer Solstice, the armies met near the present village of Cong near the pass of Benlevi. For four days groups of single combatants fought. The Tuathan king Nuada lost his hand in battle with the Fir Bolg champion Sreng. King Eochaid was killed, and the Fir Bolgs reduced to 300 men. In a peace gesture, the Tuatha De Danann offered them one-fifth of Ireland; the enemy chose Connaught.

Diancecht, physician of the Tuatha, made Nuada a marvelous silver hand that could move like a real one.

But Nuada had to step down, for no Tuatha king was allowed to have any disfigurement. In an attempt for permanent peace with the Fomors, the Tuatha council sent a message to Bress, son of King Elathan, to rule over them. Bress agreed and married Brigit, the daughter of the Dagda. At the same time Cian, son of Diancecht, married Ethniu, daughter of the Fomor Balor.

Bress promised to abdicate if his rule ever displeased the Tuatha, but he soon began to tax them into poverty. It wasn't long before Ogma had to gather firewood and the Dagda was reduced to building forts and cities for the Fomors. To add insult, Bress cut down on the food and fuel of the Tuatha.

By the time the Tuatha De Danann were suffering greatly, Nuada began to have trouble with his silver hand. An infection caused great pain to the deposed king. Diancecht's son Miach and daughter Airmid went to Nuada and by magic replaced the severed real hand, thus making the king whole again. For some reason, Diancecht killed his son for being better at magic than he was.

Meanwhile Bress was as stingy with hospitality as he was with his promises, a practice frowned upon by the Tuatha. When the chief Tuathan bard Cairpre, son of Ogma, visited him, he was treated rudely and given terrible food and quarters. As Cairpre left, he laid a magic satire on Bress which made the king break out in red blotches. The Tuatha De Danann insisted Bress abdicate.

Bress retreated under the sea to the Fomor kingdom where he complained to his father Elathan. The Fomor armies decided to run the Tuatha De Danann out of Ireland.

While Nuada was celebrating his return with a

great feast at the capital of Tara, a strange warrior came to the gates and demanded entrance. It was Lugh, son of Cian and Ethniu and grandson of Diancecht.

The porter refused him entrance, saying that no man without a skill could enter Tara. Lineage did not matter, the gatekeeper told him.

Lugh then listed his skills—carpenter, smith, professional warrior, harper, poet, sorcerer, physician, bronze worker, cup-bearer—but the man just sneered. The Tuatha De Danann had those already. So Lugh sent a message to Nuada, asking if he had a man among his people who could do all those skills.

The king still was not impressed and sent out his best fidhchell player as a challenge. (Fidhchell is a boardgame of Irish tradition.) Lugh won all the games. Nuada then admitted the young man and set him in the seat reserved for the sage, as Lugh was a sage in all skills.

Trouble with the Fomorians was getting worse. Nuada decided to give up his throne to Lugh for thirteen days of battle so that the powerful warrior could command the Tuathan armies against their enemies. Goibniu the smith promised to replace all swords and spears overnight, weapons with a guarantee that every throw would be accurate and deadly; Credne the bronze worker to make magic rivets for the spears, hilts for swords, and rims for shields. Luchtaine the carpenter promised to provide all spear shafts and shields, while the Dagda would crush the enemy with his gigantic club. Ogma laid plans to kill the Fomorian king and capture at least one-third of his army. Diancecht prepared to bring the dead back to life by putting them into a magic well or cauldron. Other deities,

Druids and sorcerers promised to hide the rivers and lakes and confuse the enemy with magical acts.

Preparations for the war took seven years. During this planning time, Lugh sent messengers all over Ireland to assemble the Tuatha. His father Cian, one messenger, was killed by the three sons of Tuirenn, son of Ogma, with whom his family had a dispute. Lugh found the body and knew who the murderers were. He demanded blood payment in the form of a long series of dangerous tasks for the three men, knowing they could not possibly survive. They died fulfilling the last task.

Just before the battle, while the Dagda was reconnoitering, he met the Morrigu, the war goddess, as she bathed in the river. In exchange for lying with her, she promised him victory in battle.

The two armies gathered on the eve of Samhain, and again engaged in a series of single combats. This time, however, the Tuatha De Danann were always healed by the next day and their swords and spears made new.

The Fomors became suspicious. They sent Ruadan, son of Bress and Brigit, to find out what was going on. Ruadan, while spying on Goibniu, decided the smith must be killed. He hurled a spear through Goibniu's body, but the great man pulled it out and mortally wounded the Fomorian. Diancecht and Airmid immediately plunged Goibniu into a healing well and cured him. In retaliation a group of Fomorians managed to fill the well with stones, destroying it forever.

The two armies at last squared off for the final battle. A council of the Tuatha, deciding that Lugh was too valuable to risk in the fighting, placed him at the rear. Lugh escaped his nine protectors and rushed to the front in his chariot. Ogma killed Indech, son of the goddess Domnu, and Balor slew Nuada and Macha.

Lugh challenged Balor of the Evil Eye, his grandfather, who was leading the enemy. When the Fomorians started to pull open Balor's eye, which could destroy everyone in his sight, Lugh drove the eye through Balor's head with a magic stone so that it looked back upon the Fomorians. It killed a whole rank of the enemy. Another version says that Lugh used his great spear to put out Balor's eye.

The Tuatha De Danann were victorious, driving the remaining Fomors back into the sea. The Morrigu and Badb went to the top of the high mountains to proclaim victory. But Badb prophesied the coming of the end of the gods. This prophecy was fulfilled when the mortal Gaelic Celts arrived, those called the Milesians.

In Aileach (Londonderry), three sons of Ogma, also the grandsons of the Dagda, ruled after Nuada's death. The first boatload of Milesians arrived and expressed a great interest in Ireland, which naturally upset the Tuatha De Danann. The Tuatha killed their leader Ith, but the other Milesians escaped to tell of the treachery. The other Milesian boats, commanded by the Druid Amergin, landed, and the newcomers marched on Tara. There were two great battles, filled with magic on both sides. Defeated, the Tuatha withdrew beneath the earth.

Even though they had retreated, the Tuatha still had power to hurt or help. The Dagda began destroying corn and milk until the Milesians made a peace treaty with the old gods. The basis of this treaty was that the Tuatha would receive homage and offerings from the Milesians.

Some of the Tuatha De Danann chose to go to an unknown island in the west, called "Land of the Young" (Tir-Nan-Og) or "Breasal's Island" (Hy-Breasil). Manannan mac Lir, the sea god, went with them but returned to visit Ireland from time to time.

Those Tuatha who stayed behind were given dwellings by the Dagda, their new king. He assigned each to a sidhe (a barrow or hillock). Each sidhe was the doorway to a beautiful underground realm. Thus, the Celtic gods became known as the Aes Sidhe (People of the Hills). Every god was a Fer-Sidhe (Man of the Hill), every goddess a Bean-Sidhe (Woman of the Hill).

Stories of the Milesian Celtic warriors list two classes of fighters. The first lived within the tribes, obeying the rules; Cu Chulainn was such a warrior. The second class was tribeless, obeying its own laws, and living in the borderlands between the real world and the supernatural. They lived and fought in groups known as Fianna Eirinn or Fenians.

Cu Chulainn was the grandson of the Dagda on his mother's side, while Lugh of the Long Hand was said to be his father. His mother, Dechtire, daughter of Maga (daughter of Angus mac Og) was the half-sister to King Conchobar.

King Conchobar ruled at Emain Macha. His warriors called themselves Champions of the Red Branch; his best warrior was Cu Chulainn (Culann's Hound). Cathbad the Druid prophesied Cu Chulainn's greatness when he was a small child. In later years, the warrior wanted to marry Emer, daughter of Forgall the Wily. In order to gain Forgall's permission, Cu Chulainn studied under the warrioress-goddess Scathach on her sacred island for a year and a day. On his return, his prospective father-in-law gave trouble. So Cu Chulainn abducted Emer from his castle and killed many of Forgall's men. After his marriage, Cu Chulainn had a son Conlaoch by Aoife, a woman of the sidhe.

Finn mac Cumhail, or Finn mac Coul, was the most famous of the Fianna. The tales of Finn and the Fianna were written in some of the very earliest of Irish manuscripts.

Cumhail was killed in battle by his enemy Goll mac Morna before Finn was born. To save the baby from death at enemy hands, Finn's mother sent him to Bodball a Druidess and Fiacal a woman-warrior. These women raised the boy in secret in the mountains of central Ireland. They taught Finn all the skills he would need to survive.

At last Finn was ready to go back into the Irish communities. For a time he served several kings, but upon discovering who he was, the kings sent him away. Everyone feared the sons of Morna, Cumhail's enemies. Finn wandered throughout Ireland, finally going to study with an old poet who lived by the river Boyne. After seven years Finn fulfilled a prophecy when he ate the salmon of knowledge.

Finn gathered 150 of the bravest Fianna and killed Goll mac Morna, his father's murderer. No one could equal Finn in daring, magic, poetry or wisdom. But there was a prophecy that Finn would die in Ireland during his 230th year. When he reached that age, Finn decided to leave the island, but his warriors persuaded him to stay with them in their homes.

The prophecy would not be denied. The first warrior to offer sanctuary was Fer-tai, son of mac Morna. Fer-li (Fer-tai's son) gathered fellow hot-heads and, first verbally, then physically, attacked Finn. Fer-li's mother stopped the fight in the hall, but Fer-li issued a personal challenge which Finn was honor-bound to accept.

The next morning the two groups met at a ford on the Boyne. All day the fighting raged. Ultimately Finn and the Fianna were outnumbered and fell. But, the legend continues, the Fianna did not die. The Otherworld People, sometimes called the fairies or the old gods (Tuatha), carried the warriors deep into their sidhe (shee) mounds, where they still lie asleep, horses and weapons beside them. If ever Ireland is in danger, trumpets will blow, and Finn and his Fianna will ride forth, armed for battle, to defend the land.

The British and Welsh legends of King Arthur and the Knights of the Round Table are a re-telling of the story of Finn and the Fianna. Excalibur, the sword drawn from the stone, is symbolic of sword-iron processed from ore and extracted by the magic smith. The war goddess the Morrigu became Arthur's sister, Morgan Le Fey. Merlin, or in Welsh Myrddin, was a combination of Druid Bard and priest who counseled the king. Many of the old Celtic deities appear in the Arthurian legends, thinly cloaked in Christian disguises.

That there was a connection between Wales and Ireland is shown by many of the similarities of deity names. The British mainland deities were divided into three families: children of Don, children of Lludd or Nudd, children of Llyr. The Goddess Don is the equivalent of Danu; Llyr equivalent to the sea God Manannan mac Lir; Lludd equivalent to Nuada.

Lludd's (or Nudd) son was Gwynn ap Nudd, the god of battle and the dead. Gwynn became known as the wild huntsman in Wales. He is still believed to ride the night skies with his pack of hounds. He was a rival with Gwyrthur ap Greidawl (Sun god) for Creiddylad or Creudylad, who was the daughter of the sea god Llyr.

Math, son of Mathonwy, was the god of money, treasure, giver of metals, wisdom. He handed on his knowledge and magical lore to his nephew and pupil Gwydion. Gwydion, son of Don, was the Druid of the mainland gods, master of illusion and fantasy, friend and helper of humankind. His brothers were Amaethon (god of agriculture) and Govannan (god of smithcraft and equivalent of Goibniu). His sister was Arianrhod; by her Gwydion had two sons Dylan (darkness) and Lleu (light). Dylan (Son of the Wave), also a sea god, was killed by his uncle Govannan.

Lleu Llaw Gyffes was the equivalent of Lugh Lamhfada in Ireland. Because of a curse by his mother, he could never have a real wife. So Gwydion and Math made a woman for Lleu out of flowers. This was Blodeuwedd, who later left Lleu and was changed into an owl for conspiring with Gronw Pebyr (god of darkness) to kill her husband.

The goddess Penardun (daughter of Don) was married to Llyr (the Sea), whose other wife was Iweridd (Ireland). Their son Manawyddan was identical to Manannan mac Lir. Llyr's children by Iweridd were a son Bran and a daughter Branwen.

Bran was a huge giant, the god of battle and the

patron of Bards, minstrels and musicians. His son Caradawc was called the Strong-armed.

Pwyll (Head of Annwn or the underworld) had a wife Rhiannon (daughter of Heveydd the Ancient) and a son Pryderi (Trouble). Pwyll and his family were hostile to the children of Don but friends of the children of Llyr. After Pwyll's disappearance for a year, Rhiannon married Manawyddan, who was the guardian of a magic cauldron of inspiration.

Pwyll, Prince of Dyfed (Pen Annwn) was a mortal man who became head of the underworld after a battle between Arawn (Silver-Tongue) and Havgan (Summer-White). Arawn lost and went to the upper world in search of a mortal ally. Pwyll was out hunting and saw a pack of hounds chasing a stag. The hounds were shining white with red ears. He ran them off and claimed the stag, only to have a horseman dressed in grey and carrying a hunting horn ride up. This was Arawn and the dogs were his. To atone for the discourtesy, Pwyll changed appearances with Arawn and went to the underworld. There he managed to kill Havgan. Then the two men returned to their own shapes and countries.

Bran, one of the Welsh deities, was the brother of Branwen and half-brother of Manawyddan. King Matholwch of Ireland came to Wales with thirteen ships to ask for Branwen in marriage. At the wedding were two other sons by Llyr's wife Penardun by another marriage: Nissyen (lover of peace) and Evnissyen or Efnisien (lover of strife), both giants like Bran.

Evnissyen felt slighted because he had not been consulted about the marriage. In spite, he mutilated and killed Matholwch's horses. Bran tried to smooth over the affair by replacing the animals with gold and silver.

Branwen sailed back to Ireland with Matholwch. But the king's relatives demanded that he take revenge on Branwen for the incident with the horses. She was banished to the kitchens and the dirtiest of work. After a year she had a son Gwern.

A long time went by before Branwen managed to get a message to her brother by fastening a letter to a bird's leg. The Welsh invaded Ireland to avenge the insult, leaving Bran's son Caradawc in charge while they were gone.

Bran, a giant, waded across the seas and forced the Irish to negotiate. The Irish agreed to turn the kingdom over to Branwen's son Gwern. At the crowning ceremonies, while the little boy was meeting Bran and his other relatives, Evnissyen grabbed him by the feet and threw him into a fire, killing him.

A great battle broke out. The Irish had an advantage, the cauldron of rebirth, a wedding gift from Bran to Matholwch. They lit a fire under it and threw in their dead warriors to revive them. Evnissyen decided he had better redeem himself or Bran would kill him when the battle was over. Evnissyen, also a giant, hid among the bodies in the cauldron of rebirth. Stretching himself out completely caused the cauldron to burst. This act of atonement cost Evnissyen his life.

The Welsh won the battle, but not without consequence. Only Branwen and a few men survived: Pryderi, Manawyddan, Gluneu son of Taran, Taliesin the Bard, Ynawc, Grudyen son of Muryel, and Heilyn son of Gwynn the Ancient.

Bran was mortally wounded when a poisoned

dart punctured his foot. He had ordered that, when he died, his head be cut off and buried on the White Mount in London with his face towards France. Branwen subsequently died of a broken heart.

Another Welsh legend tells of a young hero, Gwion Bach, who suddenly found himself at the bottom of Lake Bala in northern Wales. Here lived a giant Tegid and his wife Cerridwen, goddess of crops, poetry and great magic. The goddess owned a potent magic cauldron in which she planned to brew a special liquid.

For a year and a day Gwion Bach was made to stir the cauldron while Cerridwen gathered the necessary herbs and chanted incantations. At the end of that time, there were only three drops left. These flew out of the cauldron, burning Gwion's finger. Instinctively, the young man thrust his finger into his mouth and instantly knew the power of Cerridwen. He fled the lake in terror.

Furious, Cerridwen went after him. The two repeatedly changed forms, Gwion to escape, and Cerridwen in the attempt to capture him. At last Gwion spied a pile of wheat and, changing himself into a grain, fell down among the others. Cerridwen would not give up. She changed into a hen, scratched around until she found him, and promptly swallowed him. Upon returning to her own shape, she discovered she was pregnant. When Gwion was reborn, Cerridwen found she could not kill him, but instead cast him into the sea, leaving him to fate.

Elphin, son of a wealthy landowner, rescued the boy and called him Taliesin (radiant brow). Gwion Bach, now Taliesin, remembered all of the knowledge he had gained from Cerridwen's magic potion. He became a great Bard, magician and counselor of kings.

The Major Gods & Goddesses

The following list of Celtic deities gives a brief description of each and lists the magical powers connected with them. This list, along with the Quick References section in chapter 11, is for use in determining what powers to call upon when you are working magic.

ANGUS MAC OG/ANGUS OF THE BRUGH/ OENGUS OF THE BRUIG/ANGUS MAC OC (mak ohk): Ireland. "Young son." One of the Tuatha De Danann. He had a gold harp that made irresistibly sweet music. His kisses became birds carrying love messages. He had a brugh (fairy palace) on the banks of the Boyne. God of youth, love and beauty.

ANU (an-oo)/ ANANN/DANA/DANA-ANA: Ireland. Mother Earth; goddess of plenty, another aspect of the Morrigu; Great Goddess; greatest of all goddesses. The flowering fertility goddess, sometimes she formed a trinity with Badb and Macha. Her priestesses comforted and taught the dying. Fires were lit for her at Midsummer. Two hills in Kerry are called the Paps of Anu. Maiden aspect of the Triple Goddess in Ireland. Guardian of cattle and health. Goddess of fertility, prosperity, comfort.

ARAWN (ar-awn): Wales. King of Hell; god of Annwn, the underground kingdom of the dead. Revenge, terror, war.

ARIANRHOD (ari-an-rod): Wales. "Silver Wheel";

"High Fruitful Mother"; star goddess; sky goddess; virgin; goddess of reincarnation; Full Moon goddess. Her palace was called Caer Arianrhod (Aurora Borealis). Keeper of the circling Silver Wheel of Stars, a symbol of time or karma. This wheel was also known as the Oar Wheel, a ship which carried dead warriors to the Moonland (Emania). Mother of Lleu Llaw Gyffes and Dylan by her brother Gwydion. Her original consort was Nwyvre (Sky or Firmament). Mother aspect of the Triple Goddess in Wales. Honored at the Full Moon. Beauty, fertility, reincarnation.

BADB (bibe)/BADHBH/BADB CATHA: Ireland. "Boiling"; "Battle Raven"; "Scald-crow"; the cauldron of ever-producing life; known in Gaul as Cauth Bodva. War goddess and wife of Net, a war god. Sister of Macha, the Morrigu and Anu. Mother aspect of the Triple Goddess in Ireland. Associated with the cauldron, crows and ravens. Life, wisdom, inspiration, enlightenment.

BANBA: Ireland. Goddess; part of a triad with Fotia and Eriu. They used magic to repel invaders.

BEL/BELENUS/BELINUS/BELENOS/BELI MAWR: Ireland. "Shining"; Sun and Fire god; Great God. Similar to Apollo. Closely connected with the Druids. His name is seen in the festival of Beltane or Beltain. Cattle were driven through the bonfires for purification and fertility. Science, healing, hot springs, fire, success, prosperity, purification, crops, vegetation, fertility, cattle.

BLODEUWEDD (blod-oo-eeth)/BLODWIN/ BLANCHEFLOR: Wales. "Flower Face"; "White Flower". Lily maid of Celtic initiation ceremonies. Also known as the Ninefold Goddess of the Western Isles of Paradise. Created by Math and Gwydion as a wife for Lleu. She was changed into an owl for her adultery and plotting Lleu's death. The Maiden form of the Triple Goddess; her symbol was the owl; goddess of the Earth in bloom. Flowers, wisdom, lunar mysteries, initiations.

BOANN (boo-an)/BOANNAN/BOYNE: Ireland. Goddess of the river Boyne; mother of Angus mac Og by the Dagda.

Once there was a well shaded by nine magic hazel trees. These trees bore crimson nuts which gave knowledge of everything in the world. Divine salmon lived in the well and ate the nuts. No one, not even the high gods, was allowed to go near the well. But Boann went anyway. The well waters rose to drive her away, but they never returned. Instead they became the River Boyne and the salmon became inhabitants of the river.

Other Celtic river goddesses: Siannan (Shannon), Sabrina (Severn), Sequana (Seine), Deva (Dee), Clota (Clyde), Verbeia (Wharfe), Brigantia (Braint, Brent). Healing.

BRAN THE BLESSED/BENEDIGEIDFRAN (bran): Wales. A giant; "raven"; "the blessed". Brother of the mighty Manawydan ap Llyr (Ireland, Manannan mac Lir) and Branwen; son of Llyr. Associated with ravens. God of prophecy, the arts, leaders, war, the Sun, music, writing.

BRANWEN (bran-oo-en): Manx, Wales. Sister of Bran the Blessed and wife of the Irish king Matholwch. Venus of the Northern Seas; daughter of Llyr (Lir); one of the three matriarchs of Britain; Lady of the

Lake (cauldron). Goddess of love and beauty.

BRIGIT (breet)/BRID (breed)/BRIG/BRIGID/ BRIGHID: Ireland, Wales, Spain, France. "Power"; "Renown"; "Fiery Arrow or Power" (Breo-saighead). Daughter of the Dagda; called the poetess. Often called The Triple Brigids, Three Blessed Ladies of Britain, The Three Mothers. Another aspect of Danu; associated with Imbolc. She had an exclusive female priesthood at Kildare and an ever-burning sacred fire. The number of her priestesses was nineteen, representing the nineteen-year cycle of the Celtic "Great Year". Her kelles were sacred prostitutes and her soldiers brigands. Goddess of fire, fertility, the hearth, all feminine arts and crafts, and martial arts. Healing, physicians, agriculture, inspiration, learning, poetry, divination, prophecy, smithcraft, animal husbandry, love, witchcraft, occult knowledge.

CERNUNNOS (ker-noo-nos)/CERNOWAIN/ CERNENUS/HERNE THE HUNTER: Known to all Celtic areas in one form or another. The Horned God; God of Nature; god of the Underworld and the Astral Plane; Great Father; "the Horned One". The Druids knew him as Hu Gadarn, the Horned God of fertility. He was portrayed sitting in a lotus position with horns or antlers on his head, long curling hair, a beard, naked except for a neck torque, and sometimes holding a spear and shield. His symbols were the stag, ram, bull, and horned serpent. Sometimes called Belatucadros and Vitiris. Virility, fertility, animals, physical love, Nature, woodlands, reincarnation, crossroads, wealth, commerce, warriors.

CERRIDWEN/CARIDWEN/CERIDWEN: Wales. Moon Goddess; Great Mother; grain goddess; goddess of Nature. The white corpse-eating sow representing the Moon. Wife of the giant Tegid and mother of a beautiful girl Creirwy and an ugly boy Avagdu. Welsh Bards called themselves Cerddorion (sons of Cerridwen). The Bard Taliesin, founder of their craft, was said to be born of Cerridwen and to have tasted a potent brew from her magic cauldron of inspiration. This potion known as 'greal' (from which the word Grail probably came), was made from six plants for inspiration and knowledge. Gwion Bach (later called Taliesin) accidentally drank the remaining three drops of the liquid. Her symbol was a white sow. Death, fertility, regeneration, inspiration, magic, astrology, herbs, science, poetry, spells, knowledge.

CREIDDYLAD/CREUDYLAD/CORDELIA: Wales. Daughter of the sea god Llyr. Connected with Beltane and often called the May Queen. Goddess of summer flowers. Love and flowers.

THE CRONE: One aspect of the Triple Goddess. She represents old age or death, Winter, the end of all things, the waning Moon, post-menstrual phases of women's lives, all destruction that precedes regeneration through her cauldron of rebirth. Crows and other black creatures are sacred to her. Dogs often accompanied her and guarded the gates of her after-world, helping her receive the dead. In Celtic myth, the gatekeeper-dog was named Dormarth (Death's Door). The Irish Celts maintained that true curses could be cast with the aid of a dog. Therefore, they used the word cainte (dog) for a satiric Bard with the magic power to speak curses that came true.

THE DAGDA: Ireland. "The Good God"; "All-father"; Great God; Lord of the Heavens; Father of the gods and men; Lord of Life and Death; the Arch-Druid; god of magic; Earth God. High King of the Tuatha De Danann. He had four great palaces in the depths of the earth and under the hollow hills. The Dagda had several children, the most important being Brigit, Angus, Midir, Ogma and Bodb the Red. God of death and rebirth; master of all trades; lord of perfect knowledge.

He had a cauldron called The Undry which supplied unlimited food. He also had a living oak harp which caused the seasons to change in their order. He was pictured wearing a brown, low-necked tunic which just reached his hips and a hooded cape that barely covered his shoulders. On his feet were horse-hide boots. Behind him he pulled his massive 8-pronged warclub on a wheel.

Protection, warriors, knowledge, magic, fire, prophecy, weather, reincarnation, the arts, initiation, patron of priests, the Sun, healing, regeneration, prosperity and plenty, music, the harp. First among magicians, warriors, artisans, all knowledge.

DANU/DANANN/DANA (thana): Ireland. Probably the same as Anu. Major Mother goddess; ancestress of the Tuatha De Danann; Mother of the gods; Great Mother; Moon goddess. She gave her name to the Tuatha De Danann (People of the Goddess Danu). Another aspect of the Morrigu. Patroness of wizards, rivers, water, wells, prosperity and plenty, magic, wisdom.

DIANCECHT (dian-ket)/DIAN CECHT: Ireland. Physician-magician of the Tuatha. Once he destroyed a terrible baby of the Morrigu. When he cut open the child's heart, he found three serpents that could kill anything. He killed these, burned them and threw the ashes into the nearest river. The ashes were so deadly that they made the river boil and killed everything in it. The river today is called Barrow (boiling). Dian-cecht had several children: sons Miach, Cian, Cethe and Cu, and a daughter Airmid. God of healing, medicine, regeneration, magic, silver-working.

DON/DOMNU (dom-noo)/DONN: Ireland, Wales. "Deep sea"; "Abyss". Queen of the Heavens; goddess of sea and air. Sometimes called a goddess, sometimes a god. The equivalent of the Irish Danu. In Ireland, Don ruled over the Land of the Dead. Entrances to this Otherworld were always in a sidhe (shee) or burial mound. Control of the elements, eloquence.

DRUANTIA: "Queen of the Druids"; Mother of the tree calendar; Fir goddess. Fertility, passion, sexual activities, trees, protection, knowledge, creativity.

DYLAN: Wales. Son of the Wave; god of the sea. Son of Gwydion and Arianrhod. His symbol was a silver fish.

ELAINE: Wales, Britain. Maiden aspect of the Goddess.

EPONA: Britain, Gaul. "Divine Horse"; "The Great Mare"; goddess of horses; Mother Goddess. Fertility, maternity, protectress of horses, horse-breeding, prosperity, dogs, healing springs, crops.

ERIU (err-i-oo)/ERIN: Ireland. One of the three queens of the Tuatha Da Danann and a daughter of the Dagda.

FLIDAIS: Ireland. Goddess of forests, woodlands,

and wild things; ruler of wild beasts. She rode in a chariot drawn by deer. Shape-shifter.

GOIBNIU/GOFANNON/GOVANNON (gov-ann-on): Ireland, Wales. "Great Smith"; one of a triad of craftsmen with Luchtaine the wright and Credne the brazier. Similar to Vulcan. He forged all the Tuatha's weapons; these weapons always hit their mark and every wound inflicted by them was fatal. His ale gave the Tuatha invulnerability. God of blacksmiths, weapon-makers, jewelry making, brewing, fire, metalworking.

GREAT FATHER: The Horned God; The Lord. Lord of the Winter, harvest, land of the dead, the sky, animals, mountains, lust, powers of destruction and regeneration; the male principle of creation.

GREAT MOTHER: The Lady; female principal of creation. Goddess of fertility, the Moon, Summer, flowers, love, healing, the seas, water. The index finger was considered the "mother finger," the most magical which guided, beckoned, blessed and cursed.

THE GREEN MAN: See Cernunnos. A horned deity of trees and green growing things of Earth; god of the woodlands. In Old Welsh his name is Arddhu (The Dark One), Atho, or the Horned God.

GWYDION (gwi-dee-on): Wales. Druid of the mainland gods; son of Don; brother of Govannon, Arianrhod and Amaethon (god of agriculture). Wizard and Bard of North Wales. A many-skilled deity like Lugh. Prince of the Powers of Air; a shape-shifter. His symbol was a white horse. Greatest of the enchanters; warrior-magician. Illusion, changes, magic, the sky, healing.

GWYNN AP NUDD (gwin ap neethe): Wales. King of the Fairies and the underworld. Later he became king of the Plant Annwn, or subterranean fairies.

GWYTHYR (gwee-theer): Wales. Opposite of Gwynn ap Nudd. King of the Upper World.

HERNE THE HUNTER: See Cernunnos and the Horned God. Herne the Hunter has come to be associated with Windsor Forest and has taken on attributes of Gwynn ap Nudd with his Wild Hunt.

THE HORNED GOD: Opener of the Gates of Life and Death; Herne the Hunter; Cernunnos; Green Man; Lord of the Wild Hunt. The masculine, active side of Nature; Earth Father. His sacred animals were the stag, bull, goat, bear. Growing things, the forest, Nature, wild animals, alertness, annihilation, fertility, panic, desire, terror, flocks, agriculture, beer and ale.

LLYR (thleer)/LEAR/LIR (hlir): Ireland, Wales. God of the sea and water, possibly of the underworld. The father of Manawyddan, Bran the Blessed and Branwen.

LUGH (loo or loog)/LUGA (looga) LAMHFADA (lavada—of the Long Arm)/LLEW/LUG/LUGUS/ LUG SAMILDANACH (many skilled)/LLEU LLAW GYFFES (''bright one of the skillful hand'')/LLEU/ LUGOS: Ireland, Wales. The Shining One; Sun god; god of war; ''many-skilled''; ''fair-haired one''; ''white or shining''; a hero god. His feast is Lughnassadh, a harvest festival. Associated with ravens. His symbol was a white stag in Wales. Son of Cian and Ethniu. Lugh had a magic spear and rod-sling. One of his magic hounds was obtained from the sons of Tuirenn as part of the blood-fine for killing his father Cian.

He was a carpenter, mason, smith, harper, poet, Druid, physician and goldsmith. War, magic, commerce, reincarnation, lightning, water, arts and crafts, manual arts, journeys, martial arts, blacksmiths, poets, harpers, musicians, historians, sorcerers, healing, revenge, initiation, prophecy.

MACHA (maax-ah): Ireland. "Crow"; "Battle"; "Great Queen of Phantoms"; Mother of Life and Death; a war goddess; Mother Death; originally a Mother Goddess; one of the aspects of the triple Morrigu. Also called Mania, Mana, Mene, Minne. Associated with ravens and crows. She was honored at Lughnassadh. After a battle, the Irish cut off the heads of the losers and called them Macha's acorn crop. Protectress in war as in peace; goddess of war and death. Cunning, sheer physical force, sexuality, fertility, dominance over males.

MANANNAN MAC LIR (manan-awn mak lir)/ MANAWYDAN AP LLYR (man-au-yth-an ap thleer)/ MANAWYDDEN: Ireland, Wales. He dressed in a green cloak and a gold headband. A shape-shifter. Chief Irish sea god, equivalent of the Welsh Llyr. Son of the sea god Lir. The Isle of Man and the Isle of Arran in Firth of Clyde were under his protection. At Arran he had a palace called Emhain of the Apple Trees. His swine, which constantly renewed themselves, were the chief food of the Tuatha De Danann and kept them from aging.

He had many famous weapons: two spears called Yellow Shaft and Red Javelin; swords called The Retaliator, Great Fury and Little Fury. His boat was called Wave Sweeper, and his horse Splendid Mane. He had magic armor that prevented wounds and could make the Tuatha invisible at will.

God of the sea, navigators, storms, weather at sea, fertility, sailing, weather-forecasting, magic, arts, merchants and commerce, rebirth.

MARGAWSE: Wales, Britain. Mother aspect of the Goddess.

MATH MATHONWY (math math-on-oo-ee): Wales. God of sorcery, magic, enchantment.

MERLIN/MERDDIN/MYRDDIN (meer-din): Wales, Britain. Great sorcerer; Druid; magician. Associated with the fairy religion of the Goddess. Old Welsh traditions called him a wild man of the woods with prophetic skills. He is said to have learned all his magic from the Goddess under her many names of Morgan, Viviane, Nimue, Fairy Queen, and Lady of the Lake. Tradition says he sleeps in a hidden crystal cave. Illusion, shape-shifting, herbs, healing, woodlands, Nature, protection, counseling, prophecy, divination, psychic abilities, foreseeing, crystal reading, tarot, magic, rituals, spells, incantations, artisans and smiths.

THE MORRIGU (moor-rig-oo)/MORRIGAN (mor-ee-gan) /MORRIGHAN/MORGAN (moor-gan): Ireland, Wales and Britain. "Great Queen"; "Supreme War Goddess"; "Queen of Phantoms or Demons"; "Specter Queen"; shape-shifter. Reigned over the battlefield, helping with her magic, but did not join in battles. Associated with crows and ravens. The Crone aspect of the Goddess; Great Mother; Moon Goddess; Great White Goddess; Queen of the Fairies. In her Dark Aspect (the symbol is then the raven or crow) she is the goddess of war, fate and death; she went fully armed and carried two spears. The carrion crow is her favorite disguise. With her, Fea (Hateful), Nemon (Venomous), Badb (Fury), and Macha (Battle) encouraged fighters to battle madness. Goddess of rivers, lakes, and fresh water. Patroness of priestesses and witches. Revenge, night, magic, prophecy.

NIAMH: Ireland. "Brightness"; "Beauty". A form of Badhbh who helps heroes at death.

NUADA/NUDD/NODONS/NODENS/LUD /LLUD LLAW EREINT/LLUD (hlood) OF THE SILVER HAND: Ireland, Wales. "Silver Hand"; "He who bestows wealth"; "the Cloud-Maker"; chieftain-god. Similar to Neptune. He had an invincible sword, one of the four great treasures of the Tuatha. God of healing, water, ocean, fishing, the Sun, sailing, childbirth, dogs, youth, beauty, spears and slings, smiths, carpenters, harpers, poets, historians, sorcerers, writing, magic, warfare, incantations.

OGMA/OGHMA/OGMIOS/GRIANAINECH/ CERMAIT (honey-mouthed): Ireland. "Sun-face"; similar to Hercules; carried a huge club and was the champion of the Tuatha. Invented the Ogham script alphabet. He married Etan (daughter of Diancecht) and had several children. One son Cairpre became the professional Bard of the Tuatha. Eloquence, poets, writers, physical strength, inspiration, language, literature, magic, spells, the arts, music, reincarnation.

PWYLL (pe-ool): Wales. Ruler of the Underworld at times. Also known as Pwyll pen Annwn (Pwyll head of Annwn). Cunning.

RHIANNON (hri-an-non): Wales. "The Great Queen". Goddess of birds and horses. Enchantments, fertility, and the Underworld. She rides a swift white horse.

SCATHACH/SCOTA/SCATHA/SCATH: Ireland, Scotland. "Shadow, shade"; "The Shadowy One"; "She Who Strikes Fear". Underworld goddess of the Land of Scath; Dark Goddess; goddess in the Destroyer aspect. Also a warrior woman and prophetess who lived in Albion (Scotland), probably on the Isle of Skye, and taught the martial arts. Patroness of blacksmiths, healing, magic, prophecy, martial arts.

TALIESIN (tal-i-ess-in): Wales. Prince of Song; Chief of the Bards of the West; a poet. Patron of Druids, Bards and minstrels; a shape-shifter. Writing, poetry, wisdom, wizards, Bards, music, knowledge, magic.

TEPHI: Ireland. Goddess of Tara and co-founder with Tea.

WHITE LADY: Known to all Celtic countries. Dryad of Death; identified with Macha; Queen of the Dead; the Crone form of the Goddess. Death, destruction, annihilation.

Other Supernatural or Mortal Beings & Places

AER (air): Wales. Goddess of war and revenge; goddess of the River Dee.

AINE (aw-ne): Ireland. Fairy queen of Knockaine. Moon goddess and patroness of crops and cattle. Her rites at Midsummer Eve were for a fruitful harvest

AIRMID (air-mit): Ireland. Physician daughter of Diancecht.

AMAETHON: Wales. God of agriculture.

AMERGIN (amor-gin): Ireland. The Druid who helped the Milesians beat the Tuatha De Danann.

ANDRASTE/ANDRED/ANDATE: Britain. A war and Nature goddess whose animal was the hare. She was worshipped by Queen Boadicia.

AOIFE (eefa or oif-ee): Ireland. A fairy queen and the mother of Cu Chulainn's son.

ARTHUR/ARTH VAWR (Heavenly Bear): Wales, Britain. King and leader of the Knights of the Round Table. The Round Table symbolized the goddess Arianrhod's Silver Wheel of rebirth, and the Grail the sacred cauldron of inspiration and reincarnation.

AVALON: "Apple-isle"; Celtic paradise across the sea where the gods and heroes were fed on apples of immortality.

BALOR (bail-or): Ireland. A Fomorian who had a poisonous eye. One of his eyes became malignant to other beings when he spied on his father's sorcerers as they prepared a magic potion. The smoke from the cauldron contaminated one eye. He was allowed to live only if he kept that eye shut. The Fomors used a hook to open his eye during battle in order to kill the enemy. Balor's Castle, a cliff on Tory Island off the coast of Donegal, is supposed to have been a Fomorian outpost.

BLATHNAT (blay-nat): Ireland. Daughter of Midir, king of the Gaelic Underworld. She helped Cu Chulainn steal her father's magic cauldron.

BODB (bove) THE RED: Ireland. Son of the Dagda. He succeeded his father as king of the gods. He is connected mainly with southern Ireland, the Galtee Mts., and Lough Dearg. At Lough he had a sidhe or underground palace.

BRAN and SCEOLAN (shkeolawn or scolaing): Ireland. The two favorite hounds of Finn mac Cumhail.

BRESS (brees): Ireland. Son of Elathan of the Fomors; married Brigit.

BRIGANTIA: Britain. "High One"; pastoral and river goddess. Associated with Imbolc. Flocks, cattle, water, fertility, healing, victory.

CAIRPRE (kair-pra): Ireland. Chief Bard of the Tuatha; son of Ogma.

CAILLECH (cal-yach) BEINE BRIC: Scotland. Great Goddess in Her Destroyer aspect; called the "Veiled One". Another name is Scota, from which Scotland comes. Originally Scotland was called Caledonia, or land given by Caillech. Disease, plague.

CAMULOS/CAMULUS: Britain, Gaul. "Heaven"; war god.

CARADAWC: Wales. Son of Bran; "Strong-armed."

CIAN (kee-an): Ireland. Son of Diancecht; he married Ethniu, the daughter of Balor the Fomor. Their son was Lugh Lamhfada, or Long-hand. He was killed by the sons of Tuirenn.

COCIDIUS: N. Britain. "The Red One"; god of

war. Similar to Mars. Slaughter, wild animals, forests, strength, swiftness, war.

CONLAOCH (con-la): Ireland. Son of Cu Chulainn and Aoife.

CONANN (con-ann): Ireland. Son of Febar and a Fomor King.

COVENTINA: N. Britain. Goddess of springs and waters.

CREDNE: Ireland. Bronze-worker god of the Tuatha.

CU CHULAINN/CUCHULAIN/CUCHULLIN (koo chul-inn): Ireland. "Culann's Hound". A hero who is described as having seven pupils in each eye, seven fingers on each hand and seven toes on each foot. Cu means dog, a common title of Celtic chieftains. He received his battle skills from Scathach.

CULANN (kul-an): Ireland. An Irish chief; Cu Chulainn served him for a time as payment for killing Culann's dog.

CWN ANNWN (koon anoon): Wales. The hounds of Arawn, later called hell hounds. They often are a portent of death but do not do any actual destruction themselves.

CYHIRAETH (kerherrighth): Wales. Goddess of streams. Later she became like the Banshee.

DECHTIRE (deck-tyra): Ireland. Mother of Cu Chulainn; great grand-daughter of Angus mac Og; half-sister to King Conchobar.

ELVA (alva): Ireland. Sister-in-law of Lugh.

EMER (avair): Ireland. Daughter of Forgall the Wily; married Cu Chulainn.

EMANIA: Celtic "Land of the Moon", where the dead went. It was ruled by the Queen of Shades or Macha. Her holy city was called Emain Macha.

EOCHAID (ughy): Ireland. A Fir Bolg king; killed in the first battle with the Tuatha.

ETAIN (aideen or et-ain): Ireland. Of the Tuatha De Danann; second wife of Midir, king of the fairy hill of Bri Leith.

ETAN: Ireland. Daughter of Diancecht; a physician. Wife of Ogma.

ETHNIU: Ireland. Daughter of the Fomor Balor of the Evil Eye. Married Cian, the son of Diancecht.

EVNISSYEN/EFNISIEN (ev-ness-jen): Wales. "Lover of Strife"; half-brother of Bran; a giant.

FAND: Ireland, Manx. One wife of the sea god Manannan mac Lir, who deserted her. Goddess of healing and pleasure.

FIANNA (feen-a)/FIANNA EIRINN: Ireland. Also known as the Fenians and Champions of the Red Branch. The great fighting force serving under the Ard Righ (High King). Its last and greatest leader was Finn mac Cumhail. The Irish Fianna had a rule to never insult a woman.

FINDIAS, GORIAS, MURIAS, FALIAS: The four cities where the Tuatha De Danann lived before coming to Ireland.

FINN MAC CUMHAIL (coul or coo-al)/FINN

MAC COUL/FIONN (f-yoon): Ireland. Son of Cumhail and the last and greatest leader of the Fianna.

FIRBOLGS (fir-vulag)/FIR BOLGS: Ireland. The original inhabitants; enemies of the Tuatha De Danann. They consisted of three tribes: Domnu, Gaillion, and Bolg. They were conquered and driven into the western islands by the Tuatha De Danann.

FOMORS: Ireland. "Under the sea". A sea-dwelling race who opposed the Tuatha De Danann and lost.

HI BREASIL (hi bree-sal): Ireland. See Tir-Nan-Og.

IWERIDD (i-oo-er-ith): Wales. One of Llyr's wives.

KAI (kay): Wales. A fire and smithing god.

LIA FAIL (lee-a fail): Ireland. Stone of Fal; Stone of Destiny; it came from the city of Falias with the Tuatha and was one of their great treasures.

LUCHTAINE/LUCHTA: Ireland. Carpenter god of the Tuatha.

MABINOGION (mab-in-oh-geeon): Wales. A selection of stories from the White Book of Rhydderch, the Red Book of Hergest and the Hanes of Taliesin.

QUEEN MAB/MABH/MEDB (meev)/MEDBH/MEDHBH/MAEVE (maive or mayv): Ireland. "Drunk woman"; "Queen-wolf"; Celtic fairy queen whose name means "mead", more particularly a red drink or claret she gave to her many consorts. Also considered a queen of Connacht, a warrior queen of the Ulster cycle. Goddess of war, actually participating in the fighting; combined mother and warrior aspects of the

Goddess. Physical sexuality and fertility, revenge, war.

MARGAWSE: Mother aspect of the Triple Goddess in Arthurian legend. Elaine was the virgin, Morgan Le Fay the crone.

MIACH: Ireland. Son of Diancecht; killed by his father after he restored Nuada's hand.

MIDIR (my-tir)/MIDHIR/MIDER: God of the underworld connected with the Isle of Falga (Isle of Man) where he had his palace. He owned three wonderful cows and a magic cauldron. Angus mac Og took his wife Etain. His cows, cauldron and his daughter Blathnat were taken as spoils of war by the heroes of King Conchobar of Ulster.

MORC: Ireland. Son of Dela, a Fomor king.

MORGAN LE FAY: Welsh death-goddess; Morgan the Fate. Glamorgan in Wales is said to be her sacred territory. She can cast a destroying curse on any man. Gawaine of the Round Table bore Morgan's pentacle as a heraldic device on his blood-red shield.

NANTOSUELTA: Britain. "Winding river"; river goddess; consort of Sucellus; linked with the war goddess Morrigu. Associated with ravens. Maternity, bees, doves, domestic arts, wells, childbirth, fertility.

NEMED: Ireland. The second race of invaders to arrive.

NICNEVEN: Scotland. "Divine"; "Brilliant". A Samhain witch-goddess; a form of Diana. In Scotland she is said to ride through the night with her followers at Samhain. During the Middle Ages she was called

Dame Habonde, Abundia, Satia, Bensozie, Zobiana and Herodiana.

NIMUE: A Celtic Moon goddess; also called Viviene or Morgan.

NISSYEN (ness-jen): Wales. "Lover of peace"; half-brother of Bran; a giant.

OWEIN AP URIEN: Wales. God associated with ravens. Wisdom, magic, war, leadership, reincarnation, healing.

PARTHOLON: Ireland. First race of invaders to arrive.

PENARDUN: Wales. Daughter of the goddess Don; one wife of Llyr.

ROBIN HOOD: Britain. Wizard of the Greenwood; was a real person leading the Sherwood Forest covens in the early 14th century. His female companion held the role of Mother of the Grove. By force of arms he maintained a heathen preserve in the wildwood, a sanctuary for heretics and others persecuted by the Christian church.

SUCELLUS: Britain. "The God of the Mallet"; "Good Striker"; Father God; sky god. Bearded; similar to Jupiter. Associated with dogs and carried a mallet or hammer. God of abundance, success, strength, authority, protection, regeneration, dogs, trees, ravens; protector against a sudden turn of fortune.

TAILTIU: Ireland. Foster-mother of Lugh. Connected with Lughnassadh. Goddess of the Earth, peace and prosperity.

TARANIS: Britain. "The Thunderer"; associated

with the wheel symbol and the eagle. Similar to Jupiter. Power, movement, knowledge, magic, leadership.

TIR-NAN-OG/TIR NA-NOG (tier-nan-ohk or teer na nogue): Ireland. Land of the Young; Fairyland; Avalon; Isles of the Blest. Sometimes described as a land across the west sea where part of the Tuatha De Danann retreated. A fountain there gives the Water of Life that makes the old young again.

TOUTATIS/TOTATIS/TEUTATES: Britain, Gaul. "Ruler of the People"; one of the oldest and most powerful; god of war.

TREFUILNGID FRE-EOCHAIR: Ireland. "Triple Bearer of the Triple Key"; god of the shamrock and consort of the Triple Goddess. A trident was the symbol of any god mated with the Triple Goddess. The Irish worshipped the shamrock as a sign of their triple deities long before St. Patrick arrived.

TUATHA DE DANANN (toodha dae donnann or tootha day danan): Ireland. Race of gods who finally overthrew the Fomors. The Irish said they were giants who lived in underground chambers at Tara and built stone temples.

WEYLAND/WAYLAND/WEILAND: Britain, Germanic Celts. A smith god and consort of the Triple Goddess. The name Smith once referred to a priestly caste of metalworking Druids. An English tradition says that Weyland still lives inside a Berkshire hill marked by the White Horse of Uffington.

The Little People, Fairy Folk & Kin

Most Nature spirits, fairy folk and kindred souls can be safely befriended. One must use common sense, though. If you get a distinct feeling of uneasiness, it is best to leave their territories at once and not court trouble. Most of them can be called upon in rituals and asked, not commanded, to help.

The ritual offering of wine and cookies is a good way to gain their help and friendship. They also like certain herbs, especially ginger. The offering should be placed outside, preferably near green plants or trees. Do not expect the food and drink to be physically gone in the morning. Tradition says that fairies and such spirits take the vital essence from human food and leave the outer form behind.

BEAN SIDHE/BEAN-SIDHE (ban-shee): Ireland. "Woman Fairy"; not actually a deity, but a spirit attached to certain families. When a member's death approaches, the family will hear the banshee crying. Not always terrifying.

BROWNIE: Bwca or Bwbachod in Wales; Bodach (budagh) in the Scottish Highlands; Fenodoree in Manx; Pixies or Pisgies in the West Country of England. They are about three feet high and dress in brown clothes. They have brown faces and shaggy hair. Brownies make themselves responsible for the house where they live by coming out at night to complete unfinished work. Any offer of reward will drive them away, but they expect a bowl of milk or cream and cake to be left out. Tradition says they do not like teetotallers and ministers. If offended, brownies will create malicious mischief.

BWCA (booka)/BWBACHOD: Wales. A type of brownie.

CAOINEAG (konyack): Scotland. "Weeper"; a banshee.

COBLYNAU (koblernigh): Wales. Mine spirits, similar to Knockers. About 18 inches high, they dress like miners. Although they are ugly, they are good humored and will knock where rich ores are to be found.

CYHYRAETH (kerherrighth): Wales. A form of banshee. It usually cries or groans before multiple deaths by epidemic or accident.

DAOINE SIDHE (theena shee): Ireland. A name for the fairy people.

DRYADS: All Celtic countries. Spirits who dwell in trees, oaks in particular. The Druids contacted them for inspiration. Oak galls were known as Serpent Eggs by the Druids and used in many of their charms.

ELLYLLON (ethlerthlon): Wales. Fairies whose queen is Mab. Their food is toadstools and fairy butter, a fungus found on the roots of old trees.

ELVES: Another name for the Trooping Fairies of Britain. In Scotland they are divided into the Seelie and Unseelie Courts. The name is also applied to small fairy boys. Elf-shot describes an illness or disability supposedly caused by their arrows.

FAIRIES/FAERIES: The earlier name was Fays. The term fairy now covers Anglo-Saxon elves, the Daoine Sidhe of the Highlands, the Tuatha De Danann of Ireland, the Tylwyth Teg of Wales, the Seelie and Unseelie Courts, the Wee Folk, Good Neighbors, and many more. Some fairies are friendly, others wild and alien to humans. The subterranean fairies are those who live in lochs, lakes, streams or the sea.

While many fairies prefer to live in bands, large and small, there are also individual fairies who live alone. These individual fairies usually do not dress as grandly as those of the bands. The lone fairies wear different outfits of fox skins, leaves, green moss, flowers, moleskins, or cobwebs.

Fairies vary in size from diminutive to 18 inches. Others are three or four feet tall, while some are of human or larger size.

In Ireland, the men of the Trooping Fairies, the Daoine Sidh and the Shefro wear green coats and red caps, while the women wear green gowns and red shoes. Fairies love finery; they add feathers to their caps, decorate their gowns with gold spangles and wear small coronets, sometimes of pearls. Some of the men wear yellow breeches. Elves traditionally wear green, while the fairies of Manx like blue. White is another color that occasionally appears in fairy descriptions. Whatever their preference in clothing, they tend to dress in the costumes of the country in which they live.

Green is the favorite fairy color in Celtic countries with red next. Because of this preference, green came to be associated with death among the Celts. Fairies have been described as having hair of red, brown, black or blonde. The women wear it long and flowing.

Fairies require food and sleep, are liable to disease and can be killed. They spin and weave within their communities. Fairies have their fairs, hunts, markets, processional rides, games, inter-clan warfare (in Ireland), and revels. Hurling is a particular sport of the Irish fairies. Their horses are often speckled grey and shaggy. Fairies distinctly do not like humans spying on them.

According to J. G. Campbell in his book *Super-stitions of the Highlands and Islands of Scotland*, they have banquets of roots of silverweed, stalks of heather, milk of red deer and goats, barley meal, bread, mushrooms, honey, and dew.

Fairies are quite fond of music and dancing. Among their musical instruments are the panpipes, bagpipes, cymbals, tambourines, harps, whistles, and drums. The music of the Londonderry Air is said to have been learned from fairies.

Fairies tend to guard their real names, instead giving false ones to humans. Some are also capable of shape-shifting into birds to escape capture. Fairies often use glamour (spells) when encountering humans; in Ireland these spells are called pishogue (pish-ogue).

There are a number of ways to protect yourself from unfriendly fairies. All fairies have a dislike of cold iron. Jumping over running water will stop their pursuit. Using bread and salt, bells, iron horseshoes, whistling, snapping the fingers, or turning the clothes will also deter them. Herbs they do not like are St. Johnswort, red verbena, daisies, rowan or mountain ash. But the strongest plant against them is the four-leaf clover, which protects against fairy glamour. It is said that one can see fairies readily by looking through a stone with a natural hole in it.

Fairies value neatness, the ability to keep a secret and generosity among humans. They also like humans to leave out fresh water for washing their babies, and enjoy an offering of milk, bread and cheese.

Elphame is a Scottish version of the Norse word Alfheim, country of the elves, or Fairyland. It is said that those who are psychic can see fairies travel abroad and change their residences at Imbolc, Beltane, Lughnassadh, and Samhain. In Scottish witchcraft, the high priestess of the coven was called the Queen of Elphame.

Both the Welsh and Irish called the fairies The Mothers and considered Fairyland the Land of Women. This may harken back to the fact that the Celtic peoples were originally a matriarchal society.

In the Book of the Dun Cow, a fairy queen describes her realm under the earth. Although most Celtic fairies tend to live in hills, brughs, or barrows, some live in the deep woods and in lakes. Their favorite hour is twilight, between day and night. It is said that one can open a door into a fairy hill by walking around it three times counterclockwise.

FENODEREE/PHYNNODDEREE (fin-ord-er-ree): Manx. Brownies who are large, ugly and hairy.

FERRISHYN (ferrishin): Manx. Name for the fairy tribe.

FIN BHEARA (fin-vara)/FIONNBHARR (fyunn-varr)/FINDABAIR (finnavar): Ireland. The Fairy King of Ulster, sometimes called king of the dead. Although he was married to a fairy lady, he still courted beautiful mortal women.

THE GENTRY: An Irish name for fairies.

GNOMES: Earth Elementals. They live underground and guard the treasures of the Earth. Gnomes are wonderful metal workers, especially of swords and breastplates.

GOBLINS/HOBGOBLINS: Originally a general name for small, grotesque but friendly brownie-type creatures.

GWARTHEG Y LLYN (gwarrthey er thlin): Wales. Fairy cattle.

GWRAGEDD ANNWN (gwrageth anoon): Wales. Lake fairies.

HOUNDS OF THE HILL: The hunting dogs of the fairies. Very large, and white with red ears. Also called Cwn Annwn.

KNOCKERS: Cornwall. Mine spirits who are friendly to miners. They knock where rich ore can be found. They are also called Buccas.

LEPRACAUN (lep-ra-chawn): Ireland. A solitary fairy who makes shoes and generally guards a pot of gold.

MER-PEOPLE: Mermaids; water dwellers who are human from the waist up but with the tail of a fish. They are irresistible singers who sometimes lure fishermen to their deaths. The Irish equivalent of the mermaid is the Murdhuacha (muroo-cha) or Merrows.

OLD PEOPLE: Cornish name for fairies.

OONAGH (oona): Ireland. Wife of Fin Bheara.

PEOPLE OF PEACE: Ireland, Scotland. Another name for the Daoine Sidhe.

PEOPLE OF THE HILLS: Britain. Fairies who live under green mounds; subterranean fairies.

PHOUKA (pooka): Ireland. It can take various animal forms and is considered dangerous.

PIXIES/PISKIES/PISGIES: The name for fairies in Somerset, Devon and Cornwall.

THE PLANT ANNWN (plant anoon): Wales.

Fairies of the underworld. The entrance to their kingdom is through lakes. Their king is called Gwynn ap Nudd. Gwragen Annwn is the Welsh name for their women. Their speckled cattle are Gwartheg Y Llyn and their white hounds are Cwn Annwn (see Hounds of the Hill).

PWCA (pooka): Wales. A version of Puck; not like the Irish Phouka. They are helpful if milk is left out, but can also be mischievous.

SEELIE (Blessed) COURT: Scotland. These trooping fairies are benevolent towards humans, but will readily avenge any injury or insult.

SIDHE/SIDH/SITH/SI (shee): Ireland, Scottish Highlands. Name for fairies and their subterranean dwellings. A barrow or hillock which has a door to a beautiful underground realm of the Tuatha or fairies.

SITHEIN (sheean): Ireland, Scotland. Name for the outside of a fairy hill or knowe. The inside is called the brugh.

THE SLUAGH (slooa)/THE HOST: Scotland. The Host of the Unforgiven Dead, or pagan ancestors. The most formidable of the Highland fairies.

SUBTERRANEAN FAIRIES: Scotland. Fairies who live in brochs or hills. They travel from place to place at Imbolc, Beltane, Lughnassadh, and Samhain in order to change their residences.

TROOPING FAIRIES: They can be large or small, friendly or sinister. They tend to wear green jackets and love hunting and riding. The smaller ones make fairy rings with their circular dances.

TYLWYTH TEG (terlooeth teig)/THE FAIR FAMILY: Wales. The most usual name for fairies. If one wants to court their friendship, they are called Bendith Y Mamau (the Mother's Blessing).

UNSEELIE COURT: Scotland. Fairies who are never favorable to humans. They are either solitary evil fairies or bands of fairies called the Sluagh who use elf-shot against humans and cattle.

THE WEE FOLK: Scotland, Ireland. A name for fairies.

THE WILD HUNT: The night hunt by the Sluagh with their terrible hounds. They are said to kidnap humans they encounter during their rides.

10 Spellwork

In preparation of actually practicing spellwork, review chapter 2. Be very certain that you understand fully all the consequences of negative magic before you build karma for yourself.

Herb Magic

ALDER (*Alnus glutinosa*). A Druid sacred tree. The pith is easily pushed out of fresh green alder shoots to make whistles. Several shoots bound together side by side, one end stopped with plugs of wood, clay or sealing compound, can be used to entice Air Elementals to your area. Trim the end of each shoot to produce the notes you want. The old superstition of whistling up the wind comes from this.

APPLE, DOMESTIC. A Druid sacred tree. Cut an apple into three pieces. Rub the cut side on warts, saying: "Out warts, into apple." Bury the pieces; as the apple decays, the warts will disappear.

Use apple cider in any old spells calling for blood or wine.

ASH (*Fraxious excelsior*). A Druid sacred tree. Druid wands were often made of ash and carved with decorations. Ash wands are good for healing, general and solar magic. Put fresh ash leaves under your pillow to stimulate psychic dreams.

Gather ash leaves and take them to a place outdoors where you can work undisturbed. With your sword or knife, scratch a circle around you in the ground. Make it large enough to work in without crossing the line. Face the East, holding the ash leaves in both hands. Say: "Elementals of the East, rulers of Air, bring me knowledge and inspiration." Throw a few leaves to the East. Turn to the South, say: "Elementals of the South, rulers of Fire, bring me energy and change." Throw a few leaves to the South. Turn to the West, say: "Elementals of the West, rulers of Water, bring me healing and love." Throw a few leaves to the West. Turn to the North, say: "Elementals of the North, rulers of Earth, bring me prosperity and success." Throw a few leaves to the North. Stand in the center of the circle with both hands raised: "Blessings to all who come to my aid. Between friends is this bargain made." Rub out the cut line.

BASIL (*Ocimum basilicum*). Burn basil to exorcise negativity from the home. To do a really thorough cleansing and protection of yourself and your home, also sprinkle a little basil in each corner of each room and add to your bathwater.

BETONY (*Stachys officinalis, Betonica officinalis, Stachys betonica*). Also known as Bishopwort, Wood Betony, Purple Betony. A Druid sacred herb. This was a very magical herb to the Druids as it has the power to expel evil spirits, nightmares, and despair. It was burned at Midsummer Solstice for purification and protection. Sprinkle near all doors and windows to form a protective barrier. If troubled by nightmares, fill a small cloth pillow and place it under your regular pillow.

BIRCH (*Betula alba*). Also known as Lady of the Woods, Paper Birch, White Birch. A Druid sacred tree. Carefully gather strips of the bark at the New Moon. With red ink, write on a birch strip: bring me true love. Burn this along with a love incense, saying: "Goddess of love, God of desire, Bring to me sweet passion's fire." The specific name of a god/goddess may be added. Or cast the bark into a stream or other flowing water, saying: "Message of love, I set you free, to capture a love and return to me."

BISTORT (*Polygonum bistorta*). Also called Snake-weed, Dragonwort, Sweet Dock. Carry a piece of the dried root to conceive.

BLACKTHORN (*Prunus spinosa*). Also called Sloe. A Druid sacred tree. The thorns are used for sticking into black figure candles or poppets of enemies who will not leave you alone. Before burning the candle or poppet, attach the trouble-maker's name to it or carve it into the candle with your knife. Take three thorns and place them in the forehead, heart and abdomen of the image, saying: "Evil, return to the one who sent thee. Me and mine are now set free. No hurt nor harm can enter here. My life and way are now made clear."

BRIAR (*Rosa rubiginosa*). Also known as Wild Rose, Briar Rose, Sweet Briar, Hip Fruit. Regular scented roses may be substituted. For clairvoyant dreams, steep two teaspoons fresh or dried rose petals in one cup of boiling water. Cover and let stand five minutes. Drink at bedtime. Burn the petals with love incenses to strengthen love spells.

BROOM (*Cytisus scoparius*). Also known as Scotch Broom, Irish Broom. A Druid sacred tree; it can be substituted for furze (gorse) at the Spring Equinox. The Irish called it the "physician's power" because of its diuretic shoots. Sweep your outside ritual areas with it to purify and protect. Burning the blooms and shoots calms the wind.

WHITE BRYONY (*Bryonia alba, Bryonia dioica*). POISONOUS! Also known as English Mandrake, Briony, Ladies Heal. The roots can be substituted for the rare true mandrake root. Set a piece of the root on your money to increase prosperity.

BURDOCK (*Arctium lappa*). Also known as Cocklebur, Beggar's Buttons. Steep a handful of the herb in a bucket of water for washing floors. This wards off negativity, purifies and protects.

CATNIP (*Nepeta cataria*). Also known as Catnep, Catmint. A Druid sacred herb, chewed by warriors for fierceness in battle. Large dried leaves are powerful markers in magical books. Give to your cat to create a psychic bond with it.

CEDAR (*Cedrus libani*). Also known as Tree of Life, Arbor Vitae, Yellow Cedar. A Druid sacred tree. Ancient Celts on the mainland used cedar oil to preserve the heads of enemies taken in battle. To draw Earth energy and ground yourself, place the palms of your hands against the ends of the leaves.

CELANDINE (*Chelidonum majus*). Also known

as Tetterwort, Swallow Herb, Figwort, Pilewort. To prevent unlawful imprisonment, wear a red flannel bag filled with the herb next to the skin. Replace the herb every three days.

CHAMOMILE (*Anthemis nobilis*). Also known as Wild Chamomile, Roman Chamomile, Ground Apple. Roman Chamomile smells like fresh apples and is the most enjoyable to use. A tea made of two teaspoons of the herb steeped for five minutes in a cup of boiling water is a gentle sleep-inducer. It can be burned or added to prosperity bags to increase money.

WILD CHERRY (*Prunus serotina*). Also known as Black Cherry, Chokecherry. A Druid sacred tree. Chips of the wood or bark were burned at Celtic festivals.

CLUB MOSS (*Lycopodium clavatum*). Also known as Wolf Claw, Staghorn. A Druid sacred herb. Among the Celts, only a priest or priestess could gather club moss; it had to be cut with a silver dagger. The plants and the spores (collected in July and August) were used for blessings and protection.

COMFREY (*Symphytum officinale*). Also known as Slippery Root, Knitbone, Blackwort. Teas, tinctures and compresses of comfrey leaves or roots speed the healing of cuts, rashes and broken bones. To ensure the safety of your luggage while traveling, tuck a piece of root into each bag.

ELDER (*Sambucus nigra*). Also known as Ellhorn, Elderberry, Lady Elder. A Druid sacred tree. Sacred to the White Lady and Midsummer Solstice. The Druids used it to both bless and curse. Standing under an elder tree at Midsummer, like standing in a Fairy Ring of mushrooms, will help you see the "little people."

Elder wands can be used to drive out evil spirits or thoughtforms. Music on panpipes or flutes of elder have the same power as the wand.

EYEBRIGHT (*Euphrasia officinalis*). A Druid sacred tree. In a tightly covered pot, gently brew a handful of the herb in a pint of boiling water. Allow to stand overnight. Strain out the herb, squeezing as dry as possible. Store the liquid in a tightly sealed container away from sunlight and heat, but not in the refrigerator. Drink a half-teaspoon in half-cup of spring water or psychic herb tea to promote clairvoyance.

FERNS, especially MALE FERN (Lucky Hand, *Dryopteris filixmas*), MAIDENHAIR (*Adiantum pedatum*, native to North America and Asia), BRACKEN (*Pteridium acquilinum*), LADY FERN AND POLYPODY (Oak Fern, both native to the United States and both *Polypodium vulgare*). The Druids classed ferns as sacred trees. Uncurled fronds of Male Fern were gathered at Midsummer, dried and carried for good luck. All ferns are powerful protective plants. Burned indoors, they produce a very strong wall of protection. Burned outdoors, they produce rain.

FEVERFEW (*Chrysanthemum parthenium*). Also known as Featherfoil, Flirtwort. Travelers carried it as ward against sickness or accident during their journeys.

SILVER FIR (*Abies alba*). Also known as Birth Tree. A Druid sacred tree. The needles are burned at childbirth to bless and protect the mother and baby.

FOXGLOVE (*Digitalis purpurea*). POISONOUS! Also known as Fairy Gloves, Fairy Fingers, Dead Men's Bells. A Druid sacred herb associated with fairies and the "little people."

FURZE (*Ulex europaeus*). Also known as Gorse, Whin. A Druid sacred tree. Its golden flowers are associated with the Spring Equinox. Wood and blooms are burned for protection and preparation for conflict of any sort.

HAWTHORN (*Crataegus oxyacantha*). Also known as May Tree, White Thorn. A Druid sacred tree. Wands of this wood are of great power. The blossoms are highly erotic to men.

HAZEL (*Corylus spp.*). A Druid sacred tree. Wands of this wood symbolize white magic and healing. Forked sticks are used to find water or buried treasure. If outside and in need of magical protection quickly, draw a circle around yourself with a hazel branch. To enlist the aid of plant fairies, string hazelnuts on a cord and hang up in your house or ritual room.

HEATHER (*Calluna vulgaris*). A Druid sacred herb. Used at Midsummer to promote love and protection. Red heather is for passion, white heather for cooling passions of unwanted suitors.

HOLLY (*Ilex aquifolium*). The U.S. variety is *Ilex opaca*. A Druid sacred tree. Sacred to the Winter Solstice, when it was used for decorating. Planted near a house, holly repels negative spells sent against you. A bag of leaves and berries carried by a man increases his ability to attract women.

HOPS (*Humulus lupulus*). Also known as Beer Flavor. A Druid sacred herb. A pillow stuffed with dried hops aids sleep and healing.

IVY, ENGLISH (*Hedera helix*). POISONOUS! A Druid sacred herb. Connected with the Winter Solstice when it was used for decorating. Ivy provides protection when growing on or near a house.

JUNIPER (*Juniperus communis*). A Druid sacred tree. Its berries were used with thyme in Druid and Grove incenses for visions. Juniper grown by the door discourages thieves. The mature berries can be strung and hung in the house to attract love.

LAUREL (*Laurus nobilis*). Also known as Bay Laurel, Sweet Bay. Its leaves were burned by the priestesses of the Triple Goddesses to induce psychic visions. Placing the leaves under your pillow will also give inspiration and visions. Laurel counteracts negativity and restriction.

LILY OF THE VALLEY (*Convallaria majalis*). POISONOUS! Also known as May Bells. A liquid made by soaking the flowers in spring water can be sprinkled around the ritual area to draw peace and knowledge.

PURPLE LOOSESTRIFE (*Lythrum salicaria*). Placed in the corners of each room, this herb restores harmony and brings peace.

MARIGOLD (*Calendula officinalis*). Also known as Calendula, Holigold, Pot Marigold, Bride of the Sun. A Druid sacred herb. Marigold water is made from the blossoms. Rubbed on the eyelids, this liquid helps you see fairies. Flowers added to pillows give clairvoyant dreams.

MARJORAM (*Origanum majorana*), WILD MARJORAM (*Origanum vulgare*). Also known as Wintersweet, Sweet Marjoram, Pot Marjoram. An infusion of marjoram, mint and rosemary can be sprinkled around the house for protection. This also works for protecting specific objects.

MEADOWSWEET (*Filipendula ulmaria, Spirea ulmaria*). Also known as Queen of the Meadow, Gravel Root, Meadowwort. One of the three most sacred Druid herbs; the other two were mint and vervain (verbena). Meadowsweet can be used to decorate the altar during love spells.

WILD MINT (*Mentha piperita, M. spicata, M. crispa*). A Druid sacred herb. Poppets for healing and love can be stuffed with dried mint leaves. Added to incenses, it cleanses the house or ritual area.

MISTLETOE (*Viscum album*). Also known as Birdlime, All Heal, Golden Bough. It was the most sacred "tree" of the Druids, and ruled the Winter Solstice. The berries are POISONOUS! Bunches of mistletoe can be hung as an all-purpose protective herb. The berries are used in love incenses.

MOONWORT (*Botrychium lunaria*). The crescent-shaped leaflets and fronds are used in love bags. Put a piece of moonwort inside a locket with your lover's picture to promote lasting love.

IRISH MOSS (*Chondrus crispus*). Also known as Pearl Moss. This herb is for gaining and keeping a steady income of money. If you make poppets for luck or money, stuff this moss inside the doll. Burn it with incense during spellworkings for luck or money. Sprinkle a little inside your purse or billfold.

MUGWORT (*Artemisia vulgaris*). Also known as Sailor's Tobacco, Witch Herb, Old Man. A Druid sacred herb. Rub the fresh herb on crystal balls and magic mirrors to increase their strength. The herb's powers are strongest when picked on the Full Moon.

Soak one-quarter ounce mugwort in a bottle of wine for seven days, beginning on a New Moon. Strain out and drink a small amount to aid clairvoyance, divination and crystal reading. Gather at Summer Solstice for good luck.

MULLEIN (*Verbascum thapsus*). Also known as Hag's Taper, Candlewick Plant, Aaron's Rod, Velvet Plant, Shepherd's Club. The powdered leaves are sometimes called "graveyard dust" and can be substituted for such.

NUTS & CONES. Sacred to the Druids; highly steeped in magic. Small cones or acorns are often used to tip the wands used by Celtic priests. All nuts can be used in fertility magic.

OAK (*Quercus robur*). Also known as Tanner's Bark, White Oak. A Druid holy tree, the oak was the king of trees in a Grove. Magic wands were made of its wood. Oak galls, known as Serpent Eggs, were used in magical charms. Acorns gathered at night held the greatest fertility powers. The Druids and priestesses listened to the rustling oak leaves and the wrens in the trees for divinatory messages. Burning oak leaves purifes the atmosphere.

PINE (*Pinus spp*). Sacred to the Druids, the pine was known as one of the seven chieftain trees of the Irish. Mix the dried needles with equal parts of juniper and cedar; burn to purify the home and ritual area. The cones and nuts can be carried as a fertility charm. A good magical cleansing and stimulating bath is made by placing pine needles in a loose-woven bag and running bathwater over this. To purify and sanctify an outdoor ritual area, brush the ground with a pine branch.

ROWAN (*Sorbus aucuparia, Fraxinus aucuparia*). Also known as Mountain Ash, Witchwood, Sorb Apple. A Druid sacred tree and sacred to the goddess Brigit. It is a very magical tree used for wands, rods, amulets and spells. Its berries are especially magical, but the seeds are POISONOUS! A forked rowan branch can help find water. Wands are for knowledge, locating metal and general divination. Fires made of rowan wood serve to summon spirits, especially when facing conflicts.

RUE (*Ruta graveolens*). Also known as Herb of Grace. Ancient Celts considered rue an antimagical herb, that is a defense against spells and dark magic. A fresh sprig can be used to sprinkle sacred water for consecration, blessings, and healings. Burned in exorcism or purification incenses, it routs negativity and gets things moving.

ST. JOHNSWORT (*Hypericum perforatum*). A Druid sacred herb, the Celts passed it through the smoke of the Summer Solstice fire, then wore it in battle for invincibility. It can be burned to banish and exorcise spirits.

SOLOMON'S SEAL (*Polygonatum multiflorum, P. odoratum*). Also known as Dropberry, Sealroot. This herb can be burned as a thank-you offering to the Elementals for their help.

HOLY THISTLE (*Cnicus benedictus, Carduus benedictus*). Also known as Blessed Thistle and St. Benedict Thistle. A Druid sacred herb, it is primarily for protection and strength. Grown in the garden, it turns away thieves.

GARDEN THYME (*Thymus vulgaris*), WILD THYME (*thymus serpyllum*). Also known as Common Thyme, Mother of Thyme. A Druid sacred herb. A magical cleansing bath can be made by pouring a tea of thyme and majoram into the bathwater. A pillow stuffed with thyme cures nightmares. When attending a funeral, wear a sprig of thyme to repel the negativity of the mourners.

TREFOIL (*Trifolium spp*). Also known as Purple Clover, Shamrock, Three-Leaved Grass. A Druid sacred herb symbolizing the triple deities. Always leave something in payment when you take trefoil, because it is a favorite herb of the "little people" and fairies. A pinch of ginger or a little milk poured onto the ground are acceptable gifts. Decorations of trefoil on the altar honor all triple deities. Carry a three-leaf clover for protection and luck; a four-leaf one to avoid military service.

VALERIAN (*Valeriana officinalis*). Also known as Garden Heliotrope, Vandal Root, St. George's Herb. Use this herb in love spells, especially to reconcile troubled couples. Put in pillows to promote deep rest. Although the root of the herb has a strong, pungent scent, some cats love the odor more than catnip.

VERVAIN (*Verbena officinalis*). Also known as Enchanter's Herb, Holy Herb, Verbena, Blue Vervain. A Druid sacred herb common in their many rites and incantations. It was so highly held that offerings of this herb were placed on altars. When burned, it is powerful for warding off psychic attack, but is also used in spells for love, purification and attracting wealth. It is a powerful attractant to the opposite sex.

WILLOW (*Salix alba*). Also known as White Willow, Tree of Enchantment, Witches' Aspirin. One of the seven sacred trees of the Irish; a Druid sacred tree. The willow is a Moon tree sacred to the White Lady. Its groves were considered so magical that priests, priestesses and all types of artisans sat among these trees to gain eloquence, inspiration, skills and prophecies. For a wish to be granted, ask permission of the willow, explaining your desire. Select a pliable shoot and tie a loose knot in it while expressing what you want. When the wish is fulfilled, return and untie the knot. Remember to thank the willow and leave a gift.

WOODRUFF (*Asperula odorata*). Also known as Sweet Woodruff, Master of the Woods, Wuderove. A Druid sacred herb that acquires its scent after drying. Carry a sprig of woodruff when you want to change the course of your life and bring victory. Add to the Beltane wine as a symbol of clearing away barriers.

WORMWOOD (*Artemisia absinthium*). Also known as Absinthe. A Druid sacred herb; very magical and sacred to Moon deities. An accumulative poison if ingested! Burned with incenses on Samhain (Halloween) to aid evocation, divination, scrying and prophecy. Especially good when combined with mugwort. Strengthens incenses for exorcism and protection.

YARROW (*Achillea millefolium*). Also known as Woundwort, Seven Year's Love, Milfoil. This herb is a powerful incense additive for divination and love spells. It has the power to keep couples happily married.

YEW (*Taxus baccata*). Also known as English Yew, European Yew. A Druid sacred tree. This herb was sacred to the Winter Solstice and deities of death and rebirth. The Irish used it to make dagger handles, bows and wine barrels. The berries are POISONOUS! Yew wood or leaves were laid on graves as a reminder to the departed spirit that death was only a pause in life before rebirth.

Cauldron Magic

Remember that timing is very important in magic. Review chapters 3 and 4. Magic of increasing and gaining is done from just after the New Moon until the Full Moon, with the day or night of the Full Moon being strongest. Decreasing magic is done from just after the Full Moon until the New Moon, with the day or night of the New Moon being strongest.

To Gain Money

Fill the cauldron half-full of water and drop a silver coin into it. Position the cauldron so that light from the Moon shines into the water. Gently sweep your hands just above the surface, symbolically gathering the Moon's silver.

While doing this, say:

Lovely Lady of the Moon, bring to me your wealth right soon. Fill my hands with silver and gold. All you give, my purse can hold.

Repeat three times. When finished, pour the water upon the Earth. This is best done at the Full Moon.

To Gain Prophecies

Fill the cauldron half-full of water and place it on a table where you can see comfortably into it while seated. Light two purple candles and a good divinatory incense; a combination of mugwort and wormwood works well for divination. Arrange the candles so their light does not shine into the water or your eyes. Focus your attention on the bottom of the cauldron, your hands placed lightly on either side. Breathe gently onto the water.

Say:

> *Cauldron, reveal to me that which I seek.*
> *Great Mother, open my inner eye that I*
> *may truly see.*

Empty your mind as much as possible; remain relaxed while looking deep into the cauldron waters. The answers may come in images in the water, pictures in your mind, and strong bursts of "knowing." Review Preparing For Magic for help in this. This spell is best done during the waxing Moon.

To Rid Yourself of Negatives

Set an empty cauldron or goblet on your altar between two lit white candles. Burn a good protection or blessings incense. Robe yourself, preferably in white, and stand or sit before the altar. Breathe slowly and evenly until you are calm and centered. Take the cauldron or goblet in both hands; hold high over the altar in salute to the gods. Lower to chest level and slowly breathe into the cauldron, silently naming each habit, person or experience you wish removed from your life.

When finished, turn the cauldron or goblet upside down on the altar, saying:

> *The contents of this vessel I give to thee,*
> *Great Ones. Exchange these experiences*
> *for better.*

Place an offering of herbs and milk outside. Or at least burn the herbs in your censer. This is best done during the waning Moon.

To Gain Love

The cauldron should be on your altar between two pink candles. Inside the cauldron itself, place a magenta candle. Light a love incense and the pink candles. Tap the cauldron three times with your wand.

Say:

> *One to seek him/her, one to find him/her.*
> *One to bring him/her, one to bind him/*
> *her. Heart to heart, forever one. So say I,*
> *this spell is done.*

Tap the cauldron three more times. Light the magenta candle to speed the spell on its way. Best done during the waxing Moon.

To Bind a Trouble-Maker

Perform this spell during the waning Moon. Situate the cauldron between two black candles, with a third black candle opposite you on the far side of the altar. Burn a protection or binding incense. Have the names of your enemies written on a small piece of parchment. If the names are unknown, merely write "all my enemies." Sprinkle basil and elder flowers into the cauldron.

Say:

> *Bubble, bubble, cauldron bubble. Burn
> the evil, destroy the trouble.*

Ignite the parchment from the central candle and
drop into the cauldron. Take up the wand and stir the
air above the cauldron while chanting:

> *Darkness ended, control is done. Light has
> come. My battle's won.*

Take the ashes and herbs outside. Throw them up to
the winds and the Moon.

To Strengthen Your Psychic Shield

The night before the Full Moon, find a place
where your altar will not be disturbed for 24 hours.
Put the cauldron in the center with a red candle on
the right side, black candle on the left, and white candle in the back; but do not light them yet. Sprinkle a
mixture of equal parts of elder blossoms, marjoram,
mint and rue in an unbroken circle around the cauldron.
Into a tiny vial, measure equal drops of oils of clove,
frankincense, jasmine and lavender. Set the sealed
bottle in the cauldron and leave until the night of the
Full Moon.

On Full Moon night, take a cleansing bath and
robe yourself in white. Carry a good protective and/
or purification incense through every room in the
house. Make certain that the smoke drifts into closets.
Return to the altar and light the candles. Take up the
dagger or sword. Face the East and raise the sword in
salute. To salute in this manner, simply hold the sword
point upward in front of you.

Say:

> By the power of the rising Sun, all evil in
> my life is done.

Turn to the South, salute, say:

> By the power of the noonday blast, all
> control is mine at last.

Turn to the West, salute, say:

> By the power of darkening night, my shield
> is strong, my armor tight.

Turn to the North, salute, say:

> By Full Moon in blackened sky, I am not
> alone. My help is nigh. The Goddess' hands
> around me stay, to keep me safe by night
> and day. Begone, foul spirits, unbidden
> here. I send you back. I do not fear, for I
> have won. I am set free. You have no further
> power o'er me!

Face the altar and take up the vial of oil. Put a drop of oil on your finger and anoint your forehead, heart, solar plexus, wrists and ankles. As you do this, visualize a shining blue suit of armor slowly descending over your body until you are entirely protected. Cap the bottle and store in a safe place. Thank the Powers for their help and extinguish the candles. Apply the oil and repeat the chants whenever you feel the armor is slipping.

Stone Magic

The color significance of the stones you choose will be the same for divination as for spellwork. The meanings I use have evolved over a long period and are quite different from those promoted by others. These meanings are also much simpler. If you choose stones that contain more than one color, the predominating color will rule the power.

Keep your stones in a cloth bag large enough to get your hand inside. Until you have become attuned to the energies of the stones, handle each one frequently, mentally seeking its assistance and knowledge.

It is advisable to have more than one stone of each color, plus the specific stones I have listed. As I previously stated it is not necessary that they be cut or polished. Having several stones of a color enables you to step up specific spell-power by setting the stones at the four directions or in a circle on your altar. A piece of black or very dark blue velvet is best to lay them out on during readings, for it displays the colors to their best advantage.

Each stone can also be used alone for meditation. If you have a specific affinity for certain colors of stones and strongly want their powers in your life, consider purchasing a ring or necklace with a setting of that color. This will strengthen your aura.

To determine which, if any, colors are weak in your aura, cut small circles of paper in pure colors to match your chakra colors. Beginning with the root chakra at the base of the spine and ending at the top of the head, these colors are: red, orange, yellow, green, blue, indigo and lavender or white. While holding a pendulum in your power (dominant) hand, place a circle of color in the palm of your other hand. If the pendulum swings in a clockwise direction, that particular color is sufficient. If it swings in a counterclockwise direction, your aura is weak in that color.

Sometimes the pendulum merely stays still, if a color is adequate in your aura. It will circle only if you need that color addition.

When you feel that you are ready to accept the stones, and they accept you, take them to your altar on a Full Moon for consecration. The altar should be covered with a white cloth and a white candle set on each end. Burn a good consecration or blessings incense.

Lay your hands on the stones and say:

> Stones of power, strong stones of lore,
> Join with me, I do implore.
> Aid me in my magic spells;
> Bring me knowledge from deep wells.
> Stones of power, strong stones of lore,
> Join with me, I do implore.

Pass the stones through the incense smoke and above the candle flames. Store them in their special bag and leave on the altar overnight.

For divination, spread your velvet cloth and gently roll the stones in the bag until they are well mixed. Concentrate on the question you want answered. Without looking, reach into the bag, select a stone and lay it on the cloth to the East. The next stone is placed in the South, the next West, the next North, and the last in the center.

The East stands for ideas, thoughts, inspiration, psychic abilities. The South is for action, passion, change, perception of situations. The West represents emotions, healing, marriage or relationships, love. The

North is the region of prosperity, money, growth, success, business or employment. The center of the cloth stands for the power you are using, either negative or positive, to affect the question.

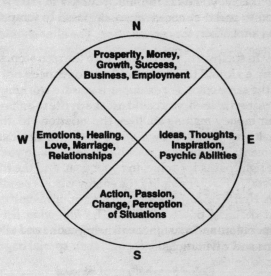

N

Prosperity, Money,
Growth, Success,
Business, Employment

W Emotions, Healing,
Love, Marriage,
Relationships

Ideas, Thoughts,
Inspiration,
Psychic Abilities **E**

Action, Passion,
Change, Perception
of Situations

S

Read each stone according to the direction in which it lies, then in relation to the other stones. For example, if a black stone is in the South, it points to rigidity in life, perhaps a fear of change. Or you may be looking at events with a negative attitude. However, if the center stone is orange, you have the power to change your luck and control the situation. A purple stone in the West would indicate success in your goals for love and healing of the mind and body. A white stone in the East points to a need for calmness before this can happen, while a blue stone in the North hints that a possible move or journey may bring the needed changes into action and benefit you financially.

You can use this layout to determine whether a proposed action will prove beneficial to you, or whether you should re-think your plans. You may need to make minor changes, or possibly scrap the idea altogether.

In spellwork, you can set up to thirteen stones in a circle around the cauldron. The stones need not be all the same color. For example, if you are working on a prosperity spell, you could use the pyrite to enhance your money-making abilities, the lodestone to draw wealth to you, a brown stone to entice the Earth Elementals to aid you, a white stone to guide you to the right paths for achieving your goal, and the rock crystal to further amplify the energy you are sending out. Herbs or candles aid the stones in magnifying and defining power sources. The following list of stone colors and meanings will help you in your selections and divinations.

Color Symbolism of Stones

WHITE: spiritual guidance; being directed into the right paths; calmness; becoming centered; seeing past all illusions. Examples: quartz, agate.

RED: courage to face a conflict or test; energy; taking action. Examples: garnet, red jasper, red agate, dark carnelian.

PINK: healing; true love; friendship. Examples: rose quartz, agate.

YELLOW: power of the mind; creativity of a mental nature; sudden changes. Examples: amber, topaz, citrine.

ORANGE: change your luck; power; control of a situation. Examples: carnelian, jacinth.

BLUE: harmony; understanding; journeys or moves. Examples: lapis lazuli, labradorite.

GREEN: marriage; relationships; balance; practical creativity, particularly with the hands; fertility; growth. Examples: jade, malachite, amazonite.

BROWN: Earth Elementals; success; amplifies all Earth magic and psychic abilities; common sense. Examples: tigereye, smoky quartz.

BLACK: binding; defense by repelling dark magic; reversing spells and thoughtforms into positive power; general defense; pessimism; feeling bound. Examples: jet, onyx, obsidian.

PURPLE: breaking bad luck; protection; psychic and spiritual growth; success in long range plans. Examples: amethyst, beryl, quartz.

INDIGO: discovering past lives; karmic problems; balancing out karma; stopping undesirable habits or experiences. Examples: turquoise, amethyst, beryl.

Additional Stones of Value

PYRITE or FOOL'S GOLD: money, prosperity, total success; Sun deities.

MOONSTONE: gaining occult power; soothing emotions; rising above problems; Moon deities.

ROCK CRYSTAL: amplifier of magical power; psychic work; help with divination; amplifies power raised during all spellwork.

LODESTONE or A MAGNET: drawing-power; ability to attract what you want.

Candle Magic

Burning candles is a very old magical art. Celtic priests and priestesses used tallow lamps or rushes, also bonfires of certain woods. Doing such today would be inconvenient and messy. Candles are a very acceptable substitute.

The most commonly used candles are about six inches long and of the taper or square-end variety. Since many candle spells require that you let the candles burn out, it is wise to invest in solid holders, non-flammable, that are wide enough to catch any dripping wax.

There is one basic major rule in candle-burning: for reversing or removing, burn during the *waning Moon* (after Full Moon until New Moon); for increasing or obtaining burn during the *waxing Moon* (after New Moon to Full Moon). The New Moon is the prime power time of the waning cycle, as the Full Moon is the prime power time of the waxing cycle.

Candles are sometimes used in conjunction with herbs and other spell aids, all geared toward one particular purpose. Select a candle to represent your goal and, with your ritual knife, carve your spell-desires into it. An appropriate oil is then used to anoint the candle. Do this by placing a little of the oil in the palm of your power hand (the hand you use most frequently), and rub the candle with a twisting motion.

If you desire something to *come* to you, rub the candle from the wick end to the bottom. If you desire to *remove* something, rub from the bottom to the wick. Roll the oiled candle in the corresponding herbs and set into the holder.

Hold your hands on each side of the candle, and mentally pour thoughts of your aim into the candle. When ready, light the candle, say:

Candle of power, candle of might,
Create my desires here on this night.
Power, stream from this candle's fire.
Bring to me my heart's desire.
My words have strength, the victory's
    won.
So say I. This spell is done.

This simple spellworking can be used for almost any goal. It is best to leave the candle or candles in a safe place to burn out entirely.

Ogham Alphabet

The Ogham (pronounced owam), or sacred Druidic alphabet, contained hidden secrets for magic and divination. Only the initiated could understand these occult meanings. The ancient Celts had a kinship with trees which is shown in this magical alphabet and in their tree calendar. Further proof of their respect for trees is in the old Celtic word for oak (Duir); the word Derwydd or Duirwydd (oak-seer) was probably the origin of the word Druid.

The Celts believed that many trees were inhabited by spirits or had spirits of their own. This idea most notably applied to any tree with a strong aura around it. They also believed that certain trees had a healing influence on humans. From this ancient respect for the power of trees came the expressions 'touch wood' and 'knock on wood.'

Oak, ash and thorn were called the fairy triad of trees. Where they grow together, it is still said that fairies live.

The Celts had rules concerning the usage of certain trees. It was unlucky to bring blossoms of the hawthorn indoors; this rule is still followed by some modern Celts and Wiccan. In fact, the only time one could break or cut branches of the hawthorn without inviting bad luck was on Beltane Eve. The elder could never be cut without asking permission of the tree. Even then, it was favorable to consider that the elder often harbored bad spirits.

The trees of the Ogham alphabet were divided into three classifications, which had nothing to do with their physical form. They merely represented their order of importance to the Druids. Chieftains came first, followed by peasants and shrubs. Two

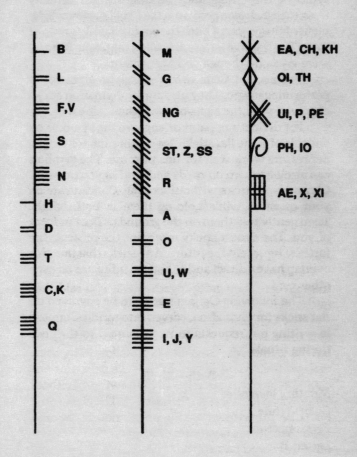

Ogham Alphabet

symbols, the Grove and the Sea, are not actually trees; their inclusion points out the Druidic acknowledgment of the power of both the sea itself and a group of trees. The last five letters are called the Crane Bag and were given by the sea god Manannan.

The ancient Celts used the Ogham alphabet in performing magic. They also threw divination sticks engraved with the signs of the Ogham alphabet.

For divination, paint or engrave the symbols on one side of some flat sticks. Ice cream sticks or tongue depressors work well for this purpose. The symbols can also be drawn on cards and read as you do tarot. Chose seven sticks without looking. Concentrate on your question while holding them in both hands. Then gently toss them on the ground or floor in front of you. The closest sticks represent the present; the farthest represent the future. Any sticks that touch or overlap have a direct and enhanced influence on each other.

The following Ogham signs can be engraved on flat sticks for divination, carved into candles, or used in writing out requests to be presented to the gods during rituals.

Beth—Birch

Month: November
Color: white
Class: peasant
Letter: B
Meaning: New beginnings; changes; purification.

Luis—Rowan

Month: December
Color: grey and red
Class: peasant
Letter: L
Meaning: Controlling your life;
protection against control by
others.

Fearn—Alder

Month: January
Color: crimson
Class: chieftain
Letter: F, V
Meaning: Help in making choices;
spiritual guidance and protec-
tion.

Saille—Willow

Month: February
Color: listed only as bright
Class: peasant
Letter: S
Meaning: Gaining balance in
your life.

Nuin—Ash

Month: March
Color: glass green
Class: chieftain
Letter: N
Meaning: Locked into a chain
of events; feeling bound.

Huathe—Hawthorn

Month: April
Color: purple
Class: peasant
Letter: H
Meaning: Being held back for a
period of time.

Duir—Oak

Month: May
Color: black and dark brown
Class: chieftain
Letter: D
Meaning: Security; strength.

Tinne—Holly

Month: June
Color: dark grey
Class: peasant
Letter: T
Meaning: Energy and guidance
for problems to come.

Coll—Hazel

Month: July
Color: brown
Class: chieftain
Letter: C, K
Meaning: Creative energies for
work or projects.

Quert—Apple

Month: none
Color: green
Class: shrub
Letter: Q
Meaning: A choice must be made.

Muin—Vine

Month: August
Color: variegated
Class: chieftain
Letter: M
Meaning: Inner development occurring, but take time for relaxation.

Gort—Ivy

Month: September
Color: sky blue
Class: chieftain
Letter: G
Meaning: Take time to soul-search or you will make a wrong decision.

Ngetal—Reed

Month: October
Color: grass green
Class: shrub
Letter: NG
Meaning: Upsets or surprises.

Straif—Blackthorn

Month: none
Color: purple
Class: chieftain
Letter: SS, Z, ST
Meaning: Resentment; confusion; refusing to see the truth.

Ruis—Elder

Month: makeup days of the thirteenth month
Color: red
Class: shrub
Letter: R
Meaning: End of a cycle or problem.

Ailim —Silver Fir

Month: none
Color: light blue
Class: shrub
Letter: A
Meaning: Learning from past mistakes; take care in choices.

Ohn—Furze

Month: none
Color: yellow gold
Class: chieftain
Letter: O
Meaning: Information that could change your life.

Ur—Heather & Mistletoe

Month: none
Color: purple
Class: heather is peasant; mistletoe is chieftain
Letter: U
Meaning: Healing and development on the spiritual level.

Eadha—White Poplar or Aspen

Month: none
Color: silver white
Class: shrub
Letter: E
Meaning: Problems; doubts; fears.

Ioho—Yew

Month: none
Color: dark green
Class: chieftain
Letter: I, J, Y
Meaning: Complete change in life-direction or attitude.

Koad—Grove

Month: none
Color: many shades of green
Class: none
Letter: CH, KH, EA
Meaning: Wisdom gained by seeing past illusions.

Oir—Spindle

Month: none
Color: white
Class: peasant
Letter: TH, OI
Meaning: Finish obligations and
tasks or your life cannot move
forward.

Uilleand—Honeysuckle

Month: none
Color: yellow-white
Class: peasant
Letter: P, PE, UI
Meaning: Proceed with caution.

Phagos—Beech

Month: none
Color: orange-brown
Class: chieftain
Letter: PH, IO
Meaning: New experiences and
information coming.

Mor—the Sea

Month: none
Color: blue-green
Class: none
Letter: AE, X, XI
Meaning: Travel

Deity Chants for Rituals

The following chants and spells are broadly classified, as many deities have more than one function in magic. As their functions change, so do the chants used to petition them. Samples of incenses are given at the beginning of this chapter. Before beginning a ritual, review the chapter on the Magic Circle if uncertain about the entire procedure.

Further information on the gods and goddesses, and their various functions, can be found in chapter 9, the Table of Deities, the Table of Elementals, and the Quick Reference Table of Deities in this chapter. The Table of Deities and the Table of Elementals give everything you need for ritual use with these chants, plus a general description of the appropriate deities.

Chants for the Creator Deities

Put a cauldron of water on the altar. Light white candles and appropriate incense.

> Open the door to my inner life; reveal the
>   past to me.
> Open the door to my inner life, that my
>   way may be made free.
> Send me the light of your cosmic fire;
>   Make my path bright clear.
> Give me a sign, that's no will of mine, to
>   show me your presence is here.

Follow this by meditation and divination with the cauldron, as discussed in cauldron magic. Sometimes this must be done for several nights leading up to the Full Moon before your "inner doors" begin to open.

Chants for the Creative & Fertility Deities

With the wand, enclose your altar and working area in an invisible circle, as you were taught in chapter 5.

> *Stones for art, stones for birth,*
> *Stones as symbols here on Earth,*
> *The Old Ones set in circles round,*
> *In lines that march across the ground.*
> *Their power still flows like a flowering*
>   *tree.*
> *O, Great Ones, send that power to me.*

Make a circle on a small piece of paper with a pen; ballpoint ink will do as well as any other. Place your name inside the circle. Anoint the center of the paper with a drop of lily oil. Leave this on the altar overnight. The next night burn it in the cauldron. Throw the ashes and herbs onto the winds.

Chants for Underworld Deities

Tap on the altar three times with your sword.

> *Life and death are yours to give,*
> *They are also yours to hold.*
> *There is no ending of this life.*
> *We are born in another mold.*
> *But all must be balanced, and so must I.*
> *This I will ask by Earth and Sky.*

Tap the altar another three times. Explain your needs carefully and precisely, for these deities take things quite literally, often creating strong results.

Chants for the Great Mother

Use the wand when requesting from the Great Mother. She answers with a softer grace to the wand. With the sword, she is an indignant protector of her children.

(Chant for the softer aspect of the Great Mother)

Mother of the comforting breast, the pro-
tecting arm,
I am your child. Keep me from harm.
Inspire me in dreams.
Give me the key
That will open the gate.
Mother, help me.

(Chant for the darker aspect of the Great Mother)

Great Mother, guardian of your children,
I stand in great need of your protection.
There are those who are against me by
thought, word, and deed.
Let their efforts fail. Let their evil return to
the lower darkness.
Great Mother, I ask for and accept your
protection.

Chants for Deities of Justice

With the wand, stir the air over your cauldron of herbs.

Little Ones, come join with me
And the Justice Deities.
Change my luck.
Make me bold.
Bring me wealth and love to hold,
Accomplishments and friendships true.
For this aid, I do bless you.

Give a special gift to the Earth Elementals to entice them to carry out your requests.

Chants for Deities of Revenge

Write your requests on a small piece of paper. Light it from an altar candle and drop it to burn away in the cauldron. Stand before the altar with the sword hilt between your hands, the point at your feet.

> *Wolf and horse, old signs of might.*
> *Lend your strength to me this night.*
> *Courage I need, and the power of steel,*
> *Energy, willpower, defense to feel.*
> *Hark to my call, great Powers all!*

Lay the tip of the sword against the cauldron. Hold that position as long as you can, soaking up the powers of these strong deities. This is very good to do when you have to face a person or situation that you dread.

Chants for Deities of Healing, Illumination & The Sun

With the wand, draw an invisible circle around the altar and your working area. Raise the wand in salute to the Sun deity.

> *Sun of power, Sun of gold*
> *Sun, O wondrous fair,*
> *Hear my words of power and grace,*
> *Winging through the air.*
> *Illuminate Deep Mysteries,*
> *Bring me favors great.*
> *Fill my life with joy and hope.*
> *Grant me wondrous fate.*
> *All-powerful, healing Deities,*
> *Guide me to high destinies.*

Kneel before the altar for a quiet time of receiving blessings.

Chants for Messenger & Teacher Deities

Set a picture or an image of a butterfly before three orange candles arranged in a triangle shape with the goblet in the center. Carve into the candles, one desire to a candle, the three things you need most from the Teacher Deities. Take up the goblet, breathing gently into it the names of every person or situation you wish to remove from your life. When finished, turn the goblet upside down in its position among the candles. Anoint and light the candles. Tap the goblet gently on the bottom with your wand.

> *I have filled this magic cup with the excesses in my life.*
> *I freely pour them upon the altar. Accept these, O Teachers.*
> *Change them into good before returning them to me.*

Tap the goblet gently again, then turn it upright.

> *Blessings to all, who come to my aid. Between friends is this bargain made.*
>
> *Ashes to gold, no more strife, for the Teachers shall guide me the rest of my life.*

Raise the goblet in a salute to the Teachers, then "drink" what they have given you.

Chants for Moon Deities

Have a goblet of white wine on the altar along with tarot cards, runes, divinatory stones, or other such aids. With the knife, trace an invisible circle around the working area. Either have a chair ready, if you can sit comfortably next to the altar, or use a pillow for sitting on the floor. With the wand, slowly circle your chosen divinatory aid three times.

> *Silver Huntress, enchanted Moon Lady,*
> *Mistress of Mysteries and the future, give*
> *me the knowledge to foretell aright.*

Lift the goblet in a salute for the Moon deities and take a sip: *One for magic.* Take another sip: *One for power.* Take a third sip: *One for 'seeing' in this hour.*

Put the goblet back on the altar along with the wand. Sit quietly for a few moments before beginning your reading of the cards, runes, or whatever chosen tool. When finished, take up the wand and gently tap the altar three times.

> *Silver Huntress, Mistress of Mysteries and*
> *the future, my thanks for your presence*
> *and instruction. Guide me whenever my*
> *hand takes up the (cards, runes, stones,*
> *whatever applies.)*

NOTE: If you have chosen a male deity, change the words in the chant from Huntress to Hunter, from Lady to Lord, from Mistress to Master.

Chants for Earth & Grain Deities

Among your altar implements, be sure to include a brown candle, some ginger, a small amount of milk, a goblet of red wine, and a few cookies or crackers. Mentally call the Elementals, asking them to join you. With the wand, touch the ginger, cup of milk, goblet of wine, cookies, saying:

> *A boon for a boon, the old words say.*
> *A boon I do bring you on this day.*

Take the goblet, face East and take a sip. Hold up the goblet in salute:

> *Sylphs and Zephrys, rulers of Air, I ask of*
> *you knowledge and inspirations.*

Turn to the South; sip the wine. Hold up the goblet:

> *Firedrakes and Salamanders, rulers of Fire,*
> *I ask of you energy and change.*

Turn to the West. Sip the wine and hold up the goblet:

> *Nymphs and Undines, rulers of Water, I*
> *ask of you healing and love.*

Turn to the North; sip the wine. Hold up the goblet:

> *Gnomes and Dwarfs, rulers of Earth, I ask*
> *of you prosperity and success.*

Be sure to leave a little wine to be put outside for the "little people."

Place the goblet on the altar. Raise your arms, say:

> *All you deities of Earth and plants and*
> *animals, what I have asked of the Little*
> *Ones, I now ask of you. Give me oppor-*
> *tunities to accomplish these desires, and*
> *the wisdom to use the opportunities. Help*
> *me to know the difference between sel-*
> *fishness and true aspiration. Grant me a*
> *balanced, growing life. For this, I give you*

all honor.

Light the brown candle, leaving it to burn out completely. Mix the remaining wine with the milk and ginger. Pour it out on the ground. Leave the cookies outside also.

Sample Spell

The best kinds of magic, rituals, and spells are those you create yourself. No good spell is cast in concrete. It is highly desirable that you write your own, if at all possible. Just remember that certain herbs, colors, etc. traditionally represent specific types of archetypal powers, those we call gods and goddesses. The more visual aids used on your altar, the easier it will be to work up the strong emotions needed to accomplish the spellworking.

A Full Love Spell

Begin by checking the list under Love Deities in the Tables of Correspondence for the supplies needed. Plan the ritual for the Full Moon since you want to increase love in your life. Place your altar so you face the West, the direction associated with Water.

Cover the altar with a green or pink cloth, and wear green or pink if you can. Light the charcoal in your censer; sprinkle in a love incense along with rose petals and elder flowers. Place a lighted pink candle at each end of the altar, and a picture or statue of a cat or dove in the rear center beside a lighted magenta candle.

Set the cauldron in the center with an unlit pink candle inside it. Sprinkle equal parts of rose petals, yarrow and thyme around the cauldron. Place your green stones along with a white, the moonstone and the lodestone on the circle of herbs. Now draw an invisible circle with your wand around the altar and your working area. If unsure about circle casting, review chapter 5.

With your ritual knife, carve your desires into the cauldron candle. Anoint it with rose oil. "Feed" this candle your desires with your hands; light it.

> *Candle of power, candle of might,*
> *Create my desires here on this night.*
> *Power, stream from this candle's fire.*
> *Bring to me my heart's desire.*
> *My words have strength, the victory's*
> *   won.*
> *So say I. This spell is done.*

Put a pinch of ginger on the altar for the Water Elementals, saying:

> *Children of Water, small ones of Light,*
> *Join with my spelling here on this night.*
> *Decreed by the Mother/Father, felt in my*
> *   heart.*
> *Bring us together, never to part.*

Raise your arms and open your heart to the deity. Speak silently with the god/goddess, explaining your need for a true love. Remember, to gain a love perfect for you, you must feel loving. This applies to men as well as to women.

A loving man, in my opinion, is not equated with the macho state. Nor does it mean he is not masculine. It means he is a balanced, caring person who desires the same in a companion. The ancient Celts were well aware of this fact, as seen by their attitude toward women.

To end the ritual, say:

> *Blessings to all who come to my aid.*
> *Between friends is this bargain made.*

Snuff out the two end candles, leaving the magenta and the cauldron candle to burn out. It is best to delay clearing the altar until the candles have burned out completely. Sprinkle the circled herbs onto the ground as an offering to the Nature spirits, or put them in a small cloth bag to carry with you. Give them to the Elementals during the next Full Moon.

11 Tables of Correspondence

Table for Incenses

The following categories will be useful in making up your own incenses, if you are so inclined. However, there are several reputable pagan businesses which can provide correctly formulated incenses for your needs. If you use oils on the charcoal, only use a drop or two at a time.

ANOINTING: acacia, angelica, carnation, cinquefoil, frankincense, jasmine, lavender, lily of the valley, lotus, myrrh, rose, rosemary, vervain.

BALANCE: jasmine, orange, rose.

BANISHING, RELEASING: cedar, clove, cypress, patchouli, rose, rue, violet, betony, elder, fern, mugwort, St. Johnswort, vervain, yarrow.

BINDING: apple, cayenne, dragon's blood, cypress, pine, pepper, rowan, wormwood.

BLESSING, CONSECRATION: carnation, cypress, frankincense, lotus, rosemary, elder, rue.

CHANGES: peppermint, dragon's blood, woodruff.

CLAIRVOYANCE, DIVINATION: cinnamon, lilac, acacia, laurel, eyebright, honeysuckle, marigold, mugwort, nutmeg, rose, thyme, wormwood, yarrow, dittany of Crete, hazel, moonwort, rowan.

CREATIVITY: honeysuckle, lilac, lotus, rose, vervain, wild cherry, savory.

CURSING: blackthorn, elder, pepper.

DETERMINATION, COURAGE: allspice, musk, rosemary, dragon's blood, mullein.

ENERGY, POWER, STRENGTH: allspice, bay, carnation, cinnamon, cinquefoil, frankincense, lotus, musk, thyme, dragon's blood, verbena, oak, holly.

EXORCISM: bay, frankincense, lavender, myrrh, pine, rosemary, vervain, basil, cedar, fern, mullein, pepper, rue, St. Johnswort, wormwood, yarrow.

GOOD LUCK, FORTUNE, JUSTICE: cedar, lotus, mint, vervain, violet, nutmeg, bayberry, cinnamon, cinquefoil, honeysuckle, chamomile, jasmine, yellow dock.

HAPPINESS, HARMONY, PEACE: apple blossom, basil, cedar, cypress, fir, jasmine, lavender, lilac, lotus, orange, patchouli, rose, rosemary, lily of the valley, purple loosestrife, valerian, vervain.

HEALING: carnation, cinnamon, cinquefoil, clove, lavender, lotus, myrrh, rose, rosemary, sandalwood, apple, laurel, wild cherry, hazel, hops, orange, peppermint, rowan, savory.

INSPIRATION, WISDOM: cinquefoil, acacia, clove,

cypress, fir, hazel, laurel, lily of the valley, oak moss, reed, rosemary, rowan, rue.

LOVE: apple blossom, birch, cinquefoil, gardenia, honeysuckle, jasmine, musk, rose, vervain, acacia, catnip, elder, fern, heather, juniper, lavender, marigold, marjoram, mistletoe, moonwort, patchouli, savory, vanilla, valerian, wormwood, yarrow.

MEDITATION: acacia, angelica, bay, cinnamon, frankincense, jasmine, myrrh, nutmeg, wisteria.

NEW BEGINNINGS: birch oil.

PROTECTION, DEFENSE: angelica, bay, bayberry, birch, cinnamon, cypress, frankincense, jasmine, lily of the valley, patchouli, pine, rue, vervain, basil, burdock, cinquefoil, club moss, dill, dragon's blood, fern, feverfew, fir, furze, hawthorn, hazel, heather, holly, juniper, marjoram, mistletoe, mugwort, mullein, oak, pepper, rosemary, rowan, St. Johnswort, thistle, wormwood, yarrow.

PSYCHIC CENTERS, OPENING: nutmeg, mimosa, wisteria, lotus, mugwort.

PURIFICATION, CLEANSING: bay laurel, frankincense, lavender, myrrh, pine, rosemary, vervain, basil, betony, burdock, cedar, dragon's blood, elder, feverfew, hyssop, marjoram, oak, peppermint, rue, salt, thyme, valerian, woodruff.

REINCARNATION: lilac, sandalwood.

VISIONS: bay laurel, frankincense, lotus, acacia, dittany of Crete, marigold, mugwort, wormwood.

WILLPOWER: rosemary, St. Johnswort.

Table of Candle Colors

RED: health, energy, strength, sexual potency, courage, will power, to conquer fear or laziness.

PINK: love, affection, romance, spiritual awakening, healing of the spirit, togetherness.

YELLOW: intellect, imagination, power of the mind, creativity, confidence, gentle persuasion, action, attraction, concentration, inspiration, sudden changes.

ORANGE: encouragement, adaptability, stimulation, attraction, sudden changes, control, power, to draw good things, change luck.

GREEN: abundance, fertility, good fortune, generosity, money, wealth, success, renewal, marriage, balance.

BLUE: truth, inspiration, wisdom, occult power, protection, understanding, good health, happiness, peace, fidelity, harmony in the home, patience.

PURPLE: success, idealism, higher psychic ability, wisdom, progress, protection, honors, spirit contact, break bad luck, drive away evil, divination.

BROWN: attract money and financial success; influence Earth Elementals, concentration, balance, ESP, intuition, study.

BLACK: reversing, uncrossing, binding negative forces, discord, protection, releasing, repel dark magic and negative thoughtforms.

WHITE: purity, spirituality and greater attainments in life, truth, sincerity, power of a higher nature, wholeness.

MAGENTA: very high vibrational frequency that

tends to work fast, so usually burned with other candles; quick changes, spiritual healing, exorcism.

INDIGO: meditation, neutralize another's magic, stop gossip, lies or undesirable competition, balance out karma.

GOLD OR VERY CLEAR LIGHT YELLOW: great fortune, intuition, understanding, divination, fast luck, financial benefits, attracts higher influences, male deity powers.

SILVER OR VERY CLEAR LIGHT GRAY: removes negative powers, victory, stability, meditation, develop psychic abilities, female deity powers.

Table of Elementals

AIR

Rulers: Sylphs, Zephyrs and Fairies who inhabit the world of trees, flowers, winds, breezes, mountains.

King: Paralda.

Attracted By: oils and incenses.

Color & Direction: red or yellow; East.

Magical Tools: wand, incense, creative visualization.

Symbols: sky, wind, breezes, clouds, breath, vibrations, plants, herbs, flowers, trees.

Ritual Work: dawn, sunrise, Spring, knowledge, inspiration, hearing, harmony, herbal knowledge, plant growth, intellect, thought, ideas, travel, freedom, revealing the truth, finding lost things, movement, psychic abilities.

EARTH

Rulers: Gnomes, Dwarfs and Trolls who inhabit the interior of the Earth and are the consciousness of precious gems, minerals and the Earth herself.

King: Ghob, Gob, or Ghom.

Attracted By: salts and powders.

Color & Direction: black or green; North.

Magical Tools: pentagram, salt, images, stones, gems, trees, cord magic.

Symbols: rocks and gemstones, mountains, plains, fields, soil, caves and mines.

Ritual Work: night, midnight, Winter, riches, treasures, surrendering self-will, touch, empathing, incorporation, business, prosperity, employment, stability, success, fertility, money.

FIRE

Rulers: Salamanders, Firedrakes, the consciousness of flames.

King: Djin.

Attracted By: candles, lamps, incense, fire.

Color & Direction: white or red; South.

Magical Tools: dagger, lamp or candles, censer, burned herbs or requests on paper.

Symbols: lightning, volcanoes, rainbow, Sun, stars.

Ritual Work: Summer, noon, freedom, change, sight, perception, vision, illumination, learning, love, will, passion, sexuality, energy, authority, healing, destruction, purification.

WATER

Rulers: Nymphs, Undines, Mermaids and Mermen who live in the sea, lakes, streams and springs, and Fairies of the lakes, ponds and streams.

King: Niksa or Necksa.

Attracted By: water, washes, solutions.

Color & Direction: gray or blue; West.

Magical Tools: cauldron, goblet, mirrors, the sea.

Symbols: oceans, lakes, rivers, wells, springs, pools, rain, mist, fog.

Ritual Work: Fall, sunset, plants, healing, emotions, taste, smell, absorbing, communion with the spiritual, purification, the subconscious mind, love, emotions, pleasure, friendships, marriage, fertility, happiness, sleep, dreams, the psychic.

Table of Deities

The deities listed in the following tables are only examples, not all of the appropriate powers are represented. Review chapter 9 with the lists of gods and goddesses, and the Quick Reference section at the end of this chapter for complete information on types of god-powers.

1. CREATOR DEITIES

Titles: Ancient of Ancients; First Cause.

Deities: Anu, Danu, the Dagda, Llyr.

Color: brilliant pure white.

Incense/Oil: wisteria, angelica.

Animals: hawk, winged dragon.

Stones: diamond, zircon.

Metal: electrum (gold & silver alloy), or piece each of gold and silver.

Plants: shamrock, clover, woad, male fern, aspen.

Wood: aspen.

Planet: Uranus.

Tarot Cards: four Aces.

Magical Tools: cauldron.

Direction: East.

Rituals Involving: divine consciousness; illumination; enlightenment; spiritual development and attainment; finding the karmic purpose in life.

2. CREATIVE & FERTILITY DEITIES

Titles: Illuminating Intelligence.

Deities: Lugh, Bran, Brigit, the Dagda, Diancecht, Goibniu, Manannan mac Lir, Nuada, Cernunnos, Bel, Mab, Macha, Nantosuelta, Ogma, Rhiannon.

Color: true pure blue.

Incense/Oil: lily of the valley.

Animals: dolphin, whale, mermaid.
Stones: azurite, turquoise.
Metal: aluminum.
Plants: carnation, honeysuckle, vervain.
Wood: bramble.
Planet: Neptune.
Tarot Cards: four Kings & four Twos.
Magical Tools: cauldron, wand.
Direction: South.
Rituals Involving: achieving equilibrium; spiritual manifestations; creative force; divine inspiration.

3. GREAT MOTHER GODDESSES; DEITIES OF THE UNDERWORLD

Titles: the Great Taskmaster; Womb of Time.
Deities: Anu, Arianrhod, Badb, Danu, Brigit, Cerridwen, the Morrigu, the Dagda, Diancecht, Don, Gwyn ap Nudd.
Color: indigo, black.
Incense/Oil: holly, juniper, yew, myrrh, cypress.
Animals: dragon, goat.
Stones: onyx, jet.
Metals: lead.
Plants: oak, yew, beech, comfrey, elm, holly, ivy, horsetail, juniper, mullein, reeds, Solomon's seal.
Wood: oak.
Planet: Saturn.
Tarot Cards: four Queens & four Threes.
Magical Tools: sword or wand.
Direction: West.
Rituals Involving: stabilization of thought and life; help with groups; comfort when in sorrow; contact with the Goddess power; developing power of faith.

4. DEITIES OF JUSTICE
Titles: the Great Helper; Scale-Balancer.
Deities: the Dagda, Danu, Lugh, Macha, Sucellus.
Color: deep purple, dark blue.
Incense/Oil: cedar, carnation.
Animals: unicorn, eagle.
Stones: amethyst, sapphire, lapis lazuli.
Metal: tin.
Plants: shamrock, clover, oak, verbena, cedar, betony, dandelion, fir, meadowsweet.
Wood: cedar.
Planet: Jupiter.
Tarot Cards: four Fours.
Magical Tools: wand, cauldron.
Direction: North.
Rituals Involving: honor, riches, health, friendship, the heart's desires, luck, accomplishment, religion, trade and employment, treasure, legal matters.

5. DEITIES OF WAR, REVENGE & SMITHING
Titles: the Warrior God.
Deities: the Morrigu, Arawn, Cerridwen, the Dagda, Lugh, Macha, Nuada, Pwyll, Scathach.
Color: red.
Incense/Oil: dragon's blood, basil, pine.
Animals: wolf, horse, bear, ram.
Stones: ruby, bloodstone, garnet, red topaz, red agate.
Metal: iron, steel.
Plants: oak, nettles, basil, broom, holy thistle, pine, wormwood, hops, woodruff.
Wood: hawthorn, furze.
Tarot Cards: four Fives.
Magical Tools: sword, cauldron.
Direction: South.

Rituals Involving: energy, courage, defense, will power, self-discipline, ridding yourself of garbage in order to attain higher aspirations, bringing rhythm and stability into life.

6. DEITIES OF THE SUN, HEALING & ILLUMINATION

Titles: the Great God.
Deities: Bel, Badb, the Dagda, Brigit, Diancecht, Ogma.
Color: gold or pale yellow.
Incense/Oil: chamomile, marigold, mistletoe, frank-incense, cinnamon, bay.
Animals: phoenix, snake.
Stones: topaz, yellow diamond, yellow jacinth, chrysolite, goldstone, zircon, pyrite.
Metal: gold.
Plants: laurel, vine, ash, chamomile, centaury, marigold, rue, mistletoe, St. Johnswort.
Wood: laurel.
Planet: Sun.
Tarot Cards: four Knights and four Sixes.
Magical Tools: wand.
Direction: East.
Rituals Involving: honor, power, life, growth, money, healing, understanding the Deep Mysteries, building intuition, energy, favor, promotion, success, friendship, hope, prosperity, confidence, personal fulfillment.

7. LOVE DEITIES

Titles: the Great Mother.
Deities: Arianrhod, Brigit, Danu, Anu, Blodeuwedd, Branwen, Angus mac Og.

Color: green, pink.
Incense/Oil: apple blossom, mugwort, elder, mint, rose, sandalwood.
Animals: cat, dove, sparrow.
Stones: emerald, amber, malachite, jade, peridot, coral.
Metal: copper.
Plants: birch, catnip, blackberry, coltsfoot, foxglove, mugwort, thyme, yarrow, feverfew, burdock, elder, pennyroyal, plantain, briar, verbena.
Wood: birch, elder.
Planet: Venus.
Tarot Cards: four Sevens.
Magical Tools: cauldron, wand.
Direction: West.
Rituals Involving: love, pleasure, the arts, music, writing, creativity, inspiration, expanding the intellect, marriage, friendship, beauty, fertility, compassion, children, spiritual harmony.

8. MESSENGER & TEACHER DEITIES

Titles: Messenger of the Gods.
Deities: Taliesin, Merlin, Angus mac Og, Branwen, Cerridwen, the Dagda, Diancecht, Gwydion, Math Mathonwy, the Morrigu, Nuada, Ogma, Scathach.
Color: orange.
Incense/Oil: dill, lily of the valley, savory, honeysuckle.
Animals: swallow, butterfly.
Stones: agate, carnelian, alexandrite.
Metal: quicksilver, alloys.
Plants: fern, lily of the valley, marjoram, savory, valerian, vervain.
Wood: hazel.

Planet: Mercury.
Tarot Cards: four Eights.
Magical Tools: goblet, wand.
Direction: East.
Rituals Involving: business, legal problems, travel, information, logic, writing, controlling runaway emotions, organization, learning, locating the proper teachers, memory, science, creativity, divination, prediction, eloquence, speech, healing nervous disorders.

9. MOON DEITIES

Titles: the Silver Huntress, Maiden of the Mysteries, Queen of Heaven.
Deities: Arianrhod, Blodeuwedd, Bran, Brigit, Cerridwen, the Dagda, Danu, Lugh.
Color: silver, lavender, pale blue, pearl white.
Incense/Oil: mugwort, lily of the valley, jasmine, lotus.
Animals: dog, hare, hart, boar, horse.
Stones: moonstone, quartz crystal, beryl, pearl.
Metal: silver.
Plants: mandrake, lily of the valley, moonwort, mugwort, water lily, willow.
Wood: willow.
Planet: Moon.
Tarot Cards: four Nines.
Magical Tools: goblet, wand.
Direction: West.
Rituals Involving: change, divination, fertility, intuition, crystal ball, tarot cards, runes or other divination aids; dreams, magic, love, plants, medicine, luck, birth, visions.

10. EARTH & GRAIN DEITIES

Titles: the Sphere of Form.

Deities: gnomes, fairies and folk, Anu, Branwen, Brigit, Cernunnos, Don.

Color: yellow, brown.

Incense/Oil: birch, cherry, cloves, lilac, rosemary.

Animals: toad, fairies, elves, gnomes.

Stones: rock crystal.

Metal: nickel.

Plants: corn, willow, lily, ivy, grains.

Wood: fir.

Planet: Earth.

Tarot Cards: four Pages and four Tens.

Magical Tools: wand, goblet.

Direction: North.

Rituals Involving: organized material manifestations; healing mental and physical illnesses; inspiration for improving life on a material basis; centering oneself; healing plants and animals; trance; any psychic work that calls for direct contact with spirits.

Quick Reference Table of Deities

ABUNDANCE: Bel, Sucellus. See Prosperity.

AGRICULTURE: Brigit, White Lady, Epona, Lugh, Bel, the Horned God, Amaethon.

AIR: See Sky.

ANIMALS: Epona, Rhiannon, Brigantia, Cerridwen, Cernunnos, Bel, Herne, Bran the Blessed, the Horned God, Cocidius, Flidais, Nuada, Anu, Manannan mac Lir, Nantosuelta.

ARCHITECTURE: Lugh, Goibniu. See Arts & Crafts.

ARTS & CRAFTS: Brigit, Cerridwen, the Dagda, Lugh, Ogma, Taliesin, Merlin, Bran the Blessed, Manannan mac Lir, Diancecht, Goibniu, Nantosuelta, Nuada.

BEAUTY: Arianrhod, Branwen, Creiddylad, Nuada, Angus mac Og.

BLACKSMITHS: See Metalworking.

BLESSINGS: Danu, Badb. See Spiritual Illumination.

BOATS: Manannan mac Lir, Nuada. See Sea.

BREWING: Goibniu, the Horned God.

CALM: Rhiannon, Branwen, Creiddylad, Arianrhod, Anu.

CARPENTERS: Lugh, Luchtaine. See Arts & Crafts.

CHANGE: Gwydion, Taliesin, Merlin. See Shapeshifter.

CHILDBIRTH: Nantosuelta, Nuada.

CIVILIZATION: Ogma, Lugh, the Dagda. See Organization.

COMMERCE: Lugh, Cernunnos, Herne, Manannan mac Lir.

COMPASSION: See Mercy.

COURAGE: Morrigu. See Strength.

CREATIVITY: Druantia. See Arts & Crafts, Music, Writing.

CREATOR GOD/DESS: Arianrhod, Danu, the Dagda.

CRONE ASPECT: Morgan Le Fay, Cerridwen, Macha.

CROSSROADS: See Journeys.

CRYSTAL READING: Merlin, Taliesin. See Psychic Abilities.

CUNNING: Pwyll, Macha.

CURSING: See Revenge.

DANCE: See Music.

DARKNESS: See Night.

DEATH: Morrigu, Creiddylad, Cerridwen, White Lady, Arawn, Gwynn ap Nudd, the Dagda, Ogma, Pwyll, Anu, Caillech, Cocidius, Don, Macha. See Underworld.

DESTINY: See Fate.

DESTRUCTION: White Lady, Macha, Caillech, Morrigu.

DISASTER: Morrigu, Macha, White Lady.

DISEASE: Caillech.

DIVINATION: Brigit, Merlin, Taliesin. See Tarot, Crystal Reading, Psychic Abilities.

DOMESTIC ARTS: Brigit, Cerridwen, Nantosuelta. See Arts & Crafts.

DREAMS: See Psychic Abilities.

EARTH: See Earth God/dess.

EARTH GOD/DESS: Cerridwen, Blodeuwedd, Creiddylad, the Dagda, Cernunnos, Anu, Tailtiu. See Great Mother, Great Father.

ECSTASY: See Passion.

ELOQUENCE: Don, Ogma.

ENCHANTMENTS: Brigit, Cerridwen, Morrigu, Rhiannon, Banba, Gwydion, Math Mathonwy, Merlin, Taliesin, Nuada. See Magic.

ENLIGHTENMENT: See Blessings.

EXORCISM: See Protection.

FAMILY: See Marriage, Motherhood.

FATE: the Dagda, Manannan mac Lir, Morrigu, Arianrhod.

FATHER GOD: the Dagda. See Great Father.

FERTILITY: Arianrhod, Brigit, Cerridwen, Brigantia, Macha, Herne, Cernunnos, Bel, Epona, Manannan mac Lir, Mab, Nantosuelta, Druantia, the Horned God, Anu, Arianrhod, Rhiannon.

FIRE: Brigit, Goibniu, Merlin, the Dagda, Bel, Kai.

FISHING: See Boats, Sea.

FLOWERS: Blodeuwedd, Creiddylad.

FORESTS: See Woodlands.

FORETELLING: Cerridwen, Danu, Macha, Morrigu, Brigit, Rhiannon, Merlin, Taliesin. See Tarot, Crystal Reading, Psychic Abilities.

GREAT FATHER: The male principle of creation; god of Winter, the Sun, woodlands, forest, animals, the sky, sexual love. Bel, the Dagda, Don.

GREAT GOD/DESS: Cerridwen, Danu, Macha, Morrigu, Brigit, Anu, Bel, Rhiannon, the Dagda, Badb. See Great Father, Great Mother.

GREAT MOTHER: The female principle of creation; goddess of fertility, the Moon, Summer, flowers, love, healing, the seas, water. Cerridwen, Danu, Morrigu, Anu, Margawse.

HARVESTS: Cerridwen. See Agriculture, Vegetation.

HEALING: Brigit, Boann, Brigantia, Cernunnos, Bel, Lugh, Merlin, Taliesin, Diancecht, Gwydion, the Dagda, Nuada, Owein ap Urien, Epona, Scathach, Airmid, Etan, Fand, Miach.

HEALTH: Brigantia, Brigit, Anu, Diancecht, Airmid, Lugh, Etan.

HEARTH: See Home, Motherhood.

HERBS: Cerridwen, Brigit, Merlin, Taliesin, Cernunnos.

HOME: Brigit.

THE HORNED GOD: Cernunnos, Herne the Hunter.

HORSES: Epona, Rhiannon, Manannan mac Lir.

THE HUNTER/HUNTRESS: Morrigu, Cernunnos, Herne the Hunter, Epona, Nicneven.

ILLNESS: See Disease.

ILLUSION: Merlin, Gwydion, Taliesin. See Shape-shifter.

INITIATION: Cerridwen, the Dagda, Lugh, Merlin, Taliesin, Blodeuwedd.

INSPIRATION: Cerridwen, Brigit, Merlin, Taliesin, Ogma, Badb.

INTELLIGENCE: See Wisdom, Knowledge.

INVENTIONS: Merlin, Taliesin, Cernunnos.

JEWELRY: Goibniu, Diancecht, Lugh. See Metal-working.

JOURNEYS: Lugh, Cernunnos.

JUDGMENT: See Retribution, Fate.

JUSTICE: See Retribution, Fate.

KARMA: See Fate, Retribution.

KNOWLEDGE: Brigit, the Dagda, Taliesin, Merlin, Cerridwen, Taranis, Druantia. See Wisdom.

LAW: Don.

LEARNING: See Knowledge, Arts & Crafts.

LIFE: Badb. See Great Mother, Great Father.

LIGHT: See Sun.

LIGHTNING: See Weather.

LOVE: Branwen, Brigit, Mab, Creiddylad, Angus mac Og.

LUCK: Danu. See Success.

MAGIC: Morrigu, Rhiannon, Cerridwen, Brigit, Danu, Banba, Lugh, the Dagda, Gwydion, Ogma, Diancecht, Manannan mac Lir, Math Mathonwy, Taliesin, Merlin, Nuada, Scathach, Taranis.

MAGIC, DARK: Morrigu, Cerridwen, Scathach.

MAIDEN ASPECT: Elaine, Blodeuwedd, Anu.

MARRIAGE: Nantosuelta. See Home, Motherhood.

MARTIAL ARTS: Brigit, Cernunnos, the Dagda, Lugh, Nuada, Scathach.

MEDICINE: Brigit, Cernunnos, Lugh, Bel, the Dagda, Diancecht. See Healing.

MEN: Cernunnos, Herne the Hunter.

MERCY: Anu. See Blessings.

METALWORKING: Brigit, Scathach, Diancecht, Goibniu, Lugh, Kai, Nuada, Weyland. See Jewelry.

MOON: Morrigu, Danu, Brigit, Mab, Blodeuwedd, Cerridwen, Cernunnos, Herne, Arianrhod, Nimue.

MOTHER ASPECT: Badb, Arianrhod, Margawse.

MOTHER GODDESS: Danu, Epona, Macha, Anu. See Great Goddess, Great Mother.

MOTHERHOOD: Brigit, Epona, Nantosuelta.

MOUNTAINS: Cernunnos.

MUSIC: Rhiannon, Cernunnos, Lugh, Ogma, Taliesin, the Dagda, Bran the Blessed, Nuada.

NATURE: See Woodlands.

NIGHT: Morrigu.

OPPORTUNITIES: the Dagda.

ORACLES: Brigit, Morrigu, Merlin, Taliesin. See Prophecy, Crystal Reading, Tarot, Psychic Abilities.

ORDER: Bran the Blessed, Owein ap Urien, Taranis.

ORGANIZATION: See Order.

PASSION: Cernunnos, Herne, Morrigu, Druantia. See Sexual Activities.

PATRON OF PRIESTS: the Dagda, Merlin, Taliesin, Lugh.

PATRON OF PRIESTESSES: Morrigu, Brigit, Epona.

PEACE: Tailtiu. See Calm.

PLEASURE: See Passion, Sexual Activities.

POETRY: See Writing.

POWER: Owein ap Urien, Taranis, Sucellus.

PROPHECY: Brigit, Morrigu, Scathach, Bran the Blessed, Tailtiu, Cernunnos, the Dagda, Lugh, Merlin, Taliesin, Gwydion.

PROSPERITY: Danu, Anu, the Dagda, Bel, Epona, Sucellus, Cernunnos, Tailtiu. See Abundance.

PROTECTION: Merlin, Taliesin, the Dagda, Sucellus, Banba, Macha, Scathach, Druantia.

PSYCHIC ABILITIES: Brigit, Morrigu, Merlin, Taliesin, Cerridwen, Cernunnos, the Dagda. See Blessings, Foretelling, Magic, Oracles, Spiritual Illumination.

PURIFICATION: Bel.

RAIN: See Weather.

REBIRTH: See Regeneration, Reincarnation.

REGENERATION: The Dagda, Diancecht, Manannan mac Lir, Cerridwen, Ogma, Owein ap Urien, Sucellus.

REINCARNATION: the Dagda, Manannan mac Lir, Cernunnos, Ogma, Owein ap Urien, Arianrhod, Cerridwen.

REST: See Peace, Calm.

RETRIBUTION: Morrigu, Lugh, Arawn, Mab, Arianrhod.

REVENGE: Morrigu, Lugh, Aer, Andraste, Mab, Pwyll, Arawn.

RITUALS: Merlin, Taliesin, Druantia, Brigit, Morrigu.

ROADS: Cernunnos, Lugh. See Journeys.

SCIENCE: Bel, Cerridwen.

SEA: Dylan, Llyr, Bel, Manannan mac Lir, Nuada, Don.

SEXUAL ACTIVITIES: Mab, Macha, Morrigu, Cernunnos, Druantia, the Horned God.

SHAPE-SHIFTER: Morrigu, Taliesin, Merlin, Manannan mac Lir, Gwydion, Flidais.

SKY: the Dagda, Don, Gwydion, Gwythyr, Anu, Arianrhod, Nuada, Sucellus.

SMITHCRAFT: See Metalworking.

SORCERER/SORCERESS: Danu, Gwydion, Manannan mac Lir, Math Mathonwy, Nuada, Merlin, Taliesin, Lugh, Cerridwen.

SPELLS: Brigit, Merlin, Nuada, Ogma, Gwydion, Taliesin, Banba, Cerridwen. See Magic, Psychic Abilities, Divination.

SPIRITUAL ILLUMINATION: Badb, Morrigu, Scathach.

SPRINGTIME: Blodeuwedd.

STORMS: Manannan mac Lir.

STRENGTH: Macha, Cernunnos, Herne, Ogma, Cocidius, Sucellus. See Power.

STUDENTS: See Knowledge.

SUCCESS: Danu, the Dagda, Sucellus, Bel.

SUMMER: Creiddylad, Gwythyr.

SUN: Bel, the Dagda, Lugh, Bran the Blessed, Nuada.

SUPREME MAGUS: Gwydion, Taliesin, Merlin, Lugh, the Dagda.

TAROT: Brigit, Morrigu, Merlin, Taliesin, the Dagda.

TERROR: Arawn, the Horned God, Cernunnos, Herne, the White Lady.

TRADE: See Commerce.

TRANSPORT: See Journeys.

TRAVEL: Lugh. See Journeys.

THE UNDERWORLD: Arawn, Pwyll, Gwynn ap Nudd, Don, the White Lady, Cerridwen, Llyr, Scathach, Rhiannon.

VEGETATION: Cerridwen, the Horned God, Cernunnos, Bel, Brigit, Sucellus, Druantia.

VICTORY: Brigantia. See Success.

WAR: Morrigu, Macha, Mab, Gwydion, Lugh, Ogma, Arawn, Bran the Blessed, Cocidius, the Dagda, Nuada, Owein ap Urien, Toutatis, Aer, Andraste, Camulos.

WATER, FRESH: Morrigu, Boann, Brigantia, Coventina, Danu, Nuada, Bel, Epona, Llyr, Nantosuelta, Cyhiraeth.

WEAPONS: Scathach, Nuada, Gwydion, Lugh, Diancecht, the Dagda, Goibniu, Credne, Luchtaine.

WINE: Cernunnos, the Horned God.

WINTER: Gwynn ap Nudd.

WISDOM: Danu, Badb, Blodeuwedd, Merlin, Taliesin, Owein ap Urien, the Dagda.

WITCHCRAFT: Morrigu, Brigit, Nicneven, Cerridwen.

WOMEN: Macha.

WOODLANDS: Blodeuwedd, Cerridwen, Creiddylad, the Horned God, Cernunnos, Herne the Hunter, Merlin, Cocidius, Flidais, the Green Man, Andraste.

WRITING: Brigit, Ogma, Lugh, Taliesin, Merlin, Bran the Blessed, Nuada, Cerridwen.

YOUTH: Nuada, Angus mac Og.

Bibliography

Alder, Margot. *Drawing Down the Moon*. Boston: Beacon Press, 1981.

Arrowsmith, Nancy and George Moorse. *A Field Guide to the Little People*. New York: Wallaby, 1977.

Batterberry, Michael and Ariane. *Fashion: The Mirror of History*. New York: Greenwich House, 1977.

Bonwick, James. *Irish Druids and Old Irish Religions*. New York: Dorset, 1986.

Boulding, Elise. *The Underside of History*. Boulder, CO: Westview Press, 1976.

Braun and Schneider. *Historic Costume in Pictures*. New York: Dover, 1975.

Brennan, J. H. *Experimental Magic*. Northamptonshire, England: Aquarian Press, 1972.

Briffault, Robert. *The Mothers*. 3 vols. New York: Macmillan, 1927.

Briggs, Katharine. *An Encyclopedia of Fairies*. New York: Pantheon Books, 1976.

Buckland, Raymond. *Practical Color Magick*. St. Paul, MN: Llewellyn, 1983.

Burton, Richard F. *The Book of the Sword*. New York: Dover, 1987.

Butler, W. E. *The Magician: His Training and Work*. Northamptonshire, England: Aquarian Press, 1959.

Butler, W. E. *Ritual Magic*. Cambridge, MA: Cambridge University Press, 1949.

Campbell, Joseph. *The Hero With a Thousand Faces*. Bollinger Series. Princeton, NJ: Princeton University Press, 1973.

Campbell, Joseph. *The Masks of God, Vol. I-IV*. New York: Penguin Books, 1977.

Campbell, Joseph. *The Mythic Image*. Princeton, NJ: Princeton University Press, 1981.

Carlyon, Richard. *A Guide to the Gods*. Wm. Morrow & Co., date unknown.

Cavendish, Richard. *Mythology: An Illustrated Encyclopedia*. New York: Rizzoli, 1980.

Ceram, C. W. *Gods, Graves and Scholars*. New York: Bantam Books, 1972.

Chant, Joy. *The High Kings*. New York: Bantam Books, 1983.

Cirlot, J. E. *A Dictionary of Symbols*. New York: Philosophical Library, 1978.

Conway, David. *Magic: An Occult Primer*. New York: E. P. Dutton & Co., 1973.

Cotterell, Arthur. *A Dictionary of World Mythology*. New York: Perigee Books, 1979.

Crossley-Holland, Kevin, Editor. *Folk Tales of the British Isles*. New York: Pantheon Books, 1985.

D'Alviella, Count Goblet. *Migration of Symbols*. Northamptonshire, England: Aquarian, 1979.

Denning, Melita and Osbourne Phillips. *Mysterica Magica, Book V*. St. Paul, MN: Llewellyn Publications, 1981.

De Paor, Maire and Liam. *Early Christian Ireland*. London: Thomas and Hudson, 1958.

Eliade, Mircea. *Shamanism*. Bollingen Series. Princeton, NJ: 1964.

Elworthy, Frederick. *The Evil Eye*. New York: Julian Press, 1958.

Frazier. Sir James G. *The Golden Bough*. New York: Macmillan, 1950.

Funk, Wilfred. *Word Origins and Their Romantic Stories*. New York: Bell Publishing, 1978.

Gantz, Jeffrey, Translator. *The Mabinogion*. Middlesex, England: Dorset Press, 1976.

Goodrich, Norma Lorre. *Medieval Myths*. New York: New American Library, 1977.

Gorsline, Douglas. *What People Wore*. New York: Bonanza Books, 1962.

Graves, Robert. *The White Goddess*. New York: Faber & Faber, 1966.

Gray, William. *Magical Ritual Methods*. York Beach, ME: Samuel Weiser, 1969.

Green, Miranda. *Gods of the Celts*. New Jersey: Alan Sutton, 1986.

Grimal, Pierre. *Larousse World Mythology*. London: Hamlyn, 1978.

Hall, Manly P. *The Secret Teachings of All Ages*. Los Angeles, CA: Philosophical Research Library, 1977.

Harris, Christie and Moira Johnston. *Figleafing Through History*. New York: Atheneum, 1971.

Hawkes, Jacquetta. *Atlas of Early Man*. New York: St. Martins, 1976.

Hawkes, Jacquetta. *World of the Past, Vol. 2*. New York: Alfred Knopf, 1963.

Hazlett, W. Carew. *Faiths and Folklore of the British Isles*. 2 vols. New York: Benjamin Blom, 1965.

Hitching, Francis. *Earth Magic*. New York: Pocket Books, 1978.

Howard, Michael. *The Magic of Runes*. New York: Samuel Weiser, 1980.

Howard, Michael. *The Runes*. Northamptonshire, England: Aquarian, 1981.

Keightley, Thomas. *The World Book of Gnomes, Fairies, Elves and Other Little People*. New York:

Avenel Books, 1978.

K'Eogh, John. *An Irish Herbal*. Northamptonshire, England: Aquarian, 1986.

Kohler, Carl. *A History of Costume*. New York: Dover, 1963.

Laing, Lloyd. *Celtic Britain*. London: Granada, 1981.

Lester, Katherine. *Historic Costume*. The Manual Arts Press, 1942.

Lippman, Deborah and Paul Colin. *How to Make Amulets, Charms and Talismans*. New York: M. Evans & Co., 1974.

MacCana, Proinsias. *Celtic Mythology*. London: Hamlyn Pub., 1970.

MacCulloch, J. A. *Celtic Mythology*. Boston: Gray and Moore, date unknown.

MacCulloch, J. A. *The Religion of the Ancient Celts*. Boston: Gray and Moore, date unknown.

MacManus, Seumas. *The Story of the Irish Race*. Connecticut: Devin-Adair, 1978.

Murray, Liz and Colin. *The Celtic Tree Oracle*. New York: St. Martins Press, 1988.

Neumann, Erich. *The Great Mother: An Analysis of the Archetype*. Princeton, NJ: Princeton University Press, 1963.

Newark, Tim. *The Barbarians*. Dorset, England: Blandford, 1985.

Newark, Tim. *Celtic Warriors*. Dorset, England: Blandford, 1986.

Norton-Taylor, Duncan. *The Celts*. New York: Time-Life Books, 1974.

Quennell, Marjorie and C.H.B. *Everyday Life in Roman Britain*. New York: G.P. Putnam's Sons, 1952.

Piggot, Stuart. *The Druids*. New York: Frederick A. Praegar, 1968.

Reed, Ellen Cannon. *The Witches' Qabala*. St. Paul, MN: Llewellyn Publications, 1985.

Rees, Alwyn and Brinley. *Celtic Heritage*. New York: Grove Press, 1961.

Ross, Anne. *Celtic Britain*. Harrisburg, PA: Historical Times Inc., 1985.

Ross, Anne. *Druids, Gods and Heroes from Celtic Mythology*. Schocken: 1986.

Ross, Anne. *The Pagan Celts*. New Jersey: Barnes & Noble, 1986.

Selbie, Robert. *The Anatomy of Costume*. New York: Crescsent, 1977.

Sibbett, Ed. *Celtic Design Coloring Book*. New York: Dover, 1979.

Spence, Lewis. *The History and Origins of Druidism*. New York: S. Weiser, 1971.

Spence, Lewis. *The Magic Arts of Celtic Britain*. London: Rider, date unknown.

Spinhoven, C. *Celtic Charted Designs*. New York: Dover, 1987.

Squire, Charles. *Celtic Myth and Legend*. Van Nuys, CA: Newcastle Pub., 1975.

Stewart, R. J. *Living Magical Arts*. Dorset, England: Blandford Press, 1987.

Stone, George. *A Glossary of the Construction, Decoration and Use of Arms and Armor*. New York: Jack Brussel, 1961.

Stone, Merlin. *Ancient Mirrors of Womanhood*. Boston, MA: Beacon, 1984.

Stone, Merlin. *When God Was a Woman*. New York: Harcourt Brace Jovanovich, 1976.

Uyldert, Mellie. *The Magic of Precious Stones*. Northamptonshire, England: Turnstone Press, 1981.

Uyldert, Mellie. *Metal Magic*. Northamptonshire,

England: Turnstone Press, 1980.

Valiente, Doreen. *ABC of Witchcraft Past and Present*. New York: St. Martins, 1973.

Valiente, Doreen. *Witchcraft for Tomorrow*. London: Robert Hale, 1978.

Walker, Barbara. *The Women's Encyclopedia of Myths and Secrets*. New York: Harper & Row, 1983.

Webster, Graham. *Celtic Religion of Roman Britain*. New Jersey: Barnes & Noble, 1986.

Wilson, Eva. *Celtic and Medieval Designs of Britain*. New York: Dover, 1983.

Yarwood, Doreen. *Encyclopedia of World Costume*. New York: Scribners, 1986.

Norse Magic

D. J. Conway

The Norse: adventurous Viking wanderers, daring warriors, worshippers of the Aesir and the Vanir. Like the Celtic tribes, the Northmen had strong ties with the Earth and Elements, the Gods and the "little people." *Norse Magic* is an active magic, only for participants, not bystanders. It is a magic of pride in oneself and the courage to face whatever comes. It interests those who believe in shaping their own future, those who believe that practicing spellwork is preferable to sitting around passively waiting for changes to come.

The book leads the beginner step by step through the spells. The in-depth discussion of Norse deities and the Norse way of life and worship set the intermediate student on the path to developing his or her own active rituals. *Norse Magic* is a compelling and easy-to-read introduction to the Norse religion and Teutonic mythology. The magical techniques are refreshingly direct and simple, with a strong feminine and goddess orientation.

0-87542-137-7
240 pp., mass market, illus.   **$5.99**

"Nice place," Nicole commented, glancing around the small room.

"Yours is much nicer," Kyle pointed out. Not to be cruel, but because it was.

But then she lifted her chin and willed herself out of it. "Thank you. It isn't what I would have chosen, but it's a decent house."

Decent.

A flash of anger ripped through him. He realized he couldn't just sit there and act as if they were casual acquaintances, like nothing had ever happened between them. As though she hadn't been his entire reason for living.

"I can't do this," he growled. "I know you've moved on, I get it. For you, it's been a long time. For me, it feels like it was just yesterday when you kissed me and told me you'd love me forever."

She took a shaky breath. "I understand," she began.

"Do you?" Though he kept his voice low so as not to disturb Jacob, he didn't bother to hide his anger or his pain. "I don't think you do. I want to be part of my son's life. But right now, I don't think I can be part of yours."

* * *

**Top Secret Deliveries:
Under extraordinary circumstances—babies!**

* * *

Dear Reader,

As a writer, every now and then it feels like a story is given as a gift from the cosmos. *The Texas Soldier's Son* is one of those books. Writing it felt like telling the story of good friends—maybe even family. I was there with them, just recounting what happened. Moved to tears with them, frightened for them, rejoicing with them and falling in love just as they did.

Sometimes life can turn on a dime. One phone call and your entire world changes. Those of us who've experienced something similar can often remember what clothes we were wearing, and replay the exact words in our mind even years later. Hold the ones you love close. Celebrate every moment you have together. Because I can promise you that you'll miss it when it's gone.

With much love and light,

Karen Whiddon

THE TEXAS
SOLDIER'S SON

———

Karen Whiddon

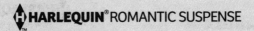

Recycling programs
for this product may
not exist in your area.

ISBN-13: 978-1-335-45639-7

The Texas Soldier's Son

Copyright © 2018 by Karen Whiddon

Printed in U.S.A.

Karen Whiddon started weaving fanciful tales for her younger brothers at the age of eleven. Amid the gorgeous Catskill Mountains, then the majestic Rocky Mountains, she fueled her imagination with the natural beauty surrounding her. Karen now lives in north Texas, writes full-time and volunteers for a boxer dog rescue. She shares her life with her hero of a husband and four to five dogs, depending on if she is fostering. You can email Karen at kwhiddon1@aol.com. Fans can also check out her website, karenwhiddon.com.

Books by Karen Whiddon

Harlequin Romantic Suspense

The CEO's Secret Baby
The Cop's Missing Child
The Millionaire Cowboy's Secret
Texas Secrets, Lovers' Lies
The Rancher's Return
The Texan's Return
Wyoming Undercover
The Texas Soldier's Son

The Coltons of Texas

Runaway Colton

The Coltons of Oklahoma

The Temptation of Dr. Colton

The Coltons: Return to Wyoming

A Secret Colton Baby

Silhouette Romantic Suspense

The Princess's Secret Scandal
Bulletproof Marriage

The Cordiasic Legacy

Black Sheep P.I.
The Perfect Soldier
Profile for Seduction

Visit the Author Profile page
at Harlequin.com for more titles.

Dedicated to my daughter, Stephanie Waters.

One of the strongest women I know.
I love you, Steph.

Chapter 1

"He's dead?" Nicole Shelton-Mabry gripped the phone so hard she thought it might break. "What do you mean, he's dead? He was fine when he left for work this morning." If by fine, one meant *hungover*. Last night her husband Bill had staggered in at 3 a.m., slurring her name, already in a rage by the time she'd hurried downstairs. The black-and-blue bruise on her upper arm had been his response to her tentative hello. Luckily, once he'd vented his anger, he'd stumbled to the couch and passed out before he could hit her again.

The pain had blossomed like an explosion. Since she had experience covering bruises, and luckily this time he hadn't got her face, she knew she needed to put ice on it. Wincing as she explored her arm and shoulder with tentative fingers, she supposed she ought to be glad he hadn't broken anything this time.

Prone on the couch, he'd let out a snore. She'd stood staring at him for a moment, hatred mingling with her pain, and wished she'd had enough guts to grab her cast-iron skillet and slam it into his skull until he'd never be able to hurt her again. Instead, she'd gone to the freezer and wrapped ice in a dishtowel, glad baby Jacob still slept in his crib upstairs.

She'd taken a deep breath, crossed the room and carefully removed Bill's wallet from his back pocket. He loved to carry wads of cash and his drinking made him careless with his money, so she'd been removing as much as she safely could each time he passed out.

This time she took an extra twenty in addition to the hundred and five. He'd never asked her about his money and she figured he probably thought he'd spent it at whatever hellhole he frequented the next town over. Topless bars were his favorite and he didn't dare go anywhere around here where someone he knew might see him. After all, he had his position as church deacon to consider.

Replacing his wallet, she'd hurried to the laundry room and shoved the bills in her hiding place, a brown envelope tucked in the pocket on the back of the washer behind the laundry detergent, fabric softener and dryer sheets. The one place Bill never went was the laundry room. Instead, he'd shove his smoke-scented, bourbon-stained clothes at her with an order to get them clean.

She'd been taking money from him for several months. Soon, she hoped to have enough to get her and Jacob on a bus that would carry them to a new life somewhere far, far away.

"Nicole? Are you there?" Yates, an older man who

worked for Bill, sounded tired. "I know this is a shock, but Dan and Theresa are too upset and I figured someone needed to let you know."

Dan and Theresa were Bill's parents. They all worked together at the trucking company Dan had started years ago.

Mabry Trucking. If they knew what kind of man their son had become, they never let on to Nicole.

"I'm here," Nicole replied, her voice shaky and her mouth dry. She knew she needed to pretend the same way she pretended in church that she, Bill and Jacob were one big, happy family, but she couldn't. Not yet, not now, with a bruise the size of a robin's egg on her cheekbone underneath her swollen black eye. "What happened, Yates? Was he in an accident?"

"Nope." Despite the somber tone, Yates didn't sound like he was grieving too much either. She imagined Bill had made his life hell as well.

"He just keeled over at his desk," Yate continued. "Cup of coffee in his hand. I called 911 and they tried to revive him, but he was already gone. I think maybe he had a massive heart attack."

After thanking him for calling, Nicole hung up. She knew she should have felt something, anything instead of this awful numbness, but digging deep, the only emotion she felt was relief.

The next several hours passed in a blur. Nicole stuck to her house as much as possible, answering the phone and trying to regain her composure. She'd thought she'd have decisions to make over her husband's funeral, but his mother had taken over all that, promising only to make sure Nicole got the details, along with the bill.

That afternoon, she'd had a few visitors, mainly from Bill's church, where she assumed none of them had truly known her husband.

Her own parents even made a token appearance to express their condolences. Her mother had brought Nicole a chicken casserole, offered a mechanical hug and didn't even ask to see the baby. Nicole went and got Jacob after his nap and brought him out, which immediately made her parents decide to leave.

Luckily, at three months old, Jacob was too young to be hurt. Nicole knew she wanted to make sure he never was. Her parents bore no love for her son. They, along with Bill himself, were the only ones who knew Bill wasn't actually Jacob's father. They'd all made sure not one word leaked about Jacob's parentage. None of them wanted to deal with the shame. As for Nicole, if she could have, she'd have shouted the truth from the rooftops.

The phone rang, Nicole answered. Bill's mother called several times and wept, sounding as if she was nearly prostrate from grief. Bill's father, a man Nicole suspected was much like Bill himself, remained stoic, saying only that he'd be supporting his wife through it all. They'd begrudgingly allowed Nicole to make a few choices as to the final arrangements. She was their son's wife after all, whether they liked her or not. She'd had Jacob after all, which helped her status in their eyes. The Mabrys doted on the infant, whom they believed to be the next Mabry heir.

Now alone in the big house, Nicole figured she'd eventually tell them the truth. She'd actually be glad to, because she'd grown weary of living such a bold-faced lie. Once, it had been a necessity. Now, as a new widow, she figured she'd be able to sell the house and combine that money with whatever was in the bank account and move far, far away from this place.

She went to bed early, slept deeply, and rose shortly after seven, when Jacob wanted his feeding.

After coffee and a shower, she debated simply unplugging the land line. But before she could, the phone rang, the shrill sound making her jump. Yesterday, she'd found the steady barrage of calls overwhelming. She'd actually stopped answering for a few hours and let the machine take care of it instead. After the sun set, the calls had died down to a trickle and then ceased altogether, giving her a quiet night.

Now with the morning, clearly they were starting up again.

Caller ID showed the Anniversary sheriff's department, so she answered. "Missus Mabry, this is Sheriff Cantrell. I'm afraid I've got some bad news for you. Your husband's parents insisted on an autopsy, so we rushed one through. The Medical Examiner put Bill ahead of everything else, considering all the Mabrys have done for this community." He took a deep breath. "Are you sitting down, ma'am?"

When she allowed that she wasn't, he gently asked her to please do so. Her stomach churned, but she did as he asked and told him she'd done so.

"Good, good." Now he cleared his throat. "The coroner's report came back and Bill didn't die of heart disease as originally believed." He paused, probably for dramatic effect. "He was poisoned. We found high concentrations of arsenic in his coffee."

"Poisoned?" Blinking, she struggled to process his

words. "You're saying someone at the office poisoned him?"

"Possibly," he agreed. "However, several of his employees claim he brought the coffee with him. I don't know if it came from home or if he stopped and bought some and poured it into his own cup. Do you have any idea?"

She shook her head before realizing he couldn't see her. "No, I don't. He usually doesn't have time to make coffee here, but I don't know where he'd stop to buy it."

"Gas station, maybe. Or fast food place." Another dramatic pause. "Listen, Nicole. Do you know if Bill had any enemies? Anyone who might want to harm him?"

He meant *murder him*, she thought. With Bill's abrasive, confrontational personality and his entitled, the-world-owes-me belief, she couldn't imagine many people liked him. But she truly didn't know. Bill kept her separated from his work life. Heck, Bill had kept her separated from everything and everyone, with the exception of the church his uncle had founded. And even there, he never allowed her to be alone with anyone. She guessed he was too worried she'd tell the truth about him.

"I'm sorry," she finally admitted. "I have no idea."

"I see." The sheriff's sigh told her he'd hoped for more. "You might want to go see your mother-in-law. She's taking her son's death pretty hard."

"I imagine," Nicole murmured. Bill had been Theresa Mabry's entire world. "Unfortunately, I don't have a car. I have no way to get over there." Bill hadn't liked her to have the freedom of her own vehicle, so they'd only owned one, which he took to work every day.

"Oh." Apparently nonplussed, Sheriff Cantrell went silent for a few seconds. "I'll have one of my guys bring your car back to you."

"Thank you," she replied, relieved when he ended the call.

Bill was dead. The words echoed over and over inside her head. Bill. Was. Dead. Never to hit her again. Never to scream invectives at her, never to force her to have sex whenever and wherever he felt like it. Gone.

She couldn't bring herself to mourn the monster Bill had been, though she empathized with the pain his parents must feel. She imagined they'd search long and hard for whoever had done this to their beloved son. Once the perpetrator had been found, the Mabrys would enact a swift and merciless vengeance.

Not sure what else to do, Nicole stuck to her usual routine, taking care of Jacob and housecleaning while he slept. She did two loads of laundry and almost caught herself ironing Bill's work shirts—he liked them well starched. She remembered in time and simply hung them up in his closet without pressing them.

One of the sheriff's deputies delivered Bill's car and keys around three. Another officer followed in a marked patrol car. Both of them expressed sympathy at her loss as they handed over the keys. Dry-eyed, she thanked them, staring at the BMW and hoping she remembered how to drive.

Once they were gone, she went back inside. Jacob's car seat was still tucked in the closet under the stairs, since Bill refused to drive around with a car seat in his car. She carried it outside, glad Jacob was napping, and placed it in the backseat the way she always did before church. Once she had it properly attached, she stood back with some satisfaction and surveyed her handiwork. This time, she wouldn't be pulling the car seat out.

After locking the car, she returned to her home and checked both her cell and the landline. No missed calls. Which meant neither of Bill's parents had felt the need to call his wife to commiserate about his death.

Which meant that she should call them. While she wasn't really close to either of Bill's parents, she'd guessed they had no idea how their son treated her or what kind of activities he enjoyed in his spare time. She wouldn't take that away from them, not in a million years.

So she took a deep breath and dialed Theresa's cell phone. Theresa picked up on the third ring.

"Nicole," she said, her voice husky from crying. "I assume you've heard. I can't believe my Billy boy is gone."

"I'm still trying to process the news," Nicole admitted. "The Sheriff said they thought someone might have poisoned him?"

Theresa sniffled. "Yes. They've asked us to make a list of possible enemies who could be potential suspects."

"That's a good idea."

"Is it?" Theresa's voice hardened. "I'm going to do you a favor and give you advance notice," she continued. "Your name will be on that list."

"What?" Nicole's heart caught in her throat. Shocked, she struggled to find a response. Any response. "Why would you say such a thing?"

"Because my son told us about you. He said you're a money-grubber, never satisfied with anything he gave you." Vicious anger warred with grief in the older woman's voice. "Now you have the house and the car and his bank account. But so help me, if we find one shred of evidence to indicate it was you, we will come after you. If you did anything to harm Bill, you will never be allowed to raise our grandson. Do you understand?"

Kyle Benning dragged his hand over his freshly-cut hair and struggled to relax the tension in his shoulders. Despite his honorable discharge from the army, he continued to wear his hair military-style. He felt more comfortable that way. Once an army ranger, always an army ranger.

That said, he couldn't wait to get home. He had no choice but to surprise Nicole and show up without a phone call, since her number had changed. Worst of all, he hadn't even had a cell phone until after he'd been discharged from the hospital. They'd flown him Afghanistan to Ramstein in Germany, where he'd remained until his condition was no longer considered critical. Months later, conscious and able to finally sit up and take solid foods, they'd deemed him on the road to recovery. Finally.

Then, they'd put him aboard another transport plane and he'd traveled from Ramstein to Walter Reed hospital in Bethesda, Maryland to continue his convalescence. Since he'd been in a medically induced coma for several months, he hadn't been aware of any of this. He wasn't even sure what had happened to him, but at least he knew who he was.

And who he wasn't. The name tags around his neck weren't his. After the enemy had taken most of the soldier's dog tags, Hank Smith had managed to hang onto one of his and had pressed it into Kyle's hand before dying.

No one would believe him at first. Then the IED had ripped their world apart in a single blaze of light. He'd learned Hank had been killed, torn apart by the blast, still wearing Kyle's dog tags. Kyle had been believed dead.

The only family of his that they could locate, the foster family back in Anniversary, Texas, who had raised him, had already been notified of his passing. Kyle doubted they'd even cared, but he'd worried himself sick about Nicole, the love of his life and the woman he'd planned to marry someday.

He tried to call her, only to learn her cell phone had been disconnected. Her parents number had also been changed and apparently was unlisted,

Briefly, he wondered if she was safe. It had been an entire year since he'd held her in his arms. Through all his seemingly endless deployment, her picture and thoughts of her love had kept him sane. Despite losing the photograph in the explosion, she'd never left his heart or his memory.

These days, he might be all messed up, but he knew she would be able to help him get through this. PTSD, they'd told him, as if that acronym could cover his nightmares and jumpiness, the irritability and constant, pressing fear. Even here, away from the constant sound of gunfire and explosions, any innocent loud sound could have him instantly on alert.

Nicole, Nicole, Nicole. He chanted her name in the

middle of night sweats, the double syllables becoming his mantra, the single thing he clung to in order to keep from falling over the edge.

She was his rock.

He hated the fact that she'd been told he was dead. And that he hadn't been able to reach out to her for so long. He took comfort in the knowledge that her parents would have at least let her know he still lived, even if he was only half the man he'd once been. At least he hoped they'd told her. Since she'd never taken the time to call him, he kind of doubted that they had.

No matter. He'd be setting things straight soon.

The 2013 Chevy Silverado he drove had been one of his lone expenditures. He'd paid cash for the used pickup, knowing he'd need something reliable for the drive west to Anniversary. Excitement jumped inside him, drowning out some of the ever-present anxiety. Excitement and, dare he say, joy. Because soon, he'd be with Nicole. He couldn't wait to see her face when he knocked on her door, to pull her into his arms and breathe the fresh strawberry scent of her shampoo, to kiss her lips until they both felt as if they were drowning.

In his pocket, he had the only other thing he'd spent part of his savings on. An engagement ring. As soon as he and Nicole got caught up, he planned to get down on bended knee and ask her formally to be his wife.

They'd talked about marrying before he'd signed up for the army. He'd even given her his high school class ring as a token, proof that he was hers and vice versa. She'd taken to wearing it with a long chain around her neck, safely tucked under her shirt so her strict parents wouldn't see.

God, he loved her. As his truck ate up the miles, he amused himself with imagining several different scenarios when they saw each other for the first time in over a year. His favorite was the one where she hopped into his truck, they drove out to the lake and made love right there in the cab.

Finally, he crossed from Louisiana into Texas. Not too much farther now. The hum of his tires on the asphalt soothed him and he felt more relaxed than he had since the explosion.

When the Anniversary city limits sign came into view, dusk had settled over the sky. The sunset colored the sky pink and orange, promising another hot East Texas day tomorrow. He remembered how everyone liked to complain about the summer heat. It would be a cakewalk compared to the temperatures in Kabul.

Instead of heading toward the small frame home he'd rented via the internet for the next six months, he drove directly to Nicole's parents' house, praying she'd be home. Parking out front, he jogged up the sidewalk, his heart pounding in his chest, and rang the bell.

A moment later, the door opened. Nicole's mother stared at him, frowning. "What are you doing here?" she asked, the rancor in her voice startling.

"I've been discharged from the hospital, ma'am," he said, figuring he'd kill her with kindness. "If you don't mind, I'd really like to see Nicole."

"Nicole?" She recoiled as violently as if he'd struck her. "Nicole doesn't live here. She's over on Broad Street in the house she shared with her husband and son." A slow, malicious smile spread across her face. "Bill Mabry? I'm thinking you might remember him?"

He hadn't gotten much past the words *husband* and

son. When he finally caught up, the name Bill Mabry made his stomach churn. That had been the same guy her parents had tried to force her to marry when he and Nicole had been together.

"Well?" The older woman stared, her gaze hard. "Is there anything else that I can help you with?"

For a moment he couldn't speak, couldn't force the words out past the huge lump in his throat. Only when she'd started to close the huge oak door in his face did he think of the one other thing he needed to know. "Did Nicole even mourn me at all?"

"Of course not," she said smoothly, without missing a beat. "Once the army notified your foster family of your death, she'd moved on. She was already married with a newborn by then. I didn't want to disrupt her life."

And then she waited, eying him with a certain mocking relish, waiting for him to reveal how devastating he found her answer. He refused to give her the pleasure.

Though his head spun, he turned on his heel, the military precision of the movement kicking in by instinctive habit. Somehow, he made it to his truck, unlocked the doors and slid inside. Turning the key, he started the engine, put the shifter into Drive and pulled away.

He started to head to the park by the lake, the same secluded place he'd intended to take Nicole, but instead he found himself heading toward Broad Street. He still couldn't believe her mother's words, couldn't accept that she hadn't waited barely any time at all before getting married and pregnant. For her to have a newborn, that meant she'd jumped into bed with this

Bill Mabry guy right after getting the erroneous news of Kyle's demise.

Had he truly meant that little to her?

Anguish turned to anger as he made the turn onto North Broad. Since he had no idea which house she lived in, he drove slowly up the street, feeling more and more like a stalker.

All his hopes, all his dreams, his *entire freaking future*, he'd pinned on her. On them. Now, she'd left him with nothing.

When he reached the intersection that separated North Broad from South, he made a decision. Why torture himself further with a confrontation? Signaling a right turn, he drove instead to his rental, the place where he'd be living for the next six months.

On the way there, he stopped at the downtown liquor mart and purchased a bottle of tequila, a twelve pack of beer and some moonshine. Thus fortified, he pulled up to his empty house, parked and took a deep breath before carrying his bags inside.

Apparently one part of his life was over. He'd need to come to terms with that before he could figure out where to go from here. Right now, he couldn't even summon up the energy to care.

Despite everything her parents had put her through, after speaking with the Bill's mom, Nicole had the overwhelming urge to call her own mother. She wasn't sure why; the older woman had never been the slightest bit supportive or even caring. But Nicole had no one else to talk to and despite their differences, she had to believe blood would win out over water and her mother would be on her side.

Or would she? Fran Shelton had always adored and fawned over Bill, even before she'd finally gotten her way and forced her own daughter to marry him. Nicole had lost count over how many times she'd gushed about how lucky she was that he'd married her daughter. The implication being that Nicole should be grateful too.

At first, she had been. She'd been single and pregnant with parents who demanded she either marry their choice or be thrown out onto the streets. They hadn't cared whether Nicole—or her baby—lived or died. And Nicole knew the only thing that kept them from demanding she get an abortion was their religion and the fact that she was a legal adult. For that at least, she was thankful. Bill had felt like her only choice to give her baby a safe start in life. Turned out she'd been wrong about that too.

In the end, Nicole decided against calling her mother. The last thing she needed right now was to hear the woman who'd given birth to her accuse her of murdering Bill.

The sniffles and soft cries coming from the baby monitor revealed baby Jacob was awake from his nap. Glad of a distraction, she hurried upstairs to get him before he started crying in earnest. He chortled when he saw her, filling her heart with so much love she thought she might burst.

For the first time, the enormity of the recent events hit her full force. She and Jacob were safe. No more beatings, her standing between him and the baby's room just in case he decided to take his drunken rage out on her son. Despite his over the top infatuation with Nicole, Bill barely tolerated the infant, well aware he wasn't the father, and had taken to referring to Jacob as that little bastard. And not in an affectionate way. He regarded Nicole as his possession and Jacob as an unfortunate addition he'd had to put up with in order to own her.

She'd dreaded the first time Bill tried to hurt her child, knowing she'd kill him if need be. Now, she no longer had to worry about that. While she knew it was morally wrong to be glad someone had been murdered, she couldn't help but feel an overwhelming sense of relief.

She hadn't had to run away to be free.

Picking up Jacob, she held him close, breathing in the baby powder scent of him, and allowed herself a smidgen of happiness. This house belonged to her now—not that she particularly liked it or wanted it—Bill had chosen it after all. But she had a roof over her head as long as she could pay the mortgage. And since Bill had loved to boast about their huge savings account, she figured she'd be okay. At least for a while. Long enough for Jacob to grow a bit. She didn't want to get a job and put him in daycare until he was a little older.

Her doorbell chimed, again and again, startling her. Still holding Jacob, she hurried downstairs and looked out the peephole to see who'd come to call. Spotting the uniformed sheriff, her stomach twisted. Now what? Had Theresa Mabry called him with her unfounded accusations?

Nicole took a deep breath and opened the door. Sheriff Cantrell was new to the job, having only replaced Bleaker a few months ago. Prior to that, he'd been a deputy for years.

"Mrs. Mabry?" The formality in his normally friendly voice was her first warning. "I'd like to talk to you about the murder of your husband, Bill. Theresa Mabry has given us reason to believe you're a potential person of interest."

Chapter 2

That night, even tequila couldn't dull Kyle's night terrors. Though he'd never been a fan of alcohol, after the explosion he'd learned that self-medicating helped. The news about Nicole had been another kind of explosion, blowing up everything he'd had left to live for. Though for Nicole, an entire year had passed and she'd gone on with her life, for him it felt like barely a few months had passed. Being in a coma for a long time had that effect on a person.

He'd never seen this betrayal coming. Not in a million years. In a shaky world full of snipers and IEDs, Nicole's love had been the one constant, the one certainty he'd believed he could count on. Clearly, their relationship had been nothing but a lie to her.

He drank enough to pass out, alternating with beer, before switching to the more potent moonshine. Once he couldn't see straight, he staggered into the bedroom and the lumpy mattress that had come with the house and let his body fall onto the bed.

He prayed and hoped for at least a couple of hours oblivion, knowing he'd be lucky to get even that. But when he sat straight up in bed with a gasp, while thunder cracked and boomed outside, he hadn't been surprised to find himself automatically reaching for his weapon. Thunder sounded like explosions. It took him a full twelve seconds to realize the flashes of light were actually lightning, accompanying the roar of steady rain.

A storm. East Texas thunder boomer. Like someone had sliced a hole in the clouds and let the water all dump out at once. It didn't rain like this in Afghanistan. Proof positive that he was home, that it all hadn't been a dream.

And then he remembered Nicole. The pain slicing through his gut had him doubling over, nausea coming in waves. Racing for the bathroom, he barely made it before retching up the contents of his stomach into the porcelain bowl.

Once he thought he was done, he rinsed his mouth out with mouthwash and went back to bed, pulling the covers over his head and trying to shut down his brain. But he couldn't stop thinking about what a cluster his life had become.

He'd rented this house for six months, paying cash in advance including the deposit. According to the rental contract, he had to stay there the entire time or forfeit the money. He supposed he could walk away, but the truth of the matter was he had nowhere else to go. Anniversary was his hometown, where he'd grown up, gone to school and planned to settle and raise his own kids someday.

Kids. Another jolt, straight to the heart. The only woman he'd ever wanted to have children with now had one of her own, with another man.

Covering his eyes, he listened to the storm raging outside, matching the emotions inside.

Finally, he must have fallen asleep. When he next opened his eyes, sunshine streamed through the bedroom windows, relentlessly cheerful. With the morning came clarity. He knew what he had to do. Find Nicole and demand an explanation. She owed him that at least.

Since he hadn't had time to stock the place with groceries, he decided he'd head downtown and have breakfast at the café. A couple of cups of coffee and some fried eggs, biscuits and gravy, and bacon would do wonders to banish the lingering nausea from the night before.

Stepping outside, the humidity and heat made him smile. Another sign he was home, because the desert heat had been brutal and dry. This was Texas, familiar and welcome.

Downtown hadn't changed a bit. He lucked out and found a parking space right in front of the café. Inside, he saw Trudy Blevins, self-dubbed nosiest woman in Anniversary, apparently interviewing customers for either her newspaper column or her radio segment. Huge, flamboyant earrings swung from her ears and she chewed gum in between talking. Though he kept his back to her, he found the sight of her oddly reassuring. Proof that some things at least, never changed.

Taking a seat at the countertop, he grinned when

the owner Jed Rodgers caught sight of him and did a double take. Jed made a beeline for him, hand out-stretched. "Let me shake your hand," the older man ex-claimed. When Kyle went to shake, instead Jed pulled him close for a quick guy hug. "I've never been so glad to see someone in my life. Everyone thought you were dead."

Kyle ducked his head. "Clearly, I'm not. What I am, though, is starving."

"Tell me what you want." Jed got out his order pad. "Whatever you get, it's on the house."

Touched, Kyle thanked him and placed his order. Jed carried it to the kitchen, returning with a mug and the pot of coffee. "Here you go. You still drink it black, right?"

"Yep." The first sip tasted like it always had, strong and rich. "I don't know what kind of coffee you brew, but it's the best I've tasted anywhere."

Jed acknowledged the compliment with a shrug. People had been after him for years to reveal his cof-fee's secret. He claimed it was a secret he planned to carry to the grave.

Since the breakfast crowd had begun to thin out, the two waitresses were able to handle the rest of the cus-tomers. Jed leaned on the counter, settling in for a chat.

"Big news going on here in our small town," Jed drawled. "The jaws are a' waggin', that's for sure."

"Because I'm back?" Kyle hoped not. The last thing he wanted or needed right now was Trudy Blevins shoving her microphone in his face and rattling off questions.

"Well, that too. But no, recently we had our first murder."

Since Jed didn't sound grief stricken, Kyle could only assume the deceased had been someone Jed didn't know well.

The cook rang the little bell to signify an order was up. Jed grabbed it and slid the plate in front of Kyle. Two fried eggs, sunny-side up. Biscuits with creamy sausage gravy. Crispy bacon and a side of grits.

"I feel like I've died and gone to heaven—for real this time," Kyle said. "We couldn't get food like this in Afghanistan. Not in the hospital either."

"Dig in, son." Jed wiped his hands on his apron and smiled, before refilling Kyle's coffee cup. "I'm going to go talk to Trudy and see if she's heard anything new about the murder."

Mouth full, Kyle waved him away. Gossip had always been a hot commodity in this town, though he figured most small communities were probably like that. As for him, he couldn't have cared less. Once he'd inhaled his breakfast and sucked down some caffeine, he planned to figure out where exactly Nicole lived and pay her a visit. She at least owed him some sort of explanation.

Luckily, everyone left him alone to eat in peace. But the second he pushed his empty plate away, Trudy Blevins hustled over.

"Kyle Benning," she trilled. "If you aren't a sight for sore eyes."

Taking a deep breath, Kyle turned to face her. "Thank you, ma'am. It's great to finally be back in town."

"I imagine it is." She wore a cat-about-to-eat-a-canary look. "And I'm guessing you probably heard about the murder."

He shrugged. "Jed mentioned something about a murder. I'm sorry to hear about that. Anniversary has always been such a safe place."

"Oh, it still is, I'm thinking." Expression turning sly, she climbed up on the stool next to him as if she meant to stay awhile. Which he supposed was fine, because he certainly did not. He signaled Jed for the check, but Jed waved him away, mouthing again that the meal was on the house.

"Word is, the killer was someone who knew the dead man all too well," Trudy continued.

Kyle gave a polite nod, keeping his expression disinterested. He made a show out of checking his watch. "I'm sorry, but I have to run," he began.

She grabbed his arm. "Wait. I'd think this story would be a particular interest to you. In fact, I'd like to report on your reaction."

"Trudy?" He stared pointedly at her hand on his forearm, making it clear her touch wasn't exactly welcome. She finally huffed and removed it.

"Trudy," he repeated. "Look, I just got back in town yesterday. While I'm sure I've got a lot to catch up on, I've got too much to do right now. I'll catch up with everything on the local news later tonight."

Was that a flash of disappointment in her gaze? But no, she shook her head, clearly undeterred. "Since this case involves your former girlfriend Nicole Shelton, I'd think you might find it a tiny bit interesting."

Nicole? A shudder of foreboding ripped through him, though he worked hard to prevent that from showing. "Are you telling me Nicole was murdered?" he asked, fighting to keep his voice steady.

Trudy cocked her head, sending those earrings of

hers swinging. "Nicole isn't dead, sugar. Nicole's husband, Bill, is. And the talk around town is that she might be the one who killed him. The sheriff has already told her not to leave town. Can you imagine?"

Stunned, he could only stare, unable to think coherently enough to hide his shock. "I…"

Her malicious smile widened. She pulled out her microphone, fumbling with her recorder before looking up at him again. "On the record, would you tell the good folks of Anniversary how you feel about this news?"

How he *felt*? He'd been through hell and back, only to return home to find the rug had not only been ripped out from under him, but set on fire as well. He used every bit of his ranger training to mentally pull himself up by his bootstraps. Squaring his shoulders, he lifted his chin and looked Trudy right in the eyes. "I've been gone a year, ma'am. And I haven't talked to Nicole at all, not in all that time. While I'm not sure why folks believe she'd be capable of murder, I can tell you this. The Nicole Shelton I know wouldn't hurt a fly. Hell, the woman even carried spiders outside if they got in the house. I can't imagine her killing another human being. Not at all."

Undeterred, Trudy licked her bright red lips. "Well, it appears you are wrong. But time will tell. The truth will come out in the end."

Kyle stood, inclining his head politely. "I'm sure it will, ma'am." With a quick wave at Jed, he strode off toward the door.

Outside, he squinted in the bright sunlight. He walked to his pickup, unlocked the doors and climbed up inside. Ignition on, AC up full blast. He had no idea where to go, just that he needed to drive.

He cruised slowly down Main Street, turning at the bank, and continued on until he'd reached a residential area. The houses here were large and well maintained, several sporting the brass historical plaques that marked them as restored homes of significance. Pulling over to the curb, he parked. Using his phone, he navigated to the county tax assessor website and put in the name *Bill Mabry*.

Bingo. Interesting, that the house title was only in Bill's name. Nicole wasn't included. And the date of purchase was a little more than one year ago, which meant he'd bought the house before he and Nicole were married.

He put the address into his GPS and punched Drive. To his surprise, the house was only a couple of blocks away. Driving slow, he went past, his heart pounding so hard he thought it might leap out of his chest. At the end of the street, he made a U-turn. This time, he parked in front of the house across the street. The two-story, rock-and-wood structure looked sleek and modern, yet somehow fit in perfectly with the restored historical homes surrounding it. The perfectly manicured lawn, numerous trees and flower gardens were all well-tended, like something out of a glossy magazine. No doubt the inside of the luxurious home was filled with expensive furniture and matching colors.

He tried to picture Nicole living there, her adoring husband at her side, her baby in her arms, and realized she'd fit right in. In fact, this kind of lifestyle was exactly what he'd wanted for her, for them, even if he'd imagined it would take a while to get to that place. While he'd saved every dollar he could from his military service, he'd planned for the two of them to start out like most young couples did, with a much more modest home.

Looks like she'd managed to skip right over all that by marrying Bill Mabry, the guy her parents had been trying to set her up with all through high school. She'd claimed to find him repulsive, describing several awkward Sunday night suppers when her parents had invited him over.

Kyle guessed she'd lied. Either that, or her parents and Bill Mabry had finally worn her down, probably while she was mourning over Kyle's supposed death. At least he hoped she'd grieved for him. He studied the house again and came to a decision. There was only one way to find out.

He hustled up the sidewalk, moving fast so he wouldn't reconsider and change his mind. He rang the bell, listening as sonorous chimes reverberated inside the house, followed immediately by a baby's loud wailing.

No one came to the door. Instead, he imagined Nicole went to comfort her infant. Heart still racing, he waited, telling himself he'd count to thirty before ringing the doorbell again.

At twenty-nine, the door opened, just a tiny crack. "Go away." Nicole's voice, making his stomach do a somersault. "I've already told you people I'm not talking to any reporters. My husband just died. Leave me alone."

"Nicole." He spoke her name, knowing she'd recognize his voice. "It's me. Kyle."

Silence. "Kyle's dead. What kind of monster would

play a cruel trick like this?" she cried out, before slamming the door shut in his face.

Still he waited, trying for patience. Even though she'd married another man immediately after his supposed death, he battled an overwhelming urge to kick the door in and yank her into his arms. Every fiber of his being, every fighting instinct to live, had been about her. Getting back to her. Holding her.

He blinked, hard, his eyes stinging. The one thing he'd never expected had been this betrayal.

When she didn't come back, he knocked. Not a quiet brush of his knuckles against the polished wood. No, this determined rapping was to let her know he wasn't going away until she faced him. She at least owed him that.

Finally, she opened the door, all the way this time. "Kyle?" she croaked. She'd gone pale as a ghost and swayed on her feet, as if on the verge of fainting. At least she wasn't holding her baby. Even though she'd borne another man's child, he didn't want her to inadvertently injure an infant.

"In the flesh." He jerked his head in a nod, emotion warring inside him. He was furious with her, as he had every right to be, but his soul rejoiced at just the sight of her. Still tiny, slender and petite, she wore her long brown hair the same way she always had. Her hazel eyes were rimmed in red, as if she'd been crying—of course she had, her husband had just died—and even now tears made the ends of her long dark lashes glisten.

Despite all this, she was still just as beautiful. This pissed him off more than it should have. Damned if he could stomach seeing her while she mourned another man. "Did you cry for me too?" he asked—no, *demanded*. "Tell me you did, because it didn't appear to be all that long after my supposed death when you went and got yourself married off to him."

"Kyle," she repeated, her voice breaking. All at once, he realized she was on the verge of shattering into a million pieces. He moved to help her without conscious thought.

At the last minute, when he would have reached her and hauled her up close against him, she stepped aside, shaking her head.

"This can't be real," she muttered. Just then, her baby began crying again and she hurried away, into the house. Though she hadn't invited Kyle to follow, she hadn't told him to leave either, so he went after her.

She picked up her son and put him to her shoulder, rubbing his back in soft circles and making soothing sounds. The baby's crying tapered off, replaced with quiet hiccupping sounds. She glanced at Kyle, her child held protectively against her, and made a strangled sound.

"You're still here? This isn't just some kind of dream?"

Before he could reply, she continued talking, almost as if to herself rather than him. "Kyle, I'm not sure how this is possible, but you're dead. And now you're not."

"Sit down," he told her, his tone gentler than she deserved. Once she had, he told her what had happened to him, all of it. Beginning with the IED exploding, the fact that he'd been holding his friend's dog tag, and the months he'd spent in a coma in a hospital. Then the rehab, learning to walk again and, finally, coming home to learn the woman he'd expected to marry had become the wife of another man. He didn't tell her the rest of it, about the PTSD he battled, because it was no longer any of her concern.

She listened quietly, tears slipping down her cheeks to be wiped away with the back of her hand. Her baby rooted around her chest, clearly seeking her breast, and finally she grabbed a baby blanket and arranged it so the infant could nurse. She looked the picture of maternal perfection, gazing lovingly at her child while her body gave sustenance.

It was almost too much for Kyle. But he'd already been to hell and clawed his way back. He'd come here for explanations and damned if he'd go without getting them.

When the baby finally finished, she rearranged her clothing and the blanket and put his tiny body against her shoulder so he could burp. Kyle continued to watch her, willing himself to feel nothing, though he failed miserably. A tempest of emotion raged inside him, ranging from a kind of joyous relief that they once again occupied the same space, to disappointment, hurt and gut-wrenching jealously. This should have been his wife, his baby. All the plans he'd made, all the hard work and sweat and tears had been supposed to culminate in this.

Instead, he'd been given the middle finger.

They both sat silently for a moment. He took a deep breath and met her gaze, steeling himself against the attraction—still—he felt when he looked at her.

"Your turn," he said, his tone harsh. "I get that your husband was murdered, but you at least owe me that."

She nodded once. "My turn," she repeated, her voice soft. "And I'll explain. But first, give me a moment to digest the fact that you're really alive, and here."

He'd bet it was a shock. She must have thought since he'd been killed, he'd never find out how quickly she'd managed to move on with her life. As if he—and what they'd had—had never mattered. A blip on her lifeline, here one day, gone the next. While for him, she'd been everything. His entire world.

With a nod, he gave her the time she requested. While she burped her baby, he prowled around the room, looking for some clue about what her life with her husband had been like. There were no photos of the two of them, none of the baby either. Just impersonal modern art prints of a type that a year ago he would have sworn didn't match her personality. She'd loved bold, vibrant colors. Not this watered-down neutral decoration surrounding her now.

In fact, the entire living room had an impersonal feel. It looked like they'd hired a decorator and let her have free rein, without any personal input. The blues and beige was tasteful; the faint touch of yellow put some color in just the right places, but none of it gave him any insight into the people who lived here.

Part of him was glad. Nicole and he had spent countless nights talking about what their first house would be like. She'd been carefree when with him, and had spoken of the bright, rich colors she'd use. She wanted, she'd said, each room to be a tapestry with a story to tell.

If this room told a story, it would be as boring as hell.

Finally, he'd had enough of the silence and turned. Her baby had finished burping and she had him in her arms, moving with a rocking motion as if to put him to sleep.

"Well?" he asked, crossing his arms.

"Let me put him down," she said. "He'll want to sleep now that he's been fed and changed."

Without waiting for a reply, she hurried off, heading toward a small room off a hallway downstairs. When she returned a moment later without the infant, she swallowed. "I keep a bassinette in the office downstairs so I'm not having to run him up to the nursery during the day. At night, since all the bedrooms are upstairs, he sleeps in his crib. Which is okay, since I have a baby monitor and am able to keep tabs on him."

Apparently realizing she was babbling, she ceased talking and sighed. Walking toward him, she stopped a few feet away and stared up at him, her expression full of wonder. "Do you have any idea what I would have given to have known you were alive? I grieved your loss deeply."

Anger blossomed inside him. Despite that, he still had to shove his hands into his pockets to keep from reaching for her. "When, Nicole?" he demanded. "Before you got married? How long did you wait after getting word I'd been killed in action? Because from where I'm standing, it doesn't seem very long at all."

Her mouth worked. Again, tears came. This time, she covered her face with her hands and wept, her shoulders shaking. The old Kyle would have rushed to console her, but she no longer belonged to him. Instead he took a step back.

He shouldn't have come here, he realized. Nothing would change. Hearing her mouth whatever explanation she came up with would do little to assuage the rawness of his pain, the aching sense of betrayal by the one person he'd believed would always have his back. Still, he couldn't seem to get his feet to moving, so he stood and watched her cry.

"I'm waiting," he finally said, the rasp in his voice in keeping with his frustration. "How long, Nicole?"

"It's not what you think," she began, her voice thick and trembling. "I really had no choice."

"Bull." He snarled the word. "Spare me the crap. I joined the army for us. So we could have a future. Every waking moment, every mission, every return to base, my first thought was of you. If the situation had been reversed, do you honestly think I'd have gotten married a month after you'd died? Do you?" He didn't shout the words, partly because he didn't want to disturb her baby, but also because volume wouldn't make any difference. She had to know he was right, yet the sorrowful look in her eyes didn't contain remorse or guilt. Just pain. Something he'd grown intimately familiar with.

"I was pregnant, Kyle," she said, her voice shaking. "My parents were going to throw me out onto the street. I had to do something to protect my baby, so I took the coward's way out and married Bill as they insisted."

He hadn't thought she could hurt him any worse, but somehow she had. "You're telling me you slept with Bill Mabry after you learned I'd been killed in action?"

If he expected her to hang her head, he was wrong. Instead, she lifted her chin and looked him square in the eyes. "No. I'm telling you I was pregnant with your child when you left me the last time. You'd gone on a mission, so I couldn't tell you. I'd planned to, the next time you called. Instead, I received word you'd been killed by an IED. Jacob is your son."

Chapter 3

Nicole waited breathlessly for his reaction. If anything, his frown deepened.

"I don't believe you," he snarled. "I never would have guessed you'd become such an opportunistic little—"

"Stop." She cut him off before he could call her whatever name he'd been about to use. It took every ounce of willpower she possessed to keep from doubling over with pain. "I can't deal with this right now. You need to go."

"Gladly." He strode to the front without a backward look. She braced herself for the noise when he slammed it, aware it would probably wake the baby, but he surprised her by closing the door with a quiet click.

Heaven help her, after inhaling so quickly it felt like

a hiccup, she found herself at the front window, hand to her aching chest, watching until he drove away. The pain was so great it felt like her heart had truly shattered. She felt almost the same as she had the day she'd learned he'd been killed. Almost.

Once he'd gone, she sank down on the couch and allowed herself to break down. She hadn't cried over Bill's passing, or over the way his horrible parents treated her. But she cried over this. The man she'd always loved was still alive. Joy and relief at knowing that Kyle Benning still walked the earth warred with sorrow and regret. Clearly, she'd managed to kill whatever he'd once felt for her. And the fact that he could honestly think she'd lie to him about something as vitally important as his own child told her how low she'd sunk in his estimation.

After crying herself out, a steadfast calm came over her. Her life might have become a crapfest, but she still had Jacob. She went into the office and watched him while he slept, letting the all-encompassing love she felt for him fill her heart, rather than pain or worry or regret.

When the doorbell chimed again an hour later, her heart skipped a beat. Now that he'd had time to think about it, had Kyle returned? Baby Jacob still slept, so she hurried to the door, her heart hammering.

Instead of Kyle, two uninformed sheriff's deputies stood on her stoop. One of them handed her a paper.

"We have a warrant to search your premises, ma'am," he said. "Please step aside."

Numb, she did as he asked. She'd only thought this day couldn't get any worse. Clearly, she'd been wrong.

Though she stood protectively over her son while

one of the men searched the office, Jacob woke when the deputy banged a file cabinet drawer shut. Nicole picked him up and soothed him, realizing he needed a diaper change, which she attended to while trying to ignore the sometimes alarming sounds the deputies were making.

They took Bill's computer and her laptop, promising they'd return it soon. They also took Bill's expensive bourbon, the used coffee pod still in the machine and several files.

With Jacob in her arms, she followed them from room to room, hating the way this search made her feel violated. They didn't speak and she didn't either, except for admonishing them to be careful when it seemed like they were growing careless with some of her perfume bottles.

They took Bill's cologne and aftershave. It finally dawned on her that they were looking for whatever poison had killed him. Which meant she'd become more than a person of interest—she'd apparently moved right into the position of primary suspect.

As they prepared to leave, the taller of the two turned to face her. "We searched his office at Mabry Trucking too," he said. Like that would make her feel better. All she could do was nod.

After they'd finally gone, she went about the business of straightening her house, finding comfort in the busywork.

Then she bathed Jacob. After drying him off and putting him in a fresh diaper and onesie, she breathed deeply, loving the clean, baby powder scent of him. Her breasts tingled, reminding her it was nearly feeding time. Jacob latched on, suckling with gusto. Filled with love and finally, a little peace, she watched him drink his fill. After burping him, she placed him in his bassinette to rest and set about making herself something for dinner.

Bill had been a meat-and-potatoes sort of guy and she'd marinated a couple of ribeye steaks. But the thought of eating that made her stomach turn, so she fixed herself a salad with tuna on top instead.

As she carried her empty bowl to the sink, the house phone rang. Caller ID showed her in-laws. After the awful conversation with Theresa before, she decided not to answer. Bill's mother could leave a voice mail. Nicole didn't need any more grief after this long and horrible day.

The answering machine picked up. "Nicole? It's Theresa. We just wanted to let you know that we intend on filing for custody of our grandson." And she ended the call.

Nicole had to remind herself to breathe. Her disbelief turned to anger. Who did these people think they were? How could they possibly believe any judge would give them custody of her son? She'd done nothing wrong. And she was a wonderful, devoted mother. On what basis did they think they could rip her baby away from her?

Then she realized the Mabrys must truly believe she'd murdered her husband. That would be the only scenario in which she could imagine a judge handing Jacob over to them. If she were convicted of murder and sent to prison, her son would need family to take care of him.

Except she hadn't killed Bill and she wasn't going

anywhere. Neither was Jacob. She'd fight to her dying breath to keep her boy by her side.

Failing that, there was one tiny fact Bill's parents were unaware of. A simple DNA test would prove that Jacob wasn't truly related to them. He carried none of their blood. Bill had known; it had been one of the conditions she'd insisted on when her parents got her to marry him. She wasn't a liar and there'd been no way she'd try to pass Kyle's child off as another man's.

Now Bill's parents—and the sheriff—clearly believed her capable of murder. Kyle was alive—and she'd rejoice in this knowledge once she could breathe again—and also considered her not only a cheat, but a liar. And she'd lived in Anniversary her entire life, so she knew soon the entire town would be talking and drawing up sides.

What a way to cap an already horrible day.

She truly didn't know how much more she could take. At least the day was almost over. Soon, she could fall into her bed and escape into the land of dreams.

Right before darkness fell, she headed out front to get the mail from the mailbox. Bill's credit card statement had arrived. He'd informed her in no uncertain terms that she was never to open his mail, so she usually left these on the kitchen counter for him to open when he got home.

Now Bill was gone and she'd be cancelling all his credit cards. Until then, she'd need to pay all outstanding bills. She slit the envelope and pulled out the statement and blinked.

The total balance was quite a bit more than she'd expected. Nearly two thousand dollars. The list of charges made her stomach clench. Flowers from a florist, three times that month. A twelve-hundred-dollar charge at Guller's Jewelry Store. Dinner at an expensive Italian restaurant, which mustn't have been for business since he'd used his personal credit card.

And the final charge was the real kicker. Two hundred and thirty dollars in lingerie at Victoria's Secret.

None of this had been for her. Bill hadn't once brought her flowers or gifted her with jewelry or lingerie.

Which meant he had a mistress. Another woman. Which would explain all those nights when he hadn't come home, claiming to have slept at the office.

A mistress. Rather than dismay or regret, all she felt was relief.

She needed to notify the sheriff. If they didn't know about this woman, they needed to. Maybe they could get a search warrant for her home too.

All the way back to his rental house, Kyle muttered a running litany of curses. He'd been hurt and angry before. Now he was furious. How could it be possible that he'd never truly known Nicole at all?

When he passed the sign for the lake, he took a sharp left, catching the turn so fast for a moment he thought his wheels might leave the pavement. He drove to the park at the top of the bluff—once his and Nicole's favorite spot, though he wouldn't think of that night.

Out of the truck, he climbed down to the water's edge, stripping off his clothes as he went. The hot Texas sun beat down on him unmercifully. Finally, clad only in his boxers, he jumped into the lake.

And swam. Clean, crisp strokes, the physical action

of using his body to move helping to clear his head. Across the lake he went, all the way to the other shore, before turning around and heading back. He did this three times, until his chest and arms were screaming in protest.

When he finally climbed up on shore, his muscles quivering, he felt better. More like himself. As if he had a snowball's chance in hell of being in control of his destiny.

Dressing, he climbed back up to his truck. He needed to get to the supermarket and stock up on provisions.

The H-E-B store looked unchanged. He parked and went inside, grabbing a cart. Though he hadn't made a list, his little rental house was totally empty, so he'd need staples including cleaning supplies, as well as food.

As he perused the choices in paper towels, someone called his name.

He looked up, breaking into a grin. "Bret Atkinson. You're a sight for sore eyes."

The two men shook hands. He and Bret had been buddies in high school. When Kyle went off after joining the army, Bret had stayed in town and gone to work at his father's boot repair shop. Bret had married his high school sweetheart, Heather.

"I was pretty damn surprised yesterday when I heard you were in town," Bret said. "Considering I went to your memorial service about a year ago."

Once again, Kyle found himself explaining what had happened to him. He figured he might ought to consider printing up his story on paper and handing them out since his appearance clearly was a shock to everyone in town.

"Wow," Bret marveled when he'd finished. "It's a shame what's happening with Nicole, isn't it?"

"I heard about her husband getting murdered." Kyle kept his tone noncommittal.

"Yeah, and she's the prime suspect."

Though Trudy had said something similar, this was his friend. Bret knew Nicole well. The two couples had spent a lot of time together.

Surely Bret didn't truly believe Nicole could do such a thing. Kyle wasn't sure how to react. He waited for Bret to laugh and say he'd been joking, but the expression on his old friend's face was serious as dirt.

"Really?" Kyle finally asked. "Are you saying the guy had no other enemies?"

"That we know of. He was a deacon at his church, a well-respected community guy, and from what I hear, an easy boss to work for at the trucking company."

Kyle nodded. "Were he and Nicole happy?" Inwardly, he winced. He hadn't meant to ask that—the words had just slipped out.

"They appeared to be." Bret shrugged. "But you know how that can be. Lots of folks just put on a happy face. No one really knows what goes on in private."

Another stab straight to the gut. Yet Kyle managed an impersonal smile. "How's Heather?"

Bret's smile slipped a notch. "We've got just about one more month. She's as big as a house, but hanging in there. She just finished decorating the nursery and says she's ready. Heck, we both are."

Then, apparently registering the stunned look on Kyle's face, he shook his head and grinned. "Sorry.

I forgot you didn't know. Heather's pregnant. It's our first. She's had a few issues, but nothing too serious. We're hoping the last month will go quickly."

"Aww, man. Congratulations!" Kyle pounded his friend on the back. "Are you having a boy or a girl?"

"Thanks." Bret shook his head. "Neither one of us wanted to know the sex of our baby, so I have no idea. All I want is healthy and strong. Heather's wavered a bit, especially when she started decorating, but she stuck with the plan."

"Wow," Kyle marveled. "This is just amazing. You and Heather will make great parents." A shadow crossed his heart as he thought of Nicole, who'd become a single parent now.

Something must have shown on his face.

"You'll get there too, Kyle," Bret said. "Look at all you've been through. Yet here you are, back home and ready to start over."

They talked a few minutes more, exchanged phone numbers and then Bret went on his way. While Kyle continued his shopping, he thought of his old friend's words. Starting over. In a way, he'd come here to pick up where he and Nicole had left off, yet when he thought of the bright and shining future he'd envisioned for them, he wanted to punch something.

On the way to the checkout line, he ran into Bret again. Bret's cart was nearly as full as his own. They shared a quick chuckle over that.

"Hey, if you get a chance, stop by for dinner sometime," Bret invited. "Maybe we can invite Nicole too, so you two can catch up. She's probably feeling pretty down, being a new widow and all. Though she has that baby of hers to keep her busy. I know Heather's been dying for some baby time."

Kyle shook his head. "I stopped by and saw her earlier today."

"Oh, you did?" Bret eyed him. "Did you get a chance to see Jacob? At first, his eyes were hazel like Nicole's, but the last time we saw him, they were changing to green. The exact same color as yours." He laughed. "Heather and I always said he could have been your son."

With a wave, Bret walked off, getting into one of the three open checkout lines.

Kyle did the same, deliberately choosing the one farthest from his friend. Nicole had said she'd gotten pregnant before he'd headed back to duty overseas. In his bitterness and hurt at her betrayal, he hadn't believed her. A wave of shame swept through him, followed immediately by anger.

Was it possible he really did have a son? A simple DNA test would prove it.

Sheriff Cantrell took a look at the Visa bill and yawned. "How do you know these charges were for a mistress?" he asked.

Nicole stared at him in disbelief. "Um, maybe because I never saw any of the things listed."

He looked again, leaning back in his chair. "Perhaps he bought them for his mother. You know he and Theresa had a close relationship."

"Victoria's Secret lingerie?" She tapped the edge of his desk. "Do you really think they had *that* close of a relationship? That's not only creepy, it's sick."

"Please, Ms. Mabry." His tone went sharp. "This

is your deceased husband we're talking about. Please show some respect."

She had to swallow twice to keep from telling him what she thought about his attitude. "Sheriff," she began, keeping her voice level and reasonable. "My husband was murdered. His credit card bill indicates he bought expensive gifts for another woman. He took her to dinner. I haven't checked his other months' bills, but I have a feeling there will be more of the same. My husband had a mistress. There was another woman involved in his life. Since you're investigating his murder, I'd think you'd want to check this out."

Glumly, he once again considered the bill. "This opens up a whole can of worms."

Oh for the love of… Deep breaths. "Do you or do you not want to find out who killed my husband?" she asked, refusing this time to curb her impatience.

"Of course I do," he answered. "That's my job. But I can't help but feel you're instigating this in order to deflect attention from you. Especially since you're a person of interest."

Shaking her head, she stood. "Sheriff, you've known me your entire life, not just since you were a deputy patrolman. I understand the pressure you're under from the Mabrys wanting a quick resolution to this investigation. But you're also our sheriff. You took an oath to uphold the law. I can't help but feel you're trying to railroad me so you can obtain an arrest. But I can assure you, I did not kill my husband. And I'd really like to know who did. So please, make a copy of the bill and look into it. Can you at least promise me you'll do that?"

His mottled complexion revealed how little he cared

for her disparaging comments. But she was right and he knew it. Moving with exaggerated slowness, he photocopied the statement and handed the original back to her. She tucked it into her diaper bag and reached down to pick up little Jacob in his infant carrier.

"Wait," Sheriff Cantrell said, motioning her to sit back down. "I understand Kyle Benning is back in town."

Holding his gaze, she waited to hear what this had to do with her.

"I was told he paid you a visit yesterday," he continued. "Mind telling me what that was all about?"

"Kyle and I are old friends," she replied. "Like everyone else in town, I was told he died in Afghanistan. He wanted to let me know that wasn't actually the case."

How stiff she sounded. Still, her meeting with Kyle was none of his business.

"I know you two were more than just friends." The faint mockery in his voice infuriated her, though she pushed it back down inside. "And now that poor Bill is out of the way, maybe now the two of you can pick up where you left off."

This was too much, even for her. "That's not only insulting," she said. "But hurtful. We haven't even buried Bill yet."

Silence. Then, very slowly, Sheriff Cantrell nodded. "My apologies. Sometimes this job makes me think the worst of people."

Except for Bill. You didn't want to even consider he might have had a mistress. Of course, she didn't voice this thought out loud.

She pushed to her feet again. "Please let me know what you find out," she said, gesturing toward the credit card statement. Jacob's carrier once again in hand, she turned to go.

The sheriff followed her to the door. "I'll give you a call if I learn anything," he said. His detached, professional tone had returned. Nicole wished she had confidence in him actually doing his job and checking the new lead out.

She didn't understand his sudden loyalty to Bill's reputation. Though they'd attended the same super-strict church, as far as she knew Bill and Sheriff Cantrell hadn't been particularly good friends. Though of course, clearly she knew next to nothing about what her husband had done when he wasn't at home with her. Anything and everything was possible. For all she knew, the two men could have gone bar hopping together. At this point, nothing would surprise her. The one thing marriage to Bill Mabry had taught her was that nothing was as it seemed on the surface.

Once she had Jacob buckled into his rear-facing infant seat, she started Bill's car and drove away. It had been a long time since she'd driven, though her driver's license hadn't expired. Bill never let her drive his BMW and after one of the deputies had delivered it to her along with the keys, she'd felt extremely nervous sitting behind the steering wheel. Now she supposed she'd get used to it eventually.

She drove to Briggses' Funeral Home. Despite not hearing anything from the Mabrys, she needed to see about making arrangements. Of course, Pastor Theodore would handle the funeral. That was a given. Her parents and Bill's parents were founding members of

The Church on Top of the Hill. Bill had been a deacon there. Of necessity, Nicole had attended as a child and then again once she and Bill had married. After the funeral, she never intended to go there again.

Since there were other things to attend to, such as choosing a casket and a burial plot, she asked to speak to the owner, Joe Wayne Briggs. His son Junior came out to greet her instead.

When she told him the reason for her visit, he led her to a tastefully decorated small office. She couldn't help but notice the box of tissues placed conspicuously close to her chair.

"Now what can I help you with today?" Junior asked, his attempt to mimic his father's sonorous tone coming off surprisingly well.

"I'm sure you know my husband, Bill Mabry, recently passed away. I need to see about selecting his casket and purchasing a burial plot."

Confusion crossed his face. "I'm sorry. I don't understand. Dan and Theresa Mabry have already made all the selections. He's going to be interred in the Mabry family plot."

Made all the selections. Without her. One more slap in the face. "I'm his widow," she began. "I should have been consulted."

Then, as he stumbled all over himself trying to explain what had happened, she realized this was okay. All of it. Bill's parents had adored their only son and mourned him, definitely far more than she did. If they knew his true character, their love for him superceded all that.

She, on the other hand, had only been married to him for one year. He'd bullied and abused her, regarded her as a possession rather than an equal part-ner, and in her heart of hearts, she felt relief rather than sorrow.

"Thank you very much," she said, interrupting him. "I assume they've also handled the obituary?"

At his nod, she exhaled. "Do you happen to have anything printed out yet?"

"We do. We do. Let me get you a copy." He scur-ried out of the room. When he returned, he handed her a sealed envelope. "Everything is in here. The casket, the burial plot number and a map to the area, and in-formation on the service." He took a deep breath and adjusted his tie. "I do apologize for not realizing we should have contacted you. I assumed you were too grief stricken to attend any planning sessions."

She let that one go. Thanking him, she once again picked up Jacob's carrier and turned to go.

When she lifted him up to buckle the carrier into the backseat, she realized his little face was bright red. His eyes were closed, and she did a panicked test, wet-ting her finger and placing it under his nose to make sure he was still breathing.

The instant she did this, he began flailing his arms about and let out a loud cry. Once he got started, his crying increased in volume and intensity, letting her know something was very wrong.

She took him out of the carrier and checked his diaper, finding it dry. No amount of rocking or sing-ing to him made any difference. When a bubbling rash of red welts appeared on his face and arms, she knew something was drastically wrong. Buckling him back into the carrier while he still wailed, she jumped into the car and drove straight for the hospital emergency room.

Chapter 4

Kyle finished unpacking his groceries, then stood back and eyed his full refrigerator. He knew he should feel some sort of satisfaction at having successfully begun his journey toward living on his own out of the military, but the best he could summon up was exhaustion.

His doorbell rang. A uniformed deputy stood outside. What now?

"Can I help you?" he asked.

"We have a warrant to search the premises," the deputy said, handing him an envelope. "Please step aside."

Stunned, Kyle didn't move. "Search for what? Don't I have the right to know what it is I've supposedly done?"

"It's all in the warrant, sir." Motioning to another

uniformed officer, the deputy let his hand hover near his holstered weapon. "Now, please. Step aside."

With a shrug, Kyle did as he was told.

While the two officers searched his small rental home—which wouldn't take them very long since Kyle had very few belongings and only the basic furniture that had come with the house—Kyle read the search warrant. The reason given, and approved by a judge, was listed as Bill Mabry's murder.

Which made absolutely zero sense. Kyle hadn't even been in town when the guy had died.

Aware that arguing with the deputies wouldn't change anything, he wandered out to his small back deck to wait until they'd finished their search. He only hoped they didn't trash the place too badly.

"Sir?" The urgent tone of the deputy's voice had him jumping to his feet. "Could you come in here please?"

Kyle hurried inside. The two deputies stood near his gun safe, one of the few purchases he'd made before driving back to Anniversary.

"Could you open this for us?"

He wondered if he could refuse. Probably not. A search warrant would definitely include firearms. Heaving a sigh, he dialed in the combination for the lock and opened it. He let the door swing wide and took a step back. "Please handle with care," he said. "Those pieces were chosen carefully and I can't afford to replace them."

To his eternal relief, they treated his small gun collection with respect. All of his weapons were clean and well taken care of, something he'd learned to do while in the army.

"Great condition," one of the deputies commented.

"And none of them have recently been fired," said the other.

Kyle simply waited until they'd finished. When they moved away from the safe, he closed the door and locked it. "Anything else you need?" he asked.

"No. I think we're done." The two men left.

Once he'd watched them drive away, he inspected his living space. They'd been thorough, he saw, straightening a sofa cushion. But not unnecessarily messy. In fact, if he weren't so meticulous about his home, he wouldn't have even known it had been searched.

He had to wonder why anyone could possibly believe he'd been involved in the murder of a man he hadn't even known. Simply because he'd visited Nicole? Did that mean she was under some sort of surveillance? Or were they probing her past for any kind of connection that might have compelled her to kill her husband?

Her husband. The words stuck in his craw. It was always supposed to be the two of them—Kyle and Nicole. Anyone who'd known them prior to one year ago would understand this. And might suspect that underneath the thin veneer of civility, strong emotions swirled and seethed.

It wouldn't be too great of a leap of faith to wonder if he had returned home to Anniversary to find his woman married to another man, whom he'd killed in a fit of jealously. Kyle supposed he ought to thank his lucky stars that the timing was all wrong. The day Bill Mabry had died, Kyle had been in Mississippi.

He had motel receipts to prove it. And Nicole had still believed him to be dead.

The sheriff had his deputies barking up the wrong tree.

His cell phone rang. "Kyle, it's Bret. I'm at the hospital ER with Heather. She's fine—it was false labor so we're heading back home. I thought you might want to know I saw Nicole come in with her baby." He paused. "If I'm bothering you, I'm sorry. I don't know how things are between the two of you. But from what I can tell, Nicole is all alone. If you're truly friends, I think she could use your help. Especially if something happens to the baby."

The baby. Possibly his son. Though his gut clenched, Kyle forced himself to breathe deeply and calmly. "What happened? Was there some sort of an accident?"

"No idea. But judging from the way they rushed her and little Jacob into the back, he's in bad shape."

"Thanks for letting me know," Kyle said, and ended the call. He wasn't a hundred percent sure why exactly Bret had decided to call him, but figured his old friend would guess Kyle still hadn't sorted out his feelings about Nicole.

And the baby. Who might or might not really be his son.

Snatching up his car keys, Kyle headed to the hospital. He didn't bother analyzing why. He just knew he had to go. Whether or not Nicole wanted him there.

By the time Nicole had pulled up in front of the emergency room, Jacob had begun wheezing, as if he couldn't suck in air.

Forcing down the panic, she'd managed to unbuckle him from his infant carrier, snatch him up and run into the ER, shouting for help. The triage nurse had taken one look at Jacob and paged for help.

She'd hustled Nicole through the double doors into the actual ER and a nurse came running. Nicole had handed over her precious baby and the nurse hustled him into a room, Nicole right on her heels.

Now someone came and asked for her insurance card, which she handed over. The doctor appeared, helping the nurse get Jacob's clothing off, including his diaper. "Nurse," the doctor ordered. "Use Broselow Tape to quickly get his weight and dose out epi based on that."

As the nurse hurriedly complied, Jacob wheezed, his eyes huge, his face red with welts. He alternated between trying to breathe and attempting to cry. Frantic to help him any way she could, she watched the doctor as he accepted the syringe and injected it into Jacob's thigh. "It's epinephrine," he told Nicole. "The nurse will start him on an IV with Benadryl and steroids."

Terrified, Nicole nodded. While the nurse bustled around, carefully inserting an IV in Jacob's wrist, the doctor turned his attention back to the infant, who squirmed and still appeared to be having a hard time breathing. His struggle broke Nicole's heart. She realized she'd never truly known abject terror until this moment.

"Help him, please," she implored the doctor.

"We're doing everything we can," he responded. "Look. He's breathing better. And those hives will subside, too."

Relieved, she clutched the side of the hospital bed to keep her knees from giving out.

"It's already working, ma'am," the nurse said, her tone soothing. "Look at him. We'll have him back to normal soon."

"Thank goodness," Nicole said, swaying with relief.

"Was he bitten by something?" the doctor asked Nicole, his voice curt, all of his focus still on Jacob. "Or did you give him something different—formula or juice? This is definitely an allergic reaction."

"There's been no change in his diet. As for a bite, I don't know," she answered. "One minute, he cried out, then the hives appeared."

"Sounds like a bee sting," the doctor said. "Let me see if I can find the stinger." He began a thorough search of Jacob's skin, which was still covered in welts.

Careful to keep out of both the doctor's and the nurse's way, Nicole moved as close as she could to her baby. To her immense relief, Jacob's wheezing disappeared. Once he could breathe again, he began crying, a confused and hurt wail that tore at her heart. She ached to gather him up and hold him close to her, but the ER doctor was busy inspecting him, searching for a sting or bite mark.

While he did this, the nurse finished hooking Jacob up to the machines. Gradually, his wailing turned into sniffles, and then little snuffling sounds. He latched his little hand on to her finger, holding on tightly. Chest tight with love, she gazed at her baby boy, aware she'd never survive losing him.

"Here it is," the doctor pronounced, glancing up at her and adjusting his glasses with one finger. "This looks like either a wasp or a bee sting. I've removed the stinger. The meds are working and I think he's going to be just fine."

"Oh, thank you so much," Nicole said. She wanted to hug the man. And the nurse too. "Can I take him home now?"

"Not yet. We're going to have to keep an eye on him for several hours."

Puzzled, she frowned. "Why?"

"We need to monitor his heart due to the epinephrine. We also need to make sure he doesn't have a rebound reaction once the epi wears off. Then, if all looks good, you can both go home."

Grateful, she nodded. "I understand."

"Good." The doctor wrote something in the chart, handed it to the nurse and left the room.

"You can hold him now," the nurse told her. "Just be careful of the IV and the other wires. Press the call button if you need anything. We'll be checking on you periodically."

Once the nurse had gone, Nicole carefully reached for Jacob. As soon as she had him in her arms, she felt the last bit of tension leave his tiny body. She climbed up to sit on his hospital bed, careful of all the apparatus, and held him close. Singing soft, she rocked him to sleep.

When the door swung open again about twenty minutes later, she looked up with a smile, assuming either the nurse or doctor had returned. Instead, Kyle stood framed in the doorway, his gaze locking on hers.

She froze, not sure what to think or say. He came into the room, closed the door carefully and quietly behind him.

"Is he all right?" he asked, his voice pitched low.

Slowly, she nodded. "I think so. Right now, they want us to stay so they can monitor him."

"What happened?"

Instead of answering his question, she frowned at him. "Why are you here?"

"One of my friends happened to see you come in and called me." He took a seat in the chair next to the bed. "I came by because…" He paused. "I don't know why I'm here. I thought maybe you could use a friend right now."

Touched despite herself, she blinked back tears. Which infuriated her. She would not cry in front of him. Never again. "Is that what you are?" She couldn't keep the bitterness from her voice. "Because you sure didn't act like it earlier."

In her arms, Jacob stirred. Instantly, she began making soothing sounds and rocking him again. Once he'd settled back into sleep, she looked up and met Kyle's intense gaze.

"I'm sorry," he said. "I was shocked. And, I'll admit, hurt. I've had some time to think about what you said."

Unsure whether or not to be appeased, she finally nodded. "You can do a DNA test, you know. It's a simple thing to prove or disprove, these days."

"I know it is." He paused, eyeing her sleeping son. "Tell me, does he have green eyes?"

"He's only three months old," she pointed out. "Babies are usually born with light-colored eyes. Around six to nine months old is when it's easier to predict their final color. I'm hoping he gets your green eyes. But it's too early to tell."

"I see." He leaned closer, resting his elbow on the edge of the bed near her knee. "Are you going to tell me what brought you here?"

She told him what had happened and what the doctor had said.

"He's allergic to bee stings?" he repeated, his expression shocked.

"Yep. Like you were as a kid. I have to find out if I need to keep an EpiPen or something with me at all times."

"I still am." His voice husky, he shook his head. "Allergic to bees. Stuff like that never goes away."

Chest tight, heart aching, she let her gaze roam over him. He had some new lines on his face, some wear and tear from whatever had happened to him in Afghanistan. He looked older, wearier, almost battle-hardened, yet he was still the tall broad-shouldered man with the bright green eyes she'd once loved.

How badly she wished they could go back in time and change some of the choices they'd made. She wouldn't have let him join the army, for one. They should have taken a chance on the future with each other, even if they were too young and broke to know better. Getting pregnant with Jacob was something she'd never give up, not for anything in the world, but how much sweeter those nine months would have been with Kyle by her side.

Since she'd learned the hard way that dwelling on the past accomplished nothing, she forced those thoughts away and focused on the here and now.

"What happened to your husband?" he asked. "I'm sorry—I know that's a personal question, but since sheriff's deputies showed up at my house with a search warrant earlier, I figure I have a right to know."

"A search warrant?" Aware her mouth had fallen open, she closed it, continuing to rock her son so he wouldn't sense her rising agitation. "Why on earth would they think you had anything to do with Bill's death?"

"That's what I'm hoping you could tell me?"

Jacob stirred in her arms, making that little mewling sound he sometimes made to indicate his hunger. He opened his eyes and nuzzled her arm, seeking his meal. A rush of milk coming in made her breast tingle. She grabbed the baby blanket she'd wrapped around her son earlier and arranged it so she could nurse him.

Once little Jacob was happily drinking, she looked at Kyle and shook her head. "I'd be happy to tell you about it, but not here. Right now I just want Jacob to be released so I can take him home."

Though he nodded, she could tell from the tightness in his jaw that he didn't care for her response.

The nurse came in then, smiling. "Well, hello there," she said. "I'm glad Daddy got to come in too. I just wanted to stop by and let you know that so far, everything is looking good. We should be able to discharge you soon."

Daddy. The word brought a lump to her throat.

Nicole glanced at the clock on the wall. Ninety minutes had passed. "Thank you."

Instead of leaving, the nurse went over to check on Jacob. Kyle pushed to his feet, moving out of the way and going to stand near the doorway. Nicole couldn't help but notice how he filled up the room with his sheer size and masculine presence. Evidently the nurse noticed as well, rolling her eyes good-naturedly at Nicole, as if to say *Men*!

"I hope it's okay that I fed him," Nicole said. "He was hungry."

The nurse chuckled. "I can see that. Nothing has changed as far as his vitals, so let me go round up the doctor and get him to sign the form so you can all go home."

Watching Nicole give the baby nourishment again stirred up a rush of complicated emotions. Kyle wasn't certain of the etiquette—should he look away—but Nicole's quiet competence and the fact that she kept herself covered put him at ease.

Though he tried unobtrusively to study Jacob, looking for some sort of resemblance, the infant looked like an infant. He supposed three months might be too young for the baby to start showing his parents' features.

Right now, it didn't really matter. He believed Nicole. After all, she had no real reason to lie to him. Especially since Jacob's parentage could be easily proven with a simple DNA test.

Which meant Kyle had a son. He wasn't sure how he felt about that yet. Children with Nicole had always been part of his long-range plans, but her marriage to another man sent those completely out the window. She'd sworn to wait for him and damned if she hadn't gotten married a month after he'd been erroneously declared dead. Kyle knew he could never get past that huge betrayal.

In addition, she'd apparently passed Jacob off as Bill Mabry's child. This both infuriated him and saddened him. Clearly, he hadn't known Nicole as well as he'd believed.

Getting Jacob released to leave took a lot longer than he'd thought. The way the nurse had talked, the doctor would sign some paper and that was that. He figured it'd take a couple of minutes, but when a half hour turned into forty-five, he could barely keep his frustration under control.

To make matters worse, someone dropped something metal out in the hall, and Kyle found himself on the floor, in full defensive cover position. While at Walter Reed hospital, they'd told him he'd need therapy to get help with his PTSD. He'd have to find someone local, once he got settled in.

Slowly, he got to his feet. Stone-faced, he hoped his expression hadn't revealed his embarrassment, but all of Nicole's attention was focused on her baby. As if she hadn't even noticed. He had a sneaking suspicion she was doing this to spare his feelings, but couldn't ask her.

Finally, after nearly an hour had passed, the nurse returned, along with the doctor. They gave Nicole instructions, what to watch for, that sort of thing, and then informed her she could go.

He followed her outside. When she reached her car, a late model shiny black BMW, she turned to face him. "I know we need to talk," she began. "But I'm exhausted and really would like to go home and get some rest. Let's plan on meeting up some time tomorrow."

"Okay." He pulled out his phone. "What's your number?"

She gave it to him and he entered it into his contacts. "I'll text you mine," he said.

"Thank you." She unlocked her car.

Feeling out of sorts, he watched her while she buckled little Jacob into his infant carrier. She barely looked at Kyle once she'd done that, getting into the driver's side, starting the engine and buckling herself in. Finally, she waved before driving away.

Fool that he was, he watched her go and wondered how he could both love and hate someone at the same time.

The next morning, while he drank a cup of strong black coffee made in his new coffeepot, he texted Nicole his number. Thirty minutes later, she texted back, asking him if he had some free time to sit down and talk. She'd prefer to come to his place. When he asked why, she texted that she had a strong suspicion someone was watching her house.

He gave her the address and told her to come over in about an hour. That'd give him time to shower and get dressed.

Exactly fifty-nine minutes later, the black BMW pulled up in front of his little house. He watched from the front window, keeping his eye on the street so he could see if she'd been followed.

When no other vehicle showed up, he opened his front door and went out to help her. She unlocked the trunk, asking him if he'd mind getting the portable Pack n' Play. While he wrestled this out onto the sidewalk, she handled the baby and a large diaper bag.

Inside the house, he set down the contraption in the middle of the living room. To his surprise, once he opened it, the thing practically set itself up.

"Thank you." Nicole smiled at him, and the entire world shifted.

He blinked, turning away until he could ground himself back in reality. "Would you like something to drink?" he asked, his voice gruffer than he intended.

Barely looking up from getting her baby settled, she responded. "Water would be great."

Listen to them. Talking in careful platitudes as if they were complete strangers. In a way, they actually were.

Except that only one year—one stinking year—had passed since he'd kissed her goodbye and gone off to serve his country. How could so much have changed in such a short period of time?

But it had. Returning with two bottled waters, he handed one to her before taking a seat in the armchair, leaving the entire couch for her.

"Nice place," she commented, glancing around the small room.

"Yours is much nicer," he pointed out. Not to be cruel, but because it was. But her smile faltered and for one second she looked sad.

But then she lifted her chin and willed herself out of it. "Thank you. It isn't what I would have chosen, but it's a decent house."

Decent.

A flash of anger ripped through him. He realized he couldn't just sit there and act as if they were casual acquaintances, like nothing had ever happened between them. As though she hadn't been his entire reason for living.

"I can't do this," he growled. "I know you've moved on—I get it. For you, it's been a long time. For me, it feels like it was just yesterday when you kissed me and told me you'd love me forever."

She took a shaky breath. "I understand," she began.

"Do you?" Though he kept his voice low so as not to disturb Jacob, he didn't bother to hide his anger or his pain. "I don't think you do. I want to be part of my son's life. But right now, I don't think I can be part of yours."

One single tear slipped down her cheek. She used her hand to swipe it away. "Won't you even let me explain?"

"Explain?" He wanted to bellow, to rant and to rave. To throw things, punch something, to use his broken, battered body to vent the overwhelming flood of emotions consuming him. Of course, he did none of this. He'd find a gym later and work out his frustration. Right now, he just needed Nicole to go. It hurt too damn much to have her so close to him and not be able to touch her.

"Yes," she whispered, her voice broken. "There were reasons for everything I did."

"I'm sure there were." He forced himself to unclench his teeth. "But I don't want to hear them. Because in the end, none of them matter. You did what you felt you had to do. You can live with yourself. That's great. I'm happy for you."

"I thought you were dead," she cried, loud enough to startle the baby, who made a few halfhearted sounds of protest. Nicole gave him his pacifier and returned her attention to Kyle. "I was pregnant. My parents threatened to toss me out on the street. I had no money, no place to go."

"So you did what you had to do," he finished for her, his heart hard. "Did your husband think you loved him?" Despite himself, his voice cracked. He forced himself to go on. "Did you pass off Jacob as his? Because that would have meant you had to sleep with him right away." The image had tormented him ever since learning of her betrayal.

"Do you really think so little of me?" Anger and anguish colored her comment. "You who know me better than anyone else."

"Knew you," he corrected. "Or thought I did."

She pushed herself up off the couch. Moving with quiet dignity, she picked up her baby and placed him where she'd been sitting so she could close up the portable crib. Once she'd accomplished that, she grabbed the diaper bag, her son and the Pack n' Play.

He expected her to storm out of there, but instead she faced him. Her beautiful hazel eyes shimmered with unshed tears. "I'm sorry to have bothered you," she said with quiet dignity. "It won't happen again."

And then she marched to the front door, opened it and exited both his house and his life.

Chapter 5

Driving home with Jacob, Nicole tried to understand. Kyle had changed. The ordeal he'd suffered through had been bad enough, but then he'd returned home to find the woman who'd promised to love him forever married to another man. When she tried to put herself in his shoes, the bitterness and anger was more than understandable, it was justified. To him, no amount of explaining would help him understand.

For herself at least, she needed to try. To make him comprehend the depths of the grief that had slayed her when she'd been informed of his death. She'd sunk so low she hadn't cared if she ever saw another sunrise. Only the knowledge that their baby grew inside her had kept her going. She'd had to force herself to eat food that had become tasteless, so their child could have nourishment.

When she'd longed to drown herself in drink, she'd abstained—because she'd known doing so would harm their baby. *Their baby.* Her only reason for continuing to draw breath.

And then, when her parents had learned of her pregnancy, the rage, shame and disappointment they'd showed her rather than unconditional love and understanding had made her desperate for an escape. She'd wanted to flee, to seek out another, better life for herself and her child. Only she had no funds. The meagre amount she'd made waitressing at the café had gone for the essentials—clothing, food, medicines— that her parents had refused to buy for her once she'd turned eighteen.

She had nothing. And no one. Just herself and her unborn child.

And the man who'd wanted to marry her since they'd been in middle school. Bill Mabry.

Terrified they'd lose standing in their church and the community, her parents had offered her a choice. Get out of their house, leave town, with no help from them, or marry Bill Mabry, the man they'd chosen for her.

In other words, they were more than willing to throw her, their own daughter, along with their unborn grandbaby, out in the street if she didn't go along with their plan.

Truth be told, she really hadn't a choice. She'd do anything to protect her child, including marry a man she didn't love.

At first, when he'd been told of her willingness to become his wife, Bill had been over the moon with happiness. But Nicole had insisted on one thing. She'd told Bill the truth. All of it. She loved Kyle Benning and would carry that love with her to her grave. And she was pregnant with Kyle's baby. It would be Bill's choice whether or not he still wanted to marry her after she told him this.

To her surprise, he listened, and agreed. Though he'd promised her earnestly he'd love and protect both her and her unborn child, Nicole believed he'd begun to hate her a little, deep inside.

This hate had begun to manifest shortly after their rushed wedding. While on the outside, Bill Mabry was a business leader and an upstanding member of the town's largest and most fervent church, at home he drank heavily. Nicole suspected that recently he'd also begun using drugs and visiting topless bars and maybe even hiring hookers.

The doorbell rang. Peering out the peephole, Nicole saw her in-laws, Theresa and Dan Mabry. Her heart skipped a beat. After that last horrible phone conversation, maybe they'd come to apologize, to say they'd changed their minds. Though Nicole doubted it.

One thing for sure, she wasn't letting the two of them anywhere near her son.

While she debated what to do, they pressed the doorbell again. And again. She realized since Bill's BMW was parked outside the garage, they knew she was home.

Finally, she took a deep breath and opened the door. Instead of inviting them in, she stepped outside. "Yes?" she asked.

Dan frowned. "Can we come inside?"

Before Nicole could answer, Theresa stepped forward. "You're showing your true colors now, aren't you? Don't worry, we know what kind of person you are. And if we find out you were the one who killed our son, we'll make sure there's not a judge in the state who will show you any mercy."

"That's it," Nicole said, surprising both herself and them. "I've had enough. I have not done a single thing for you to treat me this way. I've been a good wife to Bill and a great mother to Jacob. Yet you've called me a murderer and stated you intend to file for custody of my son. *My* son. Not yours. So excuse me for not being welcoming when you show up on my doorstep with more crazy accusations."

Theresa glared at her. If looks could kill…

Meanwhile, Dan appeared shocked. "What are you talking about?" he began. "We most certainly did not—"

"*You* didn't," Nicole interrupted. "But Theresa did. And I won't stand for it anymore."

"I want you out of this house," Theresa declared, her voice dripping venom. "Bill owned this before you were married. I don't care what state law says, we'll be taking you to court to get it back."

"Theresa!" The shock in Dan's voice revealed he truly hadn't known about any of the other phone calls. "What is wrong with you? Bill wouldn't want you to act this way."

"Wouldn't he?" She spun on her husband so fast, it reminded Nicole of a snake about to strike. "He talked to me, Dan. He wasn't happy. He wouldn't tell me why, but it wasn't hard to guess. And since he hadn't made a will, we can go to court and make sure she doesn't get a thing."

"Come on." Expression as firm as his tone, Dan

grabbed his wife's arm. "Let's go." He glanced back at Nicole and shook his head. "She's taking this hard," he said. "I'm sorry."

"Don't you dare apologize to her," Theresa screeched, allowing herself to be dragged toward the car. Before she made it even halfway, she broke down in sobs. Dan hustled her inside the car, before going around to the driver's side. He jumped in and sped off without another word.

Wow. Clearly, her son's untimely death had made Theresa go a little bit crazy. The mother/son relationship had always seemed overly close, at least as far as Nicole was concerned. But then what did she know? Her relationship with her own parents had always been strained at best.

Shaking her head, she went inside and locked the door behind her.

After Jacob's nap, Nicole bundled him up in his infant carrier and they went into town. Previously, when it was time to buy groceries, they went on Saturday since they only had the one car and Bill always insisted on accompanying her. She'd often wondered what he thought she would do there in the middle of the produce aisle. Flirt with other men over the cantaloupe?

This would be her first time since the marriage when she'd taken Jacob and gone shopping on her own.

She made a list out of habit. Bill had despised wasting time, so she'd learned to live by lists. Stores she needed to visit as well as items she wanted to purchase in each one. Then finally, the longer, more detailed grocery list. Bill had required she learn each aisle and mark those on the list as well.

Her first stop was the dry cleaners. Last week, she'd taken several of Bill's suits and dress shirts in. She'd need to pick them up, as well as let them know what had happened to her husband.

Clearly, she'd forgotten how fast news traveled in a small town. Carolyn Jenkins greeted her warmly, expressing sympathy for her loss and then exclaiming over how big little Jacob was getting. When Nicole handed her the ticket, Carolyn wasn't in a hurry to retrieve her items. Instead, she wanted to discuss the possibilities of who might have murdered Bill and why.

Of course Nicole explained she had no idea. When she reiterated that she was leaving the crime solving up to the sheriff's office, the frizzy-haired older woman looked over her glasses and sternly admonished Nicole to become more proactive. Then, while Nicole struggled with how to respond to that, Carolyn stepped into the back and returned with Bill's suits.

"Will one of these by his funeral suit?" Carolyn asked as she rung up the total.

Appalled, Nicole told her she wasn't sure yet. As soon as she paid, she grabbed her baby and the dry cleaning and fled.

At least the large grocery store would be more impersonal. But when Nicole spotted one of Theresa's friends waiting in line at the meat market, she turned and rushed off in the opposite direction. She had no idea how many people Theresa might have spewed her hate-filled accusations to, and she had no desire to find out.

Shopping, Nicole started out with checking each item off her list. This time, without Bill's disapproving gaze to deal with, she soon found herself adding extras, things she'd always loved to eat. Greek yogurt, cottage cheese and lots of fresh fruit. As for meat, she bought lean protein—chicken and fish. Bill had preferred red meat and potatoes. She bought neither of those things.

When she managed to pay the cashier, and wheel her groceries out to the car without encountering anyone, Nicole felt grateful. Some of the tension knots in her shoulders loosened the slightest bit.

She sang along to the radio as she drove home. By the time she reached the house, she felt a renewed sense of optimism. Theresa had said Bill hadn't made a will. While that might be true, she needed to educate herself in the Texas law to find out what exactly she as his widow would be entitled to. If the Mabrys truly took her to court, at least she'd have access to her and Bill's joint savings account. She'd start out by finding an attorney who could help her file probate.

After putting up all the food she buckled up Jacob again and drove to the bank. She asked to speak with an account manager. A tall dark woman with long ebony hair took Nicole back to her cubicle. "I'm Halia. What can I help you with today?"

Handing over her idea, Nicole explained her situation. "Do you have a copy of the death certificate?" Halia asked.

"Not yet. We haven't even had the funeral yet."

Halia raised one perfectly arched brow. "Okay."

"I just need to know how much money is in our savings and how much in our checking," Nicole said. "I don't have access to the online account. Here's my ID."

"Let me check." After entering all the information into her computer, Halia waited. As she peered at her screen, her eyes widened. She looked from her computer to Nicole and back again. Finally, she shook her head. "I have to be the bearer of bad news, but your husband emptied out this savings account three weeks ago and closed it. Do you think he moved it to another bank?"

Nicole's stomach dropped, though she managed to keep her composure. "Are you sure?" she asked, even though she knew Halia wouldn't have given her false information. "Maybe it's some kind of computer error?"

Expression grim, Halia typed something else. "No, not an error. He came in and did this in person. Closed this one and the checking. You might review his records at home, since it sure sounds like he might have changed banks."

"I will." Striving to sound reasonable, Nicole glanced down at her sleeping baby before meeting Halia's gaze. "If you don't mind me asking, how much money are we talking about here?" She hated to admit it, but she honestly had no idea how much had been in her and Bill's savings account, never mind checking. Bill had always simply doled out a weekly allowance to her in cash. She used it to buy groceries and diapers and whatever else she or Jacob needed.

Halia took a deep breath. "Let me print this out for you," she said. A moment later, her printer whirred. She plucked the sheet of paper from the tray and handed it to Nicole.

Reading it, Nicole gasped. Forty-five thousand dollars. "This can't be right," she muttered. When she looked up, she saw pity in the other woman's gaze.

"I'm sorry," Halia said. "Is there anything else I can do for you?"

"No. Thank you." After folding the account transaction summary, Nicole put it in her purse. She stood, collected Jacob and left the bank.

After buckling in her son, she drove home, making sure to carefully stay within the speed limit. The way things had been going, if she got stopped for speeding, instead of a simple ticket, they'd haul her off to jail.

Back at the house, little Jacob woke. He needed a diaper change, plus wanted to be fed. Glad to have this to keep her occupied, she took care of her baby. Once he'd been burped, he drifted off to sleep. As soon as she'd gotten him settled in his little bassinette, she began a thorough search of Bill's home office.

His desk had nothing out of the ordinary. Behind his desk, he had a three-drawer file cabinet that she assumed the deputies had rifled through. When she opened the top drawer, she saw row after row of alphabetically organized file folders. The labels in the top drawer were all pertaining to various years' income tax receipts.

She pulled out the one for the previous year and thumbed through it. Stock dividends and receipts. Like his credit card statement, there were several receipts from various jewelry stores and florists.

Idly, she wondered if this was all for the same mistress or if there had been a string of them.

The second drawer down was mostly empty. Except toward the back. There, inside plain manila envelopes, were CD's of various X-rated movies. Reading the titles out loud made her feel queasy. She shoved those back in place, battling the urge to go wash her hands.

She approached the third and final drawer with some trepidation. But when she went to open it, it wouldn't budge. Frowning, she studied it. It couldn't be locked, or none of the other drawers would have opened.

Just to be sure, she located the key inside the desk and turned the lock. Now none of the drawers would open.

Once she turned the lock again, she was back where she started. Two opened; the third would not.

No amount of rattling would make the thing budge. Clearly, something was jammed inside.

As she considered what to do next, her cell phone rang. Caller ID showed it was her mother. Great. Exactly what she needed to make a horrible day worse.

"Hi, Mom." Though she tried to put a little enthusiasm in her voice, she fell short. If her mother had known her better, she'd realize this, but since she rarely called or visited, she didn't notice.

"Hello, Nicole. I'm calling to discuss something with you."

No pleasantries, no asking how her recently widowed daughter might be doing, no questions about her grandson. Of course not. Nicole tried not to let her bitterness show when she spoke. "If you're calling to ask about the funeral, Theresa Mabry took care of all that."

"Oh." It was impossible to tell if her mother was surprised. "Actually, Theresa already gave me the information on the services. She notified the entire church, this past Sunday. Which you'd know, if you'd bothered to attend services."

Nicole didn't even attempt to explain her actions.

First off, there wasn't a single excuse as far as her mother was concerned for missing church, and secondly, Nicole was a grown woman and mother. She didn't have to justify her actions.

"Then why are you calling, Mother?" she asked.

"Theresa and Dan Mabry paid me a visit yesterday," Fran said. The Shelton family didn't beat around the bush. Fran in particular considered this a family motto. "They wanted me to approach you with something."

Bile rose in Nicole's throat. "And?" she prodded. Maybe this wasn't what she suspected it might be. Surely her own mother couldn't ask such a thing of her daughter.

"Now that Bill's gone." Fran paused. "You have to think about your child. Theresa and Dan want to adopt him and raise him. I'd like you to at least consider it. The boy would never want for anything."

Nicole nearly hung up the phone. Instead, she forced herself to take several deep breaths before responding. "The boy, as you put it, is my son. Your grandson. I'm perfectly capable of taking care of my own child. I can't believe you'd say such a thing." But she could. Sadly, she could.

"Theresa told me you'd be unreasonable. Nicole, the Mabrys are respected members of our church and community. You need to rise above your selfishness and do what's best for Jacob."

Selfishness. In any other world, selfishness would mean abandoning a baby rather than nurturing him. Not in her mother's.

"Mother, you know full well that Jacob isn't Bill's son. Why didn't you tell Theresa Mabry that? I'm sure once she learns the truth, she'll give up this ridiculous idea."

Fran gasped. "I'd never tell her that. Think about the gossip! We'd all become the objects of gossip and ridicule."

"If you won't, I will." Nicole hardened her voice. "Because the best thing for Jacob is staying with the mother who loves him."

"You don't have the resources," Fran pushed right back. "The Mabrys do."

"I'll manage," Nicole responded dryly. "At least I know I have you and Daddy to count on for support."

Her mocking statement was met with absolute silence. If Nicole hadn't been so used to her mother's rejection, she would have cried.

"If you turn down the Mabrys' kind offer, don't come running to us for help when you run out of money. In fact, don't bother coming to us at all. Am I clear?"

"As clear as mud." And then, because it childishly made her feel better, Nicole ended the call first.

After all this time, her mother's words should have lost the power to wound her. But in the end, Fran was still her mother—the only one she had. For one reason or another, Nicole had been made to feel she'd never been good enough to be loved. Deep down inside, she supposed she'd never lost that hope that someday, her mother would.

But the night Nicole had gone into labor, Theresa and Dan Mabry had joined Nicole and Bill at the hospital. Bill had called Nicole's parents, who'd claimed to be busy or ill or something, so they hadn't come.

Nicole had delivered her child without her own mother's presence.

She'd refused to let that hurt overshadow the joy of giving birth to a healthy baby boy. She hadn't realized that slight would but be the beginning of many.

In all of three months of life, Jacob had met his maternal grandparents exactly once. Neither Nicole's mom or dad had wanted to hold the baby. Instead of being enthralled by him as Nicole was, they mostly tried to pretend he didn't even exist.

Jacob cried and she went to get him. She'd work on the stuck file cabinet drawer later.

After waking up in the hospital with burns over seventy percent of his body, Kyle had believed he would never feel pain like that again. Skin grafts and treatments had proved him wrong, and then had come physical therapy.

The nightmares were bad too, especially the ones that brought chills and night sweats. Panic attacks, where his heart would race and he couldn't breathe. They'd noticed this there in Walter Reed and a compassionate nurse had given him a flyer addressing PTSD. She'd suggested therapy once he got out. He'd promised to look into it and had tucked the flyer away, promptly forgetting about it. He figured once some time had passed since the explosion, he'd be fine.

Only he wasn't. If anything, he'd gotten worse. Jumpy, nervous, even driving had become a trial by fire and ice. Teeth clenched, he found himself gripping the wheel and hoping he wouldn't overreact.

A car backfiring, fireworks, any loud, sudden sound or movement had him cringing, jumping, even hitting the floor. He despised the person he'd become, a coward too afraid of his own shadow.

And he'd pinned all his hope for redemption on stepping into the life he had planned with Nicole.

Only that, too, had turned out to be impossible. When he found himself obsessively cleaning his pistol and wondering if he ought to end it, he considered the possibility that he needed help. Except he couldn't make himself ask for it. He was an army ranger, after all. Sua Sponte. Of Their Own Accord.

He could deal with this. He would deal with this. It would, he reasoned, take time. And time was the one thing he had a lot of.

Driving around downtown Anniversary, he impulsively decided to visit the Army Recruiting Office. The same place where he'd originally signed up, shortly after graduating high school. How much had changed since then.

The recruiter behind the metal desk looked up when Kyle entered. As soon as Kyle introduced himself, the other man broke into a wide grin.

"Kyle Benning," he exclaimed. "Let me shake your hand. It's not every day one of my recruits becomes a ranger."

They shook. "Thank you, John." He got the name from the name tag the recruiter wore. "Though my time was cut short, I was glad to serve. I'm also glad to be home."

"Understandable. I heard what happened to you." John shook his head. "Still, it's better than what we were originally told. The whole town went into mourning when we were told you were dead."

Not sure of how to respond to that, Kyle simply

nodded. He looked around. The office seemed a lot smaller and dingier than he remembered. "How's business?"

"About what you'd expect in a small town." John shrugged. "Guys graduate high school, look around at the limited prospects if they can't afford to go to college and enlist. They want to see the world, serve their country and learn a marketable skill. Sometimes it's right after graduation, sometimes it takes a few months. But I'm busy enough."

They exchanged a few more pleasantries. Finally, Kyle turned to go. "If you're ever hiring, even part-time," he said. "Give me a call. I'd definitely be interested."

John's bushy brows rose. "I'll keep that in mind. I've been wanting to take my wife on vacation, but haven't had anyone who could fill in."

"Just say the word." Grabbing a sticky note off an empty desk, Kyle jotted down his number and handed it to John. "Take care."

Once back in his vehicle, Kyle felt pleased. He hadn't intended on immediately looking for work, but something like this—even part-time—would be perfect. He had quite a bit of money saved from his salary, plus he received a decent military disability compensation monthly. He had more than enough to live on. Working as a recruiter would perfectly fit his skill set, as well as be a way to occupy his time.

Since returning home, nothing had gone as planned. Again, he thought of Nicole, and of the baby boy who most likely was his son. His family, the first real blood relative he'd ever had. He'd been in foster care since he'd been a toddler. Child Protective Services had removed him from his drug-addicted parents' home and he'd been told both parents had overdosed and died while he'd been a small child. The only thing they'd given him had been his name.

Since no other relatives—grandparents or aunts or uncles—ever stepped forward to take over his care, he'd never seen the point in doing any kind of research to see if he had any living kin. He probably never would.

No matter what, he planned to have a relationship with his son. With Jacob. And to do that, he'd need to figure out a way to get along with Nicole. He'd need to let go of the bitterness and the hurt. Someday, he hoped he'd be able to do just that. Right now, he felt as if he had an open wound right there on his chest above his heart, still bleeding.

Later that afternoon, Bret called and invited him over for dinner. "Heather can't wait to see you," he said. "She was very excited when I mentioned running into you at the grocery store. We'd love for you to come eat tomorrow night."

"Sounds good," Kyle replied. "What should I bring?"

"Just yourself."

After the call ended, Kyle went out to his small backyard. He felt surprisingly ambivalent about going to his old friend's for dinner and he wasn't sure why. Maybe because Bret had accomplished exactly what Kyle had planned—he'd married his high school sweetheart and begun a life together with her.

Again, the bitterness, this time tempered with envy. Such thoughts and emotions were unfitting an army ranger, so Kyle did his best to shake them off. He went to bed early, hoping to at least catch a couple of hours of decent sleep instead of tossing and turning all night.

Unfortunately, the instant he finally managed to doze off, he woke up shaking and drenched in sweat. He got up and paced, finally jumping in the shower to rinse his body off. He changed the sheets, but didn't lie back down. Instead, he sat in the ancient recliner that had come with the house, turned on the television and hoped for the best.

When he woke again, his neck stiff and his arm numb, he pushed to his feet and stretched.

That afternoon, he made a run into town and picked up a bottle of wine just in case. Here in Anniversary, one never showed up for dinner at a friend's house empty handed. Even a kid from a foster home knew that.

He arrived at the address Bret had given him exactly on time. As he went up the sidewalk, he reflected on the nicely trimmed hedges, the bright flowers and the lush green lawn. Before he could ring the bell, Heather threw open the door and wrapped him in a perfume-scented hug, her belly huge, her complexion glowing. "You look amazing," he said. "Pregnancy certainly agrees with you."

"Thank you! We're so glad to see you," she said, smiling. "Come in. Come in. Make yourself at home. Can I get you a beer?"

"Sure," he agreed. He followed her through the living room, into the kitchen and then outside to the back patio.

Where he stopped. Nicole sat in one of the lawn chairs, laughing at something Bret had said. Baby Jacob sat in an infant carrier at her feet, brightly colored plastic toys strung in front of him. Kyle couldn't help but stare, struck dumb by her beauty. When she looked up and saw Kyle, all the color leached from her face. Her huge hazel eyes widened and her lips parted, though no sound came out.

He couldn't move, couldn't breathe, couldn't think.

Though he'd made a resolution to reach some sort of compromise with Nicole, he hadn't expected to see her this soon.

Chapter 6

Nicole's stomach lurched when she saw Kyle walk into the backyard. He wore a baseball cap over his short dark hair. From the stunned look on his handsome face, he hadn't expected to see her here either.

Neither spoke.

Bret looked from one to the other, his brow wrinkled, clearly puzzled. "You two don't seem particularly happy to see each other. I thought you were friends."

"Friends?" Nicole repeated weakly. "Um, I'm not sure…"

"Of course they're friends," Heather insisted, the cheerfulness in her voice not the tiniest bit forced. Her broad smile never wavered, not even when she took Kyle's arm and led him to the empty chair next to Nicole.

As their gazes locked, Nicole wondered if he'd bolt and run and how she should react if he did. Instead he lowered himself into the chair after greeting Bret. A moment later, he accepted the beer Heather brought him before she headed back inside the kitchen. Earlier, Nicole had refused Heather's offer of wine since she was still breastfeeding Jacob. Heather had given her a cucumber-flavored water instead.

Despite the way her heartbeat had gone wonky, Nicole felt strangely removed from the entire situation, as if she were watching from somewhere else and not actually involved. A coping mechanism, she felt quite sure. No way did she have it in her to initiate some kind of chitchat. Instead, she eyed the play of sunlight on Kyle's muscular arm, her mouth dry as she battled an intense need to reach out and touch him. Even a sip of her water didn't help.

"Hi," he finally said, greeting her. His smile, though a bit strained, seemed genuine enough. The brim of the hat put shadows over his face, hiding his startling emerald eyes. "Funny meeting you here."

Bret laughed at that, the sound too loud and clearly forced. Nicole didn't respond. Bret looked from Kyle to Nicole. He shrugged. "I think I'll go see if there's anything Heather needs," he said, and fled.

It took every ounce of self-restraint Nicole possessed not to ask him to stay. Leaving her alone with Kyle was a recipe for disaster, at least judging by what had happened in the ER. She debated getting up and following her host inside, but she knew if she did that, it would generate questions she didn't want to have to answer.

"Talk about uncomfortable," she mused out loud, once Bret had gone, keeping her voice low.

Kyle sighed. When he removed his hat and looked at her, his eyes were full of regret. "I'm sorry for what happened at the hospital," he said, low voiced. "I was completely out of line. If it's okay with you, I think we should start over. I'd like for us to be friends, especially since I'm going to want to be involved in Jacob's life."

Friends. Inwardly, she winced. Never in her life would she have imagined she and Kyle could have any sort of platonic relationship. Heat sparked like lightning whenever they were around each other. Even now, her entire body felt electrified, her blood humming. He wanted to be friends.

While that was infinitely better than enemies, she knew how difficult a simple, uncluttered friendship would be for her. She loved him. She always had, even when she'd believed he'd died. She'd never once doubted his would be the first face she'd see once her own life had ended, and that they'd be together in eternity until the end of time.

Inside she understood that she'd spend the rest of her life loving him. Even though right now, he didn't feel the same way.

Jacob fussed a little, drawing both their attention. He settled back down, concentrating on his pacifier as well as the brightly colored plastic toys on the bar in front of him. Already he resembled his father, from the dimple in his chin to the greenish tint of his eyes. She just knew once Jacob's eyes finally became their permanent color, they'd be the same emerald green as Kyle's.

"Nicole?" Kyle leaned closer, his breath tickling her ear. This sent a jolt of longing straight to her core. "What do you think? Can we be friends?"

Truly, she didn't know. But for her son's sake, she knew she had to try. They had to keep things amicable between them for Jacob. Her son would grow up with the love of two devoted parents, even if they lived separate lives. And who knew? Maybe once Kyle got to know her again, he'd realize she hadn't truly betrayed his trust.

"I'd like that," she answered softly, steeling herself not to visibly quiver when he smiled at her.

"Good." Kyle held out his hand, as if they were sealing the bargain with a handshake. "Friends."

"Friends," she repeated. The instant her fingers connected with his, she wondered how it was that he didn't know she'd lied. Couldn't he feel what she felt when they touched? He'd always be more than a friend to her. She supposed she'd better get used to hiding her feelings where Kyle was concerned.

Heather and Bret finally appeared, both gamely trying to pretend nothing was amiss. Bret carried a platter of thick steaks. He'd put on an apron with the words "Will grill for sex" emblazoned across the front.

"We're about ready to start grilling," Heather said with a casual smile. "Are you all hungry?"

"Let me help." Kyle jumped up. "Though it's been a long time since I've grilled anything."

"I'm a pro." Bret grinned. "Hang with me and I'll show you how it's done."

The two men moved off, backslapping and cutting up.

Watching them go, Nicole struggled to conceal her

longing. When she realized Heather had noticed, she shook her head. "I still have to pinch myself," she admitted. "I'm so happy he's alive."

"I can imagine." Heather didn't probe or push Nicole to admit anything. "I've got to go make sure everything else is ready." She winked. "But what I need the most is to sit down. My ankles are really swelling in this heat."

"Let me help you." Getting to her feet, Nicole picked up Jacob's carrier and followed the other woman into the house. Heather waddled, which made Nicole smile, since not too long ago she'd done the same.

"There's really nothing to do," Heather said, laughing slightly. "I made potato salad and some baked beans. The beans are in the crockpot." She eased herself into a chair, one hand protectively on her large stomach. "I can't wait to have this baby."

"I remember feeling like that." Nicole picked up her son, crooning softly to him. Jacob responded with a chortle, his hands waving furiously.

"He's absolutely adorable," Heather said. "May I hold him?"

"Of course."

Heather made a huge fuss over the baby, talking baby talk and making sounds, finally eliciting a prized smile from him. Right after that, he burped.

"I saw you two at the ER," Heather said. "I was having some Braxton Hicks contractions. I'm so sorry I didn't get a chance to check on you. What was the problem?"

Nicole explained. "So I've got to keep bees and wasps away from him," she concluded. "I've already purchased an EpiPen Jr, just in case, even though he's too young for it right now."

The two women chatted, Heather still holding Jacob, until the two men reappeared bearing the platter of cooked steaks, which smelled delicious.

As the foursome sat around the kitchen table, sharing the meal, Nicole found herself relaxing. No one here acted as if they needed to handle her with kid gloves since she was newly widowed. In fact, after a brief expression of sympathy for her loss, neither Heather or Bret mentioned Bill at all. Instead, it felt almost as if they'd picked up right where they'd been back in high school.

When Nicole was ready to leave, Kyle actually walked her to her car. He waited quietly, watching as she buckled Jacob into his infant carrier in the backseat. Once that was done, he eyed her.

Terrified he might actually try for an impersonal hug, Nicole sidestepped him, sliding into the driver's seat and buckling in. "Take care," she told him, summoning up what she hoped was a brilliant smile.

"You too." He smiled back, though his gaze remained watchful and serious. "We'll talk again soon."

Then, before she could stop him, he leaned in and kissed her cheek.

As she drove home, she kept reaching up and touching her cheek, feeling like a besotted schoolgirl. She couldn't help but imagine what might have happened if she'd turned her head just slightly, so that his lips had brushed hers instead.

After getting Jacob settled in for the night, Nicole went downstairs to get a glass of water. Once she had, she checked the locks and turned out the lights, before heading back upstairs.

Halfway up the stairs, the crash of glass breaking made her freeze. She'd left her cell phone on the nightstand next to the bed. And she didn't have a gun or even know how to use one. Her best option would be to barricade herself in the baby's room and call 911.

She sprinted up the remaining stairs, into her bedroom, where she snatched up her phone. The nursery—and Jacob—was the next room, so she ran in there, quietly closing the door. Though she knew turning the knob lock wouldn't deter anyone who was really determined, it was a start. Next, she pushed the rocking chair and the changing table up against the door. Then she called 911, letting them know she had an intruder inside her house. The dispatcher insisted she stay on the line, but Nicole felt strongly the less noise, the better, so she ended the call.

Heart pounding, she stationed herself between the crib and the door, looking around frantically for something she could use as a weapon. Just in case.

But aside from a package of diapers, some towels and assorted baby lotion and powder, she saw nothing. So all she could do was huddle in the dark with her heart pounding, hoping the police would arrive soon.

Time seemed to crawl. She couldn't hear anything else besides Jacob's even breathing as he blissfully slumbered. If the intruder was still in the house, he was being very quiet. She shuddered to think of what might have happened if the break-in had occurred after she'd gone to bed. Most likely she wouldn't have heard the glass shattering and would have had no idea she was no longer alone in her home.

As soon as all this was over, she planned to call an alarm company and have an alarm installed. For now, she just had to stay alive until law enforcement got there.

A moment later, she heard sirens. Really? Why would the police announce their presence like that? She would have thought they'd try to arrive by stealth, which would make it easier to catch any intruder. Either way, she was glad they were here.

A moment later she heard shouting from downstairs. "Police. We're coming in."

She waited with bated breath, her entire body shaking, praying the next sound she heard wasn't gunshots.

Instead, only an awful, ominous silence. What did that mean? Had they caught the intruder or had he gotten away?

"Ma'am? It's Deputy Frankel," a man said, his voice loud and concise. "We've checked your entire downstairs and it's clear. Please let us know immediately where you are."

"I'm in the nursery upstairs with the door closed."

"Please open that door slowly and keep your hands where we can see them until we're able to verify your identity."

Which made perfect sense. Still, her heart rate kicked up yet another notch as she fumbled for the doorknob. She opened the door slowly, raising her hands above her head. "Here," she said clearly, still hoping she wouldn't wake Jacob.

Spotting her, the uniformed officer moved forward. A second one appeared at the top of the stairs. "I'm going to check the rest of this floor," he said. "Deputy Frankel will stay with you until I say clear."

She nodded. Hopefully, the intruder had gone.

Once the floor had been cleared, the two deputies wanted her to take a look around downstairs and see if anything was missing.

"Nothing appears out of order," Frankel said. "Except for in one room."

He was right. The living room, dining room and kitchen looked exactly as she'd left them. She headed toward the office. When she reached the doorway, she stopped and gasped.

"Yep," Frankel told her. "This is the room I was talking about."

Papers were strewn everywhere. The intruder had apparently gone through the file cabinet, tossing folders and their contents around the room. He'd also ransacked the desk, leaving drawers open.

"It looks like a tornado came through this room," the deputy said.

He was right. She walked over to the desk, took a look then went back to the file cabinet.

And then she realized something. The third file cabinet drawer, the one she hadn't been able to get unlocked, sat open. Whatever had been inside it was gone.

After leaving Bret and Heather's, Kyle had driven around for a few minutes instead of going straight home. Seeing Nicole had him craving her again, something he hadn't yet managed to get under control. He wondered if he ever would.

Yet he'd agreed that they'd figure out a way to be friends. Which meant he'd just volunteered to submit himself to a form of torture.

That night, when he fell asleep, once again he re-lived the worst day of his life.

They traveled in a small convoy, taking turns at who took the most exposed position as gunny. This time, Hank Smith was on the gun and inside the truck the other three of them were making jokes, laughing and trying to act casual. They always did this when heading into danger. Each and every one of them knew they could lose a limb or worse, their life. Dying sat like a heavy dark shadow on each man's shoulders.

Kyle had that dull headache that always accom-panied a hangover. He and the other guys had sat around playing poker and drinking moonshine the night before, long past the time they should have hit the sack. It was a way of blowing off steam when they knew they'd be departing on a dangerous mission the next morning.

Of course, all the missions were dangerous. They expected this. They were army rangers, after all. Highly trained, they went places no one else could go, and did things no one else could do.

So far, they'd been lucky. Or, as they preferred to call it, damned good. They hadn't lost a single man. There'd been a few injuries here and there. A gunshot wound that had led to a major infection before they got back to base camp had been the most serious. Though no one wanted to be superstitious or jinx things by speaking the words out loud, they all hoped their luck would continue to hold. The one thing everyone knew as a stone-cold fact—it would be far better to be hit by an IED than to have to watch your buddies get hit.

They were a tight-knit bunch. Any of them would

willingly die for each other. None of them wanted to be the one left behind.

A flash. Left side. After that, everything seemed to happen in slow motion. Their luck had just run out.

The blast must have knocked him unconscious. When he came to, he wasn't sure what had happened. The acrid scent of burned metal and rubber filled his nose. He tried to stand. His ears were ringing and his legs had turned to rubber. Worse, his vision had gone wonky. Black to gray, in and out.

"Hank?" Voice hoarse, he called out. "Tanner?"

No one answered.

His vision came back enough for him to realize he was on fire. Burning. Stop, drop and roll. He remembered that much. But when he dropped, it hurt so damn bad he blacked out again.

Two men speaking. Foreign tongue. Pashto or Dari, he thought. He knew enough of both dialects that he tried to make out the words. But the pain hit in waves, along with nausea as he realized his own flesh still burned.

He rolled and rolled and rolled, screaming silently, until he'd managed to extinguish the flames. He hoped. But then he'd used up all his energy. Spent, he lay facedown in the dirt, wondering if he pretended to be dead, he'd be spared.

Had his entire unit been wiped out? Maybe they'd gone on, gotten through somehow.

He blacked out again, which brought instant relief from the intense pain. The tugging on the chain he wore around his neck brought him back. His dog tags. Someone was trying to remove his dog tags.

Every soldier knew better. If they were gone, his

body would lose all identity. No one would know to notify his family, his loved ones. Nicole. Oh Christ, Nicole.

Eyes slits, he saw the other man's face. Dark skin, torn and dirty uniform. Rebel, most likely, though several had defected from the local army, joining the opposition.

It didn't matter who this guy was. What mattered was the way he tried to steal Kyle's identity.

"No," he muttered, trying to bat the hand away. "Mine."

The man laughed and then hauled off and hit him. Burned, dying, Kyle lost consciousness again.

The next time he woke, he was alone. Without his dog tags.

A guttural groan came from the left of him. Using every bit of what remaining energy he could summon, Kyle pushed to his knees and crawled in the direction. There, he found Hank, a large piece of metal lodged in his midsection.

Clearly in pain, clearly dying. Hank looked at Kyle with eyes dulled by the mist of death. "My dog tags," Smith managed to croak.

"They took mine too," Kyle said, frantically trying to figure out a way, some way, he could help his buddy.

Hank made a gurgling sound, blood seeping out the corner of his cracked and battered lips. "Here," he managed, opening his closed fist. Inside, he held one dog tag, the bottom one that was meant to be ripped off and sent back so the family could be notified. Just as Kyle reached for the tag, Hank died, his eyes wide open.

It took three attempts for Kyle to manage to close his friend's eyes. Then, taking the dog tag, Kyle crawled away on his belly, every movement excruciating. Despite the agony of his pain, despite going in and out of consciousness, he had to find out what had happened to the others. Even if he was slowly dying, he couldn't rest until he knew.

Two more dead, one headless. Both men's dog tags were gone. Kyle wasn't sure why the enemy had taken them, but he hoped he could stay alive long enough to let rescue know, when it came, who they were. It was the least he could do for the brothers who'd fought alongside him. No one wanted to be the one left behind. Kyle had been that unlucky son of a bitch.

His cell phone rang, pulling him from his nightmare. Disoriented, confused, he looked at the screen. Nicole. She'd never call this late unless it was an emergency.

"I'm sorry to bother you," she said, agitation making her voice shake. "But my house was broken into. The police just left."

"Broken into? Before you got home?"

"No." She took a deep breath. "I'd been home a little bit. I'd already put Jacob to bed. I went to get a glass of water and on the way back upstairs, I heard them break in. I called 911."

Damn. He had to force himself to loosen his grip on his phone, afraid he might break it. "I'm on my way over."

She started to protest, but he ended the call, cutting her off. No matter what had happened in the year they'd been apart, he still knew Nicole well enough to understand how terrified she had to be. Otherwise, she never would have called him.

He made it to her house in record time. As he pulled up in front, she flung the door open and waited there for him. Silhouetted in the foyer light, she wore shorts and a tank top.

As he hurried up the sidewalk, he noticed she also wore no bra. Instantly, his body sprang to attention.

"Are you all right?" he asked, training his gaze on her earlobe so he didn't look lower. "And Jacob?"

"We're fine. Sort of," she amended. "I feel so violated. A total stranger broke into my house."

As he stepped inside, she closed and locked the front door after him. "I have no idea what they were looking for," she continued. "The police said it was unusual too. As if they'd come for something specific. They went directly to Bill's office. The only thing I could find out of place was a file cabinet drawer. It was locked, but now it's not. And it's empty. I have no idea what was in it before."

"That is strange," he agreed. Nicole seemed fragile and nervous, hovering on the verge of tears. He hoped like hell she wouldn't cry, because he'd no way, no how, be able to resist comforting her then. "How'd they get in?"

"The back door glass is shattered," she said, her voice wavering. She blinked furiously, still struggling not to cry. "I can't get a glass company out here until tomorrow and I don't feel safe knowing anyone can get inside my house."

Fighting the urge to take her into his arms and comfort her, he nodded. "Let me take a look at it."

She led him into the kitchen and pointed. "That's the door that leads out to my patio."

The door had once had a window that ran the full length of it. Now there was nothing but a few shards of broken glass remaining in the frame.

"I swept up everything," she continued. "And then vacuumed just in case. I know I need to take out those last few pieces too."

But she hadn't. He suspected she'd been afraid of cutting herself.

"Do you have any plywood?" he asked.

She thought for a moment. "Bill had a workshop out back. There might be some lumber in there. Let me get a flashlight and the key and we can go take a look."

While she went to retrieve the flashlight, he couldn't help but imagine the sheer terror she must have felt, trapped in her home with an intruder and an infant to protect. He shuddered to think what might have happened.

No doubt reflecting on that would keep Nicole awake at night.

"Here we go." She reappeared, her expression hesitant. "I hope you don't mind if I send you out there by yourself. I'm not comfortable leaving Jacob alone right now, even though he's asleep."

"I don't blame you." Accepting the key and the flashlight, he followed her out onto the back patio. The porch light illuminated a good portion of the large backyard, just enough to let him make out a shed in the back right corner.

"Is there electricity in the shed?" he asked.

"Yes. And it has an outside light by the door, only

we don't keep it on." She winced, apparently realizing she'd used the plural pronoun.

Again, he battled the urge to touch her, to let her know everything was going to be okay. Except in reality, he wasn't sure it would be.

He headed out into the backyard. When he reached the shed, he used the flashlight to illuminate the keyhole and unlocked the door.

Stepping inside, he located the light switch and flicked on the lights. Instead of a true storage shed, the well-organized interior looked more like a workshop. Tools hung neatly in pegboard above the large metal workbench, with larger tools like a circular saw on their own stands. In one area, several sheets of plywood along with two-by-fours and four-by-fours were also neatly arranged. Whatever else Bill Mabry had been, he'd clearly been meticulous. The army veteran in Kyle appreciated that.

He took a piece of plywood that looked like it would work and leaned it on the wall near the door. Then he located a hammer and a box of nails, but before he grabbed those, he spied an electric nail gun.

Perfect.

Back at the house, he found Nicole waiting anxiously for him to return. "We'll get you fixed up in no time," he told her, careful not to let his gaze linger too long. That way lay only trouble.

He made short work of getting the plywood nailed over the door. "There you go," he said, placing the nail gun on the counter. "I've already locked the shed up, so if you don't mind, I'll leave this here for you to put away." Impersonal and professional, as if he were a repairman who'd been sent there to do a job.

"Okay." The distraught look she sent him made him feel another pang. Guilt or need or both, all wrapped up in longing. He actually took a step toward her this time, before gathering up his nearly shredded will-power.

"You should be all right tonight," he continued.

"Right." She nodded, the panicked look in her eyes revealing she would be anything but all right.

He wasn't sure who moved first, but he put his arms around her and held on. Meaning only to hug and offer comfort, though his body definitely had other ideas.

Everything shifted—the earth, the atmosphere and definitely him. She still smelled the same, like vanilla and peaches, and her body fit up against his as if they'd been made for each other.

This he thought dimly, trying to think past the roaring in his ears. His blood hummed and his heart pounded. Though he knew distantly that he needed to move, he could no more break away from her than he could stop breathing.

Chapter 7

The instant his lips touched hers, he went up in flames. Judging from the sultry moan she made, she did too. All the danger, danger, take evasive action warnings he'd expected to experience went abruptly silent.

Which really didn't matter. He was so lost in her that he'd never have heard them anyway.

The taste of her, familiar and beloved, intoxicated him faster than any drug. Straight to his groin, to his chest and his heart. Nicole, Nicole, Nicole.

After her initial shocked stiffening, she responded with a fervor that matched his own. They kissed each other as though they'd been starving, a sensory overload of curves pressed against muscle, silken skin and rough hands, and clothes that were in the way.

"Wait." Nicole's voice, husky with passion, but firm. "Kyle, stop."

Of course he instantly did just that, taking a few steps back to put some distance between them. Breathing hard, he eyed her, trying to collect his thoughts and regain control over his own body. He took small consolation seeing her breathing was as ragged as his.

"This solves nothing," she said. "We've got too much unresolved stuff between us."

"Unresolved stuff." He tried for a short laugh, a rough bark of sound. "That's one way of putting it."

She tilted her head, her expression serious. "No matter what, I'm glad you're alive. The world is a much better place with you in it."

Her words inexplicably made his throat tight. She'd always had the ability to slay him with a particular turn of phrase. Now though, he knew better. In his reality, actions spoke ten times louder than words.

He stared at her, unable to respond. If he tried, the roughness in his voice would let her know how much her words affected him. He saw no reason to let her have yet another unfair advantage.

"Aren't you going to say anything?" she asked. The teasing note in her voice didn't match the earnest look in her eyes.

Talk. Everyone wanted him to talk. About what had happened. About how he was dealing with it. About his PTSD. He didn't want to talk. He had no patience for words, since lies were too easily hidden.

Black and white. Since he'd been injured, he'd come to understand how much easier life was without shades of gray.

The hopeful look on Nicole's face fell. "Never mind," she said, and turned away. "Thanks for all your help. I really appreciate it. I'll let you show your-self out."

Her tone had gone formal. Distant. Though he didn't really blame her, it still managed to hurt. Damn.

Yet he couldn't make himself leave her. Not yet.

He knew better than to go after her. If he touched her again, he knew he'd lose his fragile grip on self-control.

"Are you going to be all right?" he asked her back, feeling as if the question had been torn from him.

"I'm fine," she said, without turning around, a per-fect example of how words could mask the truth. The tightness in her shoulders screamed the truth. She wasn't fine. Far from it.

Every instinct inside him—man, protector, ranger—urged him to comfort her. While every ounce of self-preservation he relied on for survival told him to simply walk away.

In the end, he turned and headed for the door, hat-ing the way leaving felt more like beating a retreat.

Nicole shouldn't have been surprised when Kyle left. But when he'd yanked her up against him and kissed her as if he never wanted to let her go again, her heart had felt as if it would explode from joy. She'd let herself hope against hope that the Kyle she'd known and loved had finally come back to her.

Of course, he hadn't. What Kyle had been through had irrevocably changed him. She doubted the old Kyle would ever be back again. The knowledge made her want to weep.

Even worse, Bill's viewing was the next morning. His family had planned it so everything—viewing, funeral and burial—would take place in one, long day. Nicole wasn't sure why. Though she'd had no say in the arrangements, she'd be expected to go to the funeral home and stand in line near the casket along with the rest of the family. His friends, relatives and acquaintances would file by, say their goodbyes and then offer their condolences to the family.

For three long hours. Nicole knew to wear comfortable shoes since she'd be standing the entire time. She had no idea what she'd say to Dan and Theresa Mabry, assuming she even spoke to them at all. Since Bill had made her sever all her friendships, she had no girlfriends to lean on for support, or to offer to watch baby Jacob while Nicole did her duty as a new widow.

After the viewing, everyone would head to the church for the actual funeral service. From there, they'd go to the cemetery, concluding with a small, graveside service limited to immediate family and any close friends. Nicole couldn't help but wonder if Bill's mistress would attend. She couldn't help but be curious about what kind of woman would have wanted to be with a man like Bill so badly they'd be willing to sneak around with him behind his wife's back.

At least once this day was finally over, Nicole could move forward with her life.

The next morning, Nicole woke up with a renewed sense of purpose. Instead of hanging over her like a dark cloud, she knew the ceremonial aspect of this would give her a sense of closure. She dreaded being forced to pretend to be comfortable around the Mabry family, but she'd do whatever she had to and put this day behind her.

Apropos of the solemnity of the day, by the time she'd finished breakfast, clouds had darkened the sky to slate. The wind had picked up, and her phone chimed to alert her to a severe thunderstorm warning posted for her area. Perfect. Bill himself would have approved. He'd always loved causing drama.

She dressed carefully, choosing a modest black dress in a severe cut, low-heeled pumps and large dark sunglasses. Hair styled, makeup carefully applied, once she was ready, she dressed Jacob in an infant onesie that resembled a suit. Though normally a quiet, happy baby, for whatever reason he took exception to the outfit and began fussing. All she could hope was that he'd settle down by the time they got to the funeral home. Once again, she wished she had a friend who could help her watch him. Since she didn't, she just had to hope she could keep him occupied and quiet. Either way, it would be a long day.

After filling her diaper bag with necessary supplies, including a change of clothes for Jacob, formula and of course more diapers, she drove herself to the funeral home. As requested, she arrived half an hour before the time the guests had been asked to arrive. A helpful attendant directed her to the room. When she walked in, only Dan and Theresa Mabry were inside. They stood gazing down at the casket, backs to her.

Nicole hesitated. She considered backing away, returning when there were a few more people to act as a buffer between her and the in-laws. But no matter what they thought, she'd been Bill's wife. They had no idea how much she'd suffered during her marriage to their son. No one did. And now that Bill was gone, no one would ever know.

Steeling herself, she approached the casket, forcing herself to look at her former husband. He appeared to be sleeping peacefully. Beside her, she heard Theresa Mabry's audible sigh, but ignored it.

Dan Mabry lightly touched Nicole's shoulder. "For today, let's put our differences aside."

Again Theresa made a sound. It could have been a strangled sort of agreement, though Nicole doubted that. More likely, the other woman had started to protest, but had been cut off by an elbow jab in the side from her husband.

Nicole managed a nod and started to turn away. Before she could, Dan grabbed her arm and pulled her close. "Do you know if Bill had any sort of will?" he asked.

Shocked, at first she couldn't find any words. Finally, she simply shook him off and moved away. Though she'd made a thorough search of Bill's office, she hadn't located anything that would indicate he'd bothered to have a will prepared. He actually had given no thought to the possibility of dying young. From the way he'd carried on, he believed himself to be invincible.

As she considered the reason for such a question, she realized Dan hoped to find something that would legally enable him and his wife to take from her everything she might have gained through her marriage to their son.

Somehow, Nicole made it through the next three hours. Even inside, she kept her huge, dark sunglasses in place. That way, no one could remark on the fact that she hadn't shed a single tear.

After the last person had trickled through, attendants removed the casket and everyone headed to their cars to drive to the church. Apparently, Dan and Theresa had opted not to use the limo provided by the

funeral home. Nicole had wondered about that, especially after the service at church. She'd been curious
to see if Dan and Theresa would be callous enough to
attempt to ride to the cemetery in a limo without her.
Of course, that would cause talk and she didn't think
they'd want that. She really hoped they'd just take their
own vehicles, as the thought of being trapped in such a
small space with two people who not only apparently
despised her but wanted custody of her son made her
feel like vomiting. The visitation had been bad enough.

Though the last hour of the wake had been quiet,
the church parking lot had already begun to fill up.
She found a parking spot and once she'd turned off
the engine, took a deep breath and got Jacob's infant
carrier out of the car. She'd fed and changed him in
the funeral home restroom before heading here, so he
dozed off and on, content.

Dread coiling low in her belly, she walked slowly
toward the door.

Though she hadn't been back to the church since
Bill died, everyone greeted her warmly, expressing
sympathy at her loss even though most of them had
been at the visitation. But many had not. She was
hugged, Jacob exclaimed over, at least six times before she made it to the sanctuary. This was her parents'
church as well, and the moment they saw her walk in,
they made a show out of hugging her and expressing
sympathy, just as they had during their very brief appearance at the visitation earlier. Full of regret, she
wondered what it might be like to have a normal family, one who didn't feel the need to constantly pretend
for appearances' sake. Too bad they couldn't do this
and mean it. With them, everything was all for show.

They even did the obligatory fussing over baby Jacob, though neither made the slightest effort to take him from his carrier and hold him. In the three months since his birth, her parents had made it clear that they wanted little to do with her son. They considered him a direct and physical result of her sin. Illegitimate children had no place in their perfect, righteous world.

Despite knowing how they were, she couldn't help but hope it would be different this time. Of course, it never was. She'd thought she'd let the bitterness go, but she felt it pressing like a heavy weight on her chest. As she looked for her in-laws, she spied them already seated in the front row. Theresa wore all back, including a veil that hid her face. Dan sat staring ahead with a stoic expression.

With her parents right behind her, Nicole moved to take her seat next to them. As she reached the pew, she made a quick decision and stepped back, beckoning her own parents to slide in before her.

Though they both gave her a quizzical look, they complied. She'd known they wouldn't want to make a show with the entire congregation watching. At least now, Dan and Theresa couldn't openly snub her. She hoped to continue to block that possibility for as long as possible.

Pastor Theodore spotted her and hurried over, hugging her and patting her back. She'd always liked him. When she'd been a child he'd always treated her kindly. Even now, with no doubt all kinds of crazy rumors swirling around about her, he gave her the respect due a recent widow. This small kindness gave her strength and had her straightening her shoulders and lifting her chin. Jacob mercifully had stopped fussing and looked around instead, as if he found the proceedings interesting. Nicole hoped he'd stay that way as long as possible.

The service started. The church choir sang hymns and then the preacher began to speak. The Bill Mabry he spoke of bore little resemblance to the cruel, vindictive man Nicole knew so well. As she listened to Pastor Theodore extol Bill's virtues, she felt slightly queasy, but kept her head high. Glad of the dark sunglasses, she stared straight ahead, expressionless. Though her parents generally went out of their way to avoid helping her, by providing a buffer between Nicole and Bill's parents, they helped more than they'd ever know.

Finally, the preacher finished, inviting anyone else who wished to speak about the deceased to come up. Only a couple of people did, both men who'd worked with him.

The rest of the day passed more quickly. The ceremony at the cemetery was short. Nicole stood alone, the last to drop her red rose on the casket once it had been lowered into the ground.

Dark glasses still in place, she scooped up Jacob and headed to her car. She'd just gotten him buckled in the back and turned the ignition when the skies opened up and it began to pour.

On the way home, she went through a coffee shop drive-through and ordered a large latte. Hot coffee and rain went a long way toward making her feel better. Even little Jacob, who'd begun to fuss a little, allowed himself to be lulled by the motion of the car. Loath to wake him, she drove around a little bit instead of going home.

* * *

Because he couldn't seem to stop thinking about her, Kyle had known this would be a long, rough day for Nicole. He hadn't known today was her husband's funeral and burial until he'd gone out for breakfast. Everyone in the café was talking about it, almost as if this funeral was the social event of the year.

As he ate his solitary meal at the breakfast counter, he listened. Nicole—pretty, popular, vivacious Nicole—had apparently been widely regarded as reclusive and antisocial. She rarely left the house, it seemed, and the few times she did, her husband was always at her side.

Kyle wondered why no one thought that sounded more like a prisoner than anything else.

For the rest of the day, he found himself thinking about Nicole. How she was doing, if she needed help with the baby and where she was at that moment. He actually debated swinging by the cemetery and watching from a distance, but that sounded way too creepy, so he talked himself out of it.

He stayed home, worked out, watched some mindless television, ate and worked out again.

When the rain came, the storm raged fast and furious, matching his mood. He seemed to have no control over his emotions these days. He could start out feeling pretty good, energetic and happy and then an hour later find himself wallowing in a kind of black despair that no matter how hard he tried, he couldn't seem to crawl out from under. The anger was the worst, right after the jumpiness and uncertainty. He'd gone and purchased a punching bag from an athletic store, figuring hitting that would be better than slamming his fist through the sheetrock.

Today it seemed he was destined to experience a complete gamut of moods. He knew some of this had to do with how badly he wanted Nicole and how much he hated himself for wanting her.

Finally, he knew he had to get out of his house. Rain or no rain, so he took himself to a nice little coffee shop midway between him and Nicole. As he always did, he ordered a large coffee, black. He'd never been one for those fancy lattes or flavored coffees.

He took a seat near the window, watching the rain come down in sheets, and felt calmer. His phone had flashed up several alerts, from a Severe Thunderstorm Warning to a Flash Flood Warning. Funny how severe weather had a way of putting things in perspective.

Inside he knew the reason he'd chosen this place to spend his late afternoon was because it was close to Nicole's. He wasn't sure how he'd be greeted after what had happened yesterday, but he knew he could no more stay away than he could stop breathing.

Finally, after getting a refill, he braved the downpour and drove slowly to her house. Yellow light shone in the windows, letting him know she was home. He parked in the driveway instead of the street as it was a shorter path to the door.

Still not even sure she wouldn't turn him away, he sprinted from his truck to her door. Luckily, the front portico blocked the rain, so he didn't have to stand there getting soaked while waiting.

At first, despite ringing the bell, she didn't answer. He waited just long enough to realize he never should have come here, especially not today, and turned away.

Facing the downpour, he eyed his truck, barely visible through the heavy curtains of rain.

Behind him, the door opened.

"Kyle?" Nicole sounded surprised, but not dismayed. He turned slowly, aware no matter how hard he tried to act like this was a casual visit, the ferocity of the storm made that excuse laughable.

So he gave her the truth. "I just wanted to check on you," he said. "Make sure you were okay after today."

She opened the door wider. "Come in. Get out of the rain."

For the first time, he realized she wore an oversized T-shirt and a pair of tattered shorts. Her feet were bare, her toenails painted bright pink. With her face scrubbed clean of makeup, she looked impossibly young, as if she hadn't aged at all since they'd started dating back in high school.

Longing warred with self-preservation. He tried, oh how hard he tried, to talk himself into declining, telling her now that he'd checked on her, he really needed to go.

But of course, he didn't. Instead, he stepped into her foyer, rain water pooling on the marble floor at his feet.

Nicole laughed, an awkward sound, and ordered him to stay put while she fetched a towel. When she returned, she handed him a fluffy white bath sheet. Sheepishly, he dried himself off as best he could. Part of him already regretted the impulse that had made him stop by. But the other part of him, heart pounding, senses electrified, knew he couldn't go. Nicole for him had begun to feel like an addiction, a powerful drug that he knew would eventually destroy him, but made him unable to get past the craving.

"I just finished bathing Jacob," she said, accepting the towel back from hm. "He's clean and fed and awake. Would you like to see your son?"

Her choice of words startled him. He supposed because he hadn't gotten used to the idea yet. "Sure," he said.

"Follow me." She walked off, hips swaying. Behind her, he couldn't help but keep from glancing around the huge house. He wondered how she lived here. Was she comfortable? He didn't think he could ever feel at home in such a formal and ornate place.

But she seemed at ease. They turned into a long hallway. She stopped in one of the rooms—a half bath—and hung the towel up on a bar, glancing back at Kyle with a slight smile. "I'll let it dry." And she turned left, which led back to the main part of the house. "Jacob's in his playpen in the kitchen. He's had a long day—we both have. I'm letting him have some play time before I put him down for the night."

"Play time?" The term puzzled him. "What kind of playing can he do at three months old?"

Her smile widened. "Not much, but he's very interested in colorful toys. He's got some wind-up ones, too, that play music—he really likes those."

Unlike the rest of the house, the kitchen seemed bright and cheerful. The walls had been painted a soft yellow, and despite the white cabinets, granite countertops and stainless steel appliances, it had an earthy, comfortable feel. In between a large island and the kitchen table, Nicole had set up a brightly colored playpen-like apparatus.

"He's really cute," he commented, gaze riveted on the smiling, kicking baby lying on his back in the center of it.

"Yes, he is." she said, smiling. "Hey there, Jacob. Look who's come to see you."

Though he wasn't entirely sure how to communicate with an infant, he figured if he followed her example, he'd be fine. He leaned down to get as close as he could. "Hi, Jacob," he said, softening his tone. "How are you doing today?"

To his surprise, Jacob looked at him, smiling and gurgling and then blowing a bubble as he waved his arms around.

"You can pick him up if you want," Nicole suggested. "You two might as well start getting used to each other."

Though she had a point, he wasn't sure he was ready. Such a little, delicate person. What if he held him wrong or dropped him. "I don't know," he started to stay. But the quick look of hurt that flashed across her expressive face stopped him short. "I don't know how," he amended. "I'm not sure I've ever held a baby this young."

"I can show you how." She scooped up Jacob, who laughed at the swooshing sound she made. "How's Mommy's little boy?" she cooed. Interestingly enough, the baby made nonsensical sounds, as if he was trying to communicate with her.

Outside, thunder boomed. Jacob jumped, startled. Kyle jumped too, dropping to the floor as if someone had just shouted *Incoming*. Adrenaline flooded through his body, followed closely by a rush of embarrassment and shame.

Slowly, he climbed to his feet, aware he was shaking. Steeling himself, he met Nicole's startled gaze and opened his mouth to speak, to attempt to explain his actions.

"Here," Nicole said, interrupting him. She started to hand him the baby, and then motioned toward one of the kitchen chairs. "Sit down first. I don't want you doing that while holding Jacob."

Bemused, his insides still quivering, he did as she asked. Once he'd settled himself as comfortably into the chair as he could, he had to grip the edge of the table, bracing himself for the next crack of thunder. "Honestly, Nicole. I think it'd be best if I wait for another time to hold him. These days, I don't do well with loud noises."

She tilted her head, considering. Still holding Jacob, she pulled out a chair and sat next to him, close enough that their knees touched.

Outside, a rumble, then a loud pop, before lightning flashed. He braced himself, and since he had the advantage of knowing it was coming, he didn't move.

"There you go," she said softly. "You're okay. Here."

To his stunned disbelief, she leaned forward. "Take him."

What could he do but clench his teeth, and try? As he relaxed his hold on the table, he let his arms come up. She placed Jacob, squirming now, his little face screwed up as if he wasn't sure whether or not to cry, into Kyle's arms.

Terrified, Kyle froze. As if she sensed this, Nicole stayed close, hovering, ready to take back their son if he couldn't do it.

Their son. He straightened his spine. And looked, really looked, into the bright, inquisitive gaze of his baby boy.

Something clicked inside him. He wasn't sure whether to call it resolve or determination or maybe even love. But in that instant, he knew he would do whatever he had to in order to keep Jacob safe. Astounded, he brought one hand near his son's hand and when Jacob wrapped his little fist around Kyle's fingers, he was lost.

"Pretty amazing, isn't he?" Nicole asked.

"He is," Kyle answered fervently. When he looked up and met Nicole's gaze, the tenderness in her expression humbled him.

"I was an army ranger," he began, feeling the need to explain, as best he could, what had made him the way he was.

Right at that moment, a boom shook the house apart. The power flickered and went out. Another sound, clearly an explosion. Instead of panic, determination filled him. Not thunder, he thought, bringing the baby closer to his chest. Something worse. Much, much worse.

Chapter 8

This time, he knew the urge to flee wasn't psychotic. "Come on," he said, pushing to his feet, Jacob cradled protectively against him. "We've got to get out. Now."

"Did lightning hit us?" Nicole asked, clearly fighting panic. "I need to grab a few things. Jacob will need diapers and formula and—"

"No time. You can buy more later."

To her credit, she didn't argue. Together they moved toward the closest door, the one that led to the back patio.

As she reached out to fumble with the doorknob, he heard another sound loud and clear—the roar and crackle of fire. Despite the rain outside, the kitchen began to fill with acrid, thick black smoke.

He shoved Nicole outside. Wide-eyed, she turned to look back at her house. Kyle hip bumped her, sending her farther away from the house. From danger.

The rain still fell heavily, so Kyle hunched over to try and keep Jacob sheltered and dry as much as he could.

Nicole let out a cry, pointing. "Look. My house is burning. That fire is out of control."

"Call 911," he told her.

"I'm trying, but my phone keeps dropping the call."

"It probably went through on their end." He had to shout to be heard over the rain. "Let's run for my pickup. We've got to get out of this rain. You can try again from there."

Both Kyle and Nicole were soaked by the time they crawled up into the cab of his truck. Baby Jacob was wet, but not as badly as they were. Which was good, because Kyle didn't want the infant to get chilled.

While Kyle moved the truck out of the driveway to put a safe distance between them and the house, Nicole called 911. This time, she spoke a few words into her phone, giving her address and stating what had happened. When she ended the call, she looked back at her house, her long wet hair hanging into her face. Brushing it away, she nodded grimly. "I got through. They're sending people now."

The fire flared up, defying the rain. "Why isn't water putting it out?" she asked. "This doesn't make sense."

He didn't have the heart to tell her it meant that some sort of accelerant had been used. The loud pop they'd heard had been some kind of explosion. This fire had been deliberately set.

The fire trucks arrived in record time, despite the rain coming down sideways in sheets.

Nicole left Jacob with Kyle in the cab of his truck and went to meet them.

Waving his chubby little arms around as if conducting an imaginary symphony, baby Jacob appeared remarkably unaffected by it all. Gazing at his son, a rush of love slammed Kyle. For the first time, he fully considered what it meant to be this boy's father. He'd get to be there for Jacob, watch him grow. He'd see all of the firsts—first crawl, first step, first words. He'd even play a large part in shaping what kind of person Jacob would become.

As he continued to hold his son, Kyle marveled that Nicole had trusted him to keep their boy safe despite Kyle's clear instability around loud noises.

But this time was different. He hadn't lost it. To his surprise, something else had kicked in at the first hint of real danger. His every sense had sharpened. He'd known he'd get Nicole and Jacob all out, away from danger safely, or die trying.

He tried to peer out the fogged-up windows through the rain. As far as he could tell, outside, organized chaos reigned supreme. Despite the steady downpour, the fire continued to rage, eating up wood and sheetrock and whatever else it could find. Firefighters wearing their full gear worked to unravel a huge hose. Quickly, they aimed it at the house. Fascinated, Kyle watched. Water combined with rain, and yet the orange flames still leapt, no doubt fueled by gasoline or kerosene. Black smoke billowed, mingling with the damp air. As soon as a small amount of headway was made, another area would flare up. He wondered if they had some kind of foam.

Nicole returned and slid into the passenger seat.

She didn't appear to notice the rain had soaked her to the skin and ran in rivulets down her face. "They told me to wait here. They didn't want me to get in the way." She sounded so defeated, he couldn't help but reach for her.

She looked up, startled, when he squeezed her wet shoulder. She had to be cold. Carefully, he put baby Jacob in his carrier in the backseat.

"Come here," he told her, his voice gruff.

"I'm drenched," she commented, but slid over anyway as much as she could, until her hip bumped up against the console. When she leaned her head on his shoulder, her wet hair quickly dampened his shirt.

But none of that mattered. He wrapped his arm around her and held her as close as he could without asking her to crawl over the console and into his lap.

"Was it lightning?" he asked, even though he pretty much already knew it wasn't.

"They don't know." The defeat in her tone tugged at his heart. "Because of the way it keeps burning, they're thinking some sort of accelerant was used. As in, this fire was not an accident."

"I thought so. That pop we heard had to be the first spark. But do you have any idea who would want to do such a thing?" he asked, genuinely puzzled. "Do you really have enemies?"

She sighed. "Not me, but it's possible Bill did. He wasn't a nice person. I found credit card receipts that showed he had a mistress. Plus, he was always complaining about people cheating him at pool or cards. Everywhere he went, he seemed to think people were out to get him." She paused, then sighed again. "But his parents appear to hate me all of a sudden. They've threatened to take away Jacob, and are actively searching for a will so they could take away my home and my car."

"What? Take away Jacob? How would that even be possible?"

She met his gaze, exhaustion making dark circles under her eyes. "They don't know he's not Bill's. We never told them. Bill knew, but he wanted to keep it a secret."

"Wow." For the first time, Kyle had conflicted feelings about the man Nicole had married. "It's nice that he wanted to protect you from gossip."

"Nice?" Her humorless chuckle made her cough. "Bill didn't have a nice bone in his body, I'm sorry to say. Unfortunately, I didn't know that until after we were married. No, his silence was one of my conditions if he wanted me to go through with the marriage."

"Go through with... Now I'm confused. Are you telling me Bill knew you didn't want to marry him?"

"Yes." She hung her head. "He knew I didn't love him, though I promised to be faithful and loyal. He was well aware that I still grieved for you."

Stunned, he wasn't sure how to react. If this was true... "That kind of thing can eat at a man."

"I know. But I couldn't lie. Despite what my parents wanted, I couldn't pretend something I didn't feel. That wouldn't have been fair to him or to me."

Aware they were on slippery ground and in need of a distraction, he pointed at the house. "It looks like they're making progress. I don't see any new flames."

"Oh, good." She appeared as happy to change the

subject as he. "Do you mind if I go check on the progress? Jacob's still asleep."

"Not at all." He watched her go, a new sort of heaviness in his chest. What had she done, once she'd truly believed he'd died? What kind of hell had her marriage been? Had she even considered how Jacob would have felt, growing up? Soon enough, he'd have figured out that there had been no love lost between his parents.

Which brought to mind another question. Had Nicole intended to eventually tell Jacob that Bill was not his father? Would she have even attempted to keep Kyle's memory alive? And how would that have gone over with Bill, especially since he'd promised to keep Jacob's true parentage a secret? So much had hinged on the capricious twists of fate.

His gut twisted at the thought of his son growing up calling another man daddy. Another man who'd already resented him because Nicole hadn't lied about loving his father. Now, in the blink of an eye, all that had changed. Kyle had lived and returned home. Now, he'd be able to love his son, watch him grow up, help take care of him. To think that he and Jacob might never have known one another...the back of his throat ached.

Nicole returned, her sodden shoulders sagging in defeat. "The entire back part of the house is gone," she said. "And most of the upstairs too. They're saying it's not safe to go inside." When she turned toward him, rain running in rivulets down her face, at first he didn't see the tears. "Jacob and I have nowhere to go."

"I can take you to your parents' house," he offered. She started shaking her head before he'd even finished speaking. "They've made it clear that we're not welcome there."

Stunned, he gaped at her. "But Jacob's their grandson. And you're their daughter. Blood." How many times in his youth had he, the foster child with no real family, envied his friends who had blood ties.

"That doesn't matter to them." Her sad grimace tugged at his heart. "They've already let me know that to them, Jacob will always be an illegitimate bastard, proof of my sinning, harlot ways."

If he hadn't known her and her family so well, he would have thought she was joking. Unfortunately, he knew she was not.

"And your in-laws are out," he continued. "What about friends? Surely you have some girlfriends who'll help you out."

This time, she didn't even look at him. Instead, she continued to gaze out the window, as though engrossed in watching the firefighters as they began to put up their equipment.

"I have no friends," she finally said, her voice flat. "Bill made sure of that."

They sat in silence for a moment, and then one of the firefighters came and tapped on the window. "I'll be right back," Nicole murmured, before getting out of the truck.

In the small backseat of his king cab, baby Jacob made a sound in his sleep. Kyle turned, letting his gaze drink in the sight of his son, and knew what he had to do. Having Nicole stay with him in such close proximity would be rough, but he'd done more difficult things. He couldn't turn her and Jacob away with no place to stay.

A few minute later, she returned. "They won't even let me go inside for formula or diapers. My purse is in there too, so I don't have my credit cards or even my ID. I can't even get a hotel room." She turned to face him, her expression pleading. "Please, Kyle, can I—"

"You can stay with me," he said, cutting her off. No way was he going to make her beg. "You and Jacob are welcome for as long as you need. And on the way there, we'll make a Walmart run and pick you up whatever supplies and clothes you need to tide you over."

She sat so still he almost wondered if she'd heard him. And then, she nodded. "Thank you," she whispered. "I really, really appreciate it." She took a deep breath. "Jacob's infant carrier is in the backseat of the BMW. Let's just hope I forgot to lock the car."

Nicole had. Since the BMW was unlocked, Kyle removed the infant car carrier in the pouring rain. It took a few minutes, but he was able to get it installed in the backseat of his truck. She transferred a sleepy and grumpy baby Jacob into it and buckled him in. Once that was done, Kyle drove them to the huge discount store a few miles away.

Nicole knew she needed to ask to wait in the truck while Kyle shopped for her in the brightly lit superstore, but she didn't want to push her luck. However, she also was aware she had no choice. She wore a soaking-wet T-shirt, nursing bra and exercise shorts, flip-flops and little else. For the first time, she wondered how much of her body had been visible to the firefighters. Hopefully, due to the darkness, not too much.

Kyle, however, might be another story. She winced, thinking of how brightly lit her house had been. If he'd noticed her appearance, he hadn't commented. Of course he hadn't. Despite his rough upbringing, Kyle had always possessed a gentleman's manners. He also had always been observant, missing little. She had no doubt he'd seen exactly what she did and didn't have on.

Nothing she could do about it now. Jacob needed supplies. He'd require frequent diaper and clothing changes, but damned if she could go into a store in a wet T-shirt and give total strangers an eyeful.

She had no choice but to ask Kyle for one more favor.

"Kyle," she began. "I just need a few things for now, to get Jacob through the night. I can get more later. If I write them down, would you mind buying them for me while I wait in the truck with Jacob?"

He gave her a puzzled look. "Why? Wouldn't you rather pick everything out yourself?"

Though she thought she might die of shame, she forced herself to lift her chin. "My clothes are wet. And I'm not wearing anything underneath except my nursing bra."

Silence.

The atmosphere changed instantly. Charged, heavy, like static electricity would spark if they touched. His breathing changed, became rougher, harsher, and she realized her words had aroused him.

Despite everything she'd been through, this realization turned her on too. Great. How the hell was she going to manage to share a living space with him and not want to constantly rip off his clothes?

"Sure, I'll do it," he finally said, his voice husky. "I've got a notepad and pen in the console. Write down exactly what you need and the sizes, and I'll take care of getting it." He turned on the interior light and, carefully avoiding looking directly at her, fetched the paper and pen.

Relieved, she accepted the pad and jotted down a few things. One box of diapers, a pacifier, several onesies and his size, and some diaper rash cream.

When she handed it back to him, he looked it over. "What about you?" he asked. "All of this is for Jacob."

"I…" About to say she thought she'd go back and get her own supplies tomorrow, she realized she'd at least need a change of clothes and some undergarments. Her face heating, she jotted down her own sizes, asking for just one nursing bra, some panties, a T-shirt and a pair of shorts. And some flip-flops, since she couldn't run around in her bare feet. At the last moment, she changed the bra to two, because she'd need a spare.

He accepted the list again. "I'll be right back," he said. "At least the rain has stopped."

Surprised, she glanced at the windshield and the brightly lit parking lot. "That's good. At least you won't get soaked again."

After he left, she watched him until he disappeared inside.

When Kyle returned after about thirty minutes, he was pushing a cart. After loading a large box into the back of his pickup, he climbed in the cab and handed her two full shopping bags. He also had a package of diapers, which he placed in the backseat next to the once again sleeping baby.

"All set," he declared, a forced cheerfulness in his

tone. Still carefully avoiding looking at her, he started the engine.

When they reached his house, he grabbed the diapers and the bags. "You get Jacob," he said. "I'll meet you inside." And he hurried off.

Bemused, she unclicked the car carrier, hoping not to wake her son. Feeling more self-conscious than before, she kept the carrier strategically placed in front of her, hoping it would act as a shield. At least her T-shirt had begun to dry—no longer ringing wet, she hoped it provided a bit more coverage.

Once inside, Kyle turned on lights as he went. His movements were efficient and confident, just like they'd always been. She'd always wondered how someone who'd had the kind of childhood he had could still have so much optimism, but nothing had ever seemed to get Kyle down for long. This was one of the things she'd always admired about him.

"Follow me," he said, not even turning to glance her way. His house seemed spartan, more like an impersonal hotel room or barracks than a home. She could tell from the mismatched furniture that it had come furnished. Kyle probably hadn't the time or the inclination to do any decorating to reflect his tastes.

Not sure whether to be relieved or amused, she did as he asked. He stopped in front of a doorway. "Here's the guest room. I'll need to get some sheets for the bed." Dropping the plastic bags on the floor, he turned away. "Make yourself comfortable. There's a bathroom across the hall." With that, he disappeared.

The small room held a double bed, a nightstand with a lamp, and a dresser and mirror. There were no pictures on the walls. Slowly, Nicole made her way to the bed, where she placed a still-sleeping Jacob's carrier. She knew she'd been blessed to have such a calm baby, especially now when everything else in her life seemed so to have gone crazy.

After retrieving the bags and emptying their contents on to the bed, she saw Kyle had purchased two T-shirts for her, along with two pairs of shorts, a package of panties and the two nursing bras she requested. Though she blushed at the thought of him choosing such intimate items for her, she wasn't surprised to see that they were exactly the no-frills kind she liked to wear. He'd also thoughtfully purchased her a toothbrush, toothpaste, deodorant and shampoo and conditioner. He'd even put in a small bottle of the perfume she'd worn back in high school. This made her smile.

Next, she wanted a hot shower. She smelled like smoke and rain and fear. Afraid to leave Jacob alone, even though he still slept and was still securely buckled in his carrier, she brought him with her to the bathroom across the hallway. Like everything else in Kyle's house, this room was neat and clean, with nothing to mark his personality. There were already clean towels hanging on the rack.

Ten minutes later, as she stood drying herself off, she glanced in the mirror and shook her head. While outwardly, her appearance hadn't changed, her insides had been shaken up, spit out and put back in.

One week ago, her life had been entirely different. She'd been miserable, fearful, saving up in the hopes of leaving her abusive husband. Kyle had been, at least as far as she knew, dead. Her love for him had never died, and she'd known her grief at losing him would shadow her for the rest of her days.

Now her husband had been murdered, unexpectedly giving her a freedom she hadn't expected so soon, but Kyle had returned from the dead. Instead of the joyous reunion she'd have expected if she'd known he still lived, he wanted to be friends. She'd learned Bill had a mistress, had emptied their savings account and she'd lost her house. Oh, and her in-laws now hated her, the police had made it clear they considered her a suspect in Bill's murder and she'd managed to lose the respect and love of the only man she'd ever loved.

Yep. Her life had become as dramatic as one of the soap operas her mother had used to watch.

But she still had Jacob and that was all that mattered, right? Maybe some way, somehow she could find it in her to squash her feelings and become platonic friends with Kyle. She'd have to, since he'd made it clear he wanted to be a part of their son's life.

After her shower, she returned to the bedroom to find Kyle had set up a brand new portable bassinette. That must have been what was in the box. To her dismay, tears filled her eyes. How kind, how thoughtful and how unexpected. Grateful, she changed Jacob and fed him. After burping him, she placed him in the bassinette and went looking for Kyle.

She found him in the kitchen, sitting at the table drinking a beer and scrolling on his phone.

"That was really kind of you," she told him, her throat aching with emotion. "I hadn't thought about where he'd sleep tonight. I promise you, I'll repay you as soon as I can."

"No worries." He shrugged. "Do you want a beer?"

"No thank you. I can't, because I'm breastfeeding

Jacob and I don't take chances with passing anything along to him."

Immediately, his gaze went to her breasts. Full of milk, they were swollen larger than normal. She fought the urge to cross her arms.

"How about some water or tea?" Without waiting for an answer, he got up and retrieved a bottle of water from the fridge and handed it to her. To her surprise, it was the brand she preferred, which made her wonder if he'd known that or if it was just coincidence.

Feeling awkward, she took it. "I'll try to stay out of your way as much as possible," she said. "Tomorrow I'm going to call my insurance company and talk to the fire department to see when I can get into my house. I'll keep you posted."

"Sounds good." He nodded, his impersonal gaze sliding over her before returning to his phone.

Though she'd basically been dismissed, she lingered another moment, not sure if she should. Finally, she mumbled something about going to bed early before beating a hasty retreat.

Once inside her room, she closed the door and sat down on the edge of the bed. Talk about uncomfortable. The sooner she could get out of here and back in her own home, the better.

In the middle of the night, a tortured cry startled her awake. She sat up in bed, blinking, wondering if she'd imagined it. First, she checked on little Jacob, finding him still peacefully sleeping. Since she had no pajamas, she'd slept in the nude. She pulled on her sundress and opened her bedroom door. Then she stood in the doorway and peered out into the dark house, listening.

When nothing else happened, she left the door open a crack and padded back to bed. Climbed beneath the sheets, fluffed her pillow and closed her eyes, willed herself to sleep.

She'd just about dozed off when she heard something again. More sounds, muffled this time. A grunt, a moan and another cry. Someone was in agony. Or badly hurt.

Kyle.

Panic flooded her. Not completely sure where he might be, she rushed down the hallway in the dark, looking for his bedroom. She found it at the end of the hall, but he wasn't there. The room was empty, the bed covers twisted as though he'd tried to sleep but couldn't.

Then where had he gone?

She found him in the dark living room, curled up in a ball in the chair, his head down, his body shaking.

"Kyle?" She called his name softly. He didn't react.

The moonlight streaming in through the window revealed the fine sheen of perspiration on his skin.

She took a step, reaching out for him. The instant her hand connected with her shoulder, he exploded out of the chair, knocking her down.

When she hit the floor, she hit hard. Crying out, she reacted instinctively, crawling on her hands and knees away from him.

Chapter 9

"Hell's bells." Horrified, Kyle froze as he realized what he had done. Nicole still scuttled on her hands and knees to get away from him, as if she thought him some kind of monster.

She was right to think that way. He *was* a monster.

"Nicole, wait." He started to go after her, then thought better of it. Instead, he stood with his knees locked in place, forcing himself to relax the hands he'd balled into fists. "I'm sorry. I didn't know you were there. When I get like that, it's all pure reaction."

Though she didn't respond, at least she stopped crawling away.

He dared to take a step toward her. "Nicole, are you hurt? Can you stand?" He had no idea if he'd simply bumped her or if he'd done worse, and hit her. He prayed it wasn't the latter.

Instead of answering, she slowly pushed to her feet, keeping her gaze averted. When she finally turned to face him, instead of the tears he'd feared he'd see in her eyes, she appeared solemn, even thoughtful. He'd have done better with furious. Anything but this thoughtful, numb sort of detachment, as if she'd already succeeded in distancing herself from him.

"I'm okay," she said, surprise echoing in her voice. He studied her face, relieved that he saw no fear in her eyes.

"I'm glad."

"Yeah." She crossed her arms. "Would you mind telling me exactly what just happened there? It was kind of like when you startle someone who's asleep and they react in self-defense."

"That's a good analogy," he said, ashamed. He looked away, but then forced himself to give her his full attention. "I'm working through a few things since Afghanistan. The IED explosion apparently was the final straw. Though it's not an excuse—there is no excuse—I've been told I have PTSD." He swallowed, forcing out the words he really didn't want to say. "I'm not sure I'm entirely on board with that."

She stared at him, her eyes wide, but didn't speak. He couldn't help but notice her defensive posture, arms crossed.

"Sometimes I get like that, like the way you found me. It's… I'm…in a dark place. I'm not fully conscious of what's going on around me." Taking a deep breath, he hoped his desperation didn't show. "I don't know what exactly is wrong with me, but I'm working on getting better. Nicole, you know I'd never hurt you. I swear I didn't know who you were or what you were doing."

Finally, finally, to his relief, she nodded. "I believe you. And I think I understand. But Kyle, I know there's help available for servicemen with PTSD. Have you tried to get some assistance?"

"I'm dealing with it myself," he replied, even as he had to force himself to unclench his teeth. "If it ever gets to a point where I don't think I can, I'll seek help." Which it never would. He'd done and seen things in the service of his country that would make any other man shudder. Some stupid, psychological thing like PTSD didn't stand a chance against an army ranger like him.

But Nicole, all she knew was the old Kyle. The one she'd gone to school with, made plans with and loved. That Kyle, well, he might have allowed himself to exhibit weakness and seek help from a shrink.

The new Kyle, way stronger, didn't need help. Nicole should understand that, but how could she?

Judging from the way she eyed him, she was carefully considering saying something else. He knew her still, and recognized the look on her face. He braced himself, because Nicole had always been honest, sometimes blunt, at least when it came to him.

"I think you should look into it," she finally said, almost as an afterthought, pretending she didn't care. Or maybe she wasn't really pretending. Because while his life had frozen in place, she'd gone on with hers.

She'd moved on. He wondered if he'd ever be able to do the same.

Kyle in pain. As she padded back to her room, the thought tormented her. He might not have realized she'd been there, but the image of him, strong, fearless Kyle, curled into a ball and shaking, would haunt her as long as she lived.

What the heck had happened to him over there? While she knew the last thing, the IED explosion that had seriously wounded him and killed his buddy, she understood that there had been more.

And his refusal to get help seemed textbook too. She'd read enough about veterans with PTSD to know that a lot of them thought, like Kyle, that they could heal themselves.

After checking on Jacob, she stepped out of her sundress, got back in her bed and pulled up the covers. In the morning she resolved to do more research. If there was any way she could help Kyle, she'd find it.

Jacob woke early, crying with hunger. Nicole stepped into the same sundress, picked him up, got him changed and then fed him. While he nursed, she gazed down at his perfect little face in wonder. How did no one see Kyle when they looked at her son?

Once Jacob had his fill, she burped him and then rocked him in her arms. His little eyes drifted closed so she placed him back in his bassinette. Her cell phone rang just as she'd finished getting herself dressed.

When her in-laws' number showed in the display, she almost didn't answer it. But then, knowing they'd leave a message, she decided to simply get the call over with. Who knew, maybe they'd learned what had happened to her house and were calling to offer support, even though she highly doubted it.

"Hello?"

"I know what you did." Theresa's voice dripped

venom. "You knew we were investigating to see if you really had any right to Bill's house, so you set it on fire. The fire chief told me it looked like a bomb went off."

A bomb. Nicole shivered. "You do realize my son was there?" she asked, her tone frosty. "How dare you call me and act as if I am capable of such a thing? Despite what you might choose to believe, that is my home. Mine and Jacob's."

"Did you burn the will?" Theresa asked, as if Nicole hadn't spoken. "Because you should know if he had a will drawn up somewhere, I will find it. I know in my mother's heart that he wouldn't have wanted you to have everything."

"Do you?" Nicole now regretted answering. "Because no matter what kind of crazy thoughts are running through your head, your son and I were married when he died. We were not separated, and neither of us had filed for divorce."

"And now you've already taken up with another man," Theresa continued. "My son is barely in the ground and you're running around with your old high school sweetheart. For all I know, you and he were carrying on before Bill died. That's no kind of environment for a baby."

"How dare you." Though Nicole shook from anger, she kept her voice level. "Do not even presume to insinuate such nasty untruths against me. You have no idea what you're talking about."

"Don't I? Then why don't you explain exactly what you're doing living with that man?"

"Though I owe you absolutely nothing, least of all an explanation, I will tell you this. I'm doing what I have to in order to take care of my son. We have a roof over our heads now. Jacob will be cool and dry and fed."

She thought about informing Theresa about the credit card statement of Bill's that she'd found, and the clear indication that Bill had a long-term mistress. Also, she wondered if Theresa actually knew how much her son drank and gambled, or that Nicole suspected he might have even started using illegal drugs.

But that would be stooping to the other woman's level, and Nicole would never do that.

"I'm tired of defending myself to you," Nicole said.

Theresa started to speak, but Nicole wasn't finished. "I'm not sure what happened between us, or why you're willing to believe such terrible things about me. But whatever the reason, I don't need this kind of drama in my life. I'm going to have to ask you not to call me again unless you can be civil." Finger shaking, she pressed the red icon on her phone and ended the call.

While she and Bill's mother had never been remotely close, her heart sank at the realization that Bill's words had clearly made Theresa willing to believe the worse of her without actual proof.

"You did what you had to in order to have a roof over your head?" Kyle asked. She turned to find him standing about five feet away from her. "Mind telling me what the hell is going on?"

Shame made her flush, even though she knew she had absolutely nothing to feel ashamed about. "That was my ex-mother-in-law. Apparently, the town gossips are really going at it. She practically accused me of having an affair with you before Bill died."

"That would have been really difficult to do, considering I was in the hospital," he mused.

"True. But now she thinks I'm sleeping with you in order to have a place to stay."

"Interesting." He leaned one shoulder against the doorframe.

Though his bland tone seemed impersonal, the spark in his green eyes made warmth blossom inside her. Suddenly flustered, she realized she probably looked like a mess. "I, uh…" She grabbed her clothes off the dresser and gave him a pointed look. "If you don't mind moving, I need to get into the bathroom."

"Sorry." Sounding anything but, he pushed himself off and ambled away. "Coffee in the kitchen whenever you're ready."

After attending to her usual morning routine sans shower since she'd taken one last night, she returned to her room, teeth brushed, fully clothed. The smell of fresh coffee drifted down the hallway, tantalizing her.

When she reached the kitchen, he jumped up from his chair and poured her a cup, adding one sugar and some creamer, just the way she liked it. Bemused, she accepted the coffee, pulling out the chair opposite him and dropping into it.

"What's all this about with your mother-n-law?" he asked. "Why is she so antagonistic?"

She grimaced and shook her head. "No idea. I married her son, I guess. I mean, she's never really been friendly, but after Bill died, she declared out-and-out war. So far, she's accused me of murdering him, destroying his will and carrying on an affair. Oh, and threatened to try to get custody of my son. She planned the funeral without even consulting me, and is acting as if her son should be sainted or something."

The coffee tasted wonderful. As she sipped, she found herself telling Kyle all about the credit card statement she'd found and turned over to the police.

"Did you mention that to Theresa?" he asked.

"No. Until there's something absolutely certain, I'm reluctant to destroy her memory of her son."

Kyle's brows rose as he eyed her over the brim of his coffee cup. "That's weirdly noble of you."

Those words hurt. Once, Kyle had known her so well he would have been able to predict what she'd do.

"Maybe." Gazing at him, she begged him silently to see her, really see her, the way he used to. "There's enough evil and hatred in this world. I see no need to add to it."

His eyes narrowed. "You have no idea," he said, his tone flat. "While you've been living here in your perfect little world, I've seen and done things that would make you sick."

For a second, she bowed her head, summoning all her inner strength and composure. Lifting her chin, she kept her voice as measured and emotionless as she could. "You have no idea what my life was like. Despite the fact that everyone in town believes Bill Mabry was a perfect saint of a man, he wasn't. He drank too much and when he did, he liked to use me as his punching bag. He made sure I had no friends and I'm sure if I hadn't already been isolated from my family, he would have done that too. I just found out he had a mistress, so I'm going to have to take myself to the doctor and get tested for an STD. In fact, I was putting aside every dollar I could, because one day I hoped to take Jacob and leave him."

When she finished, with both her voice and her body shaking, she had to struggle to catch her breath. "So don't you dare speak to me about how wonderful you think my life was, because it was the opposite."

For the space of a heartbeat, they stared at each other. Her throat ached, her soul exhausted.

"Christ, Nicole." He crossed the space between them and yanked her up against him. His mouth covered hers, possessive, demanding, hungry. Like a match to dry tinder, she went up in flames, as she knew she always would with this man. Again, and again.

Until she realized he *pitied* her.

Horrified, she pushed at him. Hard. When he released her, she stumbled back away from him, fist against her mouth.

He opened his mouth to speak, but she forestalled him. "Don't," she ordered. "I don't want your pity."

"Pity?" His lips twisted. "Can't you see what you're doing to me? How badly I want you? This isn't pity, Nicole, I can promise you that."

"We can't," she said, even as her traitorous body curved toward him.

He caught her, or pulled her, or both and they ended up in each other's arms again. Mouth on mouth, on skin, her curves fitting into his hollows, thrilling at his body's hardness. Too far gone to take it slow, mindless with need and desire, they tore at each other's clothes, eager to more fully connect, skin to skin.

Finally, still standing, her back against the wall, he pushed himself into her. Ready, her body moist, she arched her back, accepting his hardness, thrilling at how familiar and yet how new he felt. *Kyle. Kyle.* He filled her, completed her, and she climaxed moments after that first thrust.

"Oh," she cried out, surprised and then not surprised, her release washing over her like an East Texas thunderstorm.

Jaw tight, he held himself perfectly still while her body clenched around his. Then, just as she sagged against him, he began to move. Slowly, watching her as he made love to her, until she reached up to him and pulled him close, so she could kiss him.

The instant their lips met, he took over. She fell into his kiss, drowning in the taste of him. Familiar, so achingly, intoxicatingly familiar. When his mouth left hers, blazing a path down her neck to her breasts, she arched her neck and moaned.

The strokes of his tongue, the movement of his lips as he tasted her skin, sent a shiver through her core. It had always been like this between them, instantly combustible.

Her knees went weak as he began to move again, pushing himself deep into her, filling her. With each stroke, her body shuddered. He made a sound, a groan, a guttural cry, and she opened her eyes and watched as he battled to keep his tenuous grip on self-control.

She saw the instant he abandoned all restraint, and felt it a second later, when the pace of his movement increased.

When she felt herself begin to shatter, she struggled to hold on, to wait for him, but could not. Finally she let go, abandoning herself to the pleasure. He followed her a moment later.

With him still inside her, they held on to each other until their breathing evened out and their heartbeats slowed. She wondered if his reality had shifted the same way hers had. How could it have not? After lovemaking like this, how could he not see that they'd always been meant to stay together?

After another moment, he carefully disentangled himself from her. As he turned away, his entire body rigid, she read anger in the tightness of his jaw.

Though he didn't say a word, she knew what that meant.

"Don't," she said, the single word stopping him in his tracks. "Don't you dare turn this into something wrong. Because as far as I'm concerned, this is not only right, but something beautiful."

"Beautiful?" Finally, he looked at her. The tortured, self-reproach in his eyes made her stomach twist. "We can't keep hanging on to the past, Nicole. Do you know why?"

She shook her head. "Why?"

"It can't be changed. What happened since then is the new reality. You can't expect the two to mesh all perfect and neat."

"Why not?" She challenged him. "Who says we don't deserve a second chance at happiness?"

The anger faded from his face, replaced by something worse. Sadness. "Let me ask you something. Are you the same person you were when you said goodbye to me that last time?"

Of course she wasn't. She was a mother now, a widow. She'd mourned the death of the only man she'd ever loved, believing she'd never survive the grief. Her marriage had been intolerable, but she'd hung in there and been the best wife she could. Her son had been her only reason for living.

"No, I'm not the same," she finally answered. "I've weathered a lot of storms in the year since you left."

"Exactly." He said this with grim satisfaction. "You're not the same person you were. And Nicole, neither am I."

Her heart squeezed, though she kept her face expressionless. "All we can do is try the best we can," she told him. "Maybe if we take it day by day, we might be able to see our way to…" She stopped, wondering if speaking of a possible future together would be the wrong thing to do. Yet.

"Let me know what your insurance company says," he finally said, once again impersonal. "I'd like an idea how long it will be before you can go back home."

With that, he turned, grabbed his clothes off the floor and left the room.

Gathering up her scattered clothing along with the remnants of her pride, she took an extra-long, hot shower, an unabashed attempt to wash away the hold he had on her heart and body.

While she didn't know what all had happened to him while in Afghanistan, she'd read enough to understand how that could change a man. She knew some soldiers never found their way back.

If she had a say in it, Kyle would not be one of those men. Welcome or not, she'd do her best to try and help him.

After showering, she bathed and changed Jacob and fed him. Settling into a new routine here in a different house felt strange, but she took comfort in the fact that she and Jacob had survived the fire intact.

With Jacob on the sofa next to her, she made a few phone calls, one to her insurance agent to turn in a claim, another to the fire department to see if they'd reached any sort of determination. Though she didn't get to speak directly to the fire department captain, the firefighter she spoke with told her someone from the arson investigation office would be in touch with her shortly. And no, she was still not allowed inside her own house.

Arson. Just as the firefighters had suspected. But why? She had to believe that even the Mabrys, as senselessly furious with her as they were, wouldn't do something like this.

Which begged the question of who would? One of Bill's enemies? His mistress? A disgruntled employee? She had to hope both the fire department and the police would find out.

Kyle came through on his way out shortly after she'd ended the call. She told him what the firefighter had said. "I thought so," he said, perching on the edge of the sofa. As usual, her mouth went dry at the sight of him.

"I was hoping the investigation would prove otherwise." She shook her head. "Who would do such a thing and why?"

"I'd start making a list to give to the police. It can't hurt."

He had a point.

"I've got some things to do today," he told her. "Feel free to hang out here if you want. You can use my laptop if you need to access the internet, and you're welcome to help yourself to anything you want in the pantry or fridge."

"Thank you." She summoned a smile from somewhere. His remote expression and the impersonal pleasantry of his tone made her heart ache.

And then, hating herself for doing so, she stood and watched out the front window as he got into his truck and drove away.

Waiting on the fire department to call, she put Jacob down for a nap and grabbed the laptop. She began scouring the internet for articles on PTSD. She learned that all over the country there were various innovative programs helping vets overcome this disorder. From farming to camps, volunteering and therapy, each seemed to help in their own way. But it was the final article that caught her attention and seemed the most doable. An organization that provided service dogs for veterans with PTSD.

Kyle had always liked dogs. In fact, in all the numerous discussions between the two of them about the future, he'd always said he wanted a dog. He was a natural—every canine he'd ever met had taken to him instantly. And now, he had a house with a yard. She figured his landlord would be amenable; in fact he'd have to be if the dog were a service animal.

The only problem she could see in all this was that Kyle would have to apply. Not only did she suspect he wouldn't be a fan of this idea, but she knew there probably would be a huge waiting list.

Maybe they could find a dog and work with it themselves. Not only would this give Kyle something to focus on, but owning a pet would help him realize he wasn't all alone.

She sat back, feeling as if, in the middle of chaos,

she'd managed to accomplish one small thing. Helping Kyle. If only he would let her.

Kyle had no idea why he pulled into the used car lot after spotting the motorcycle for sale. Maybe it was because, in his younger days, he'd longed for a bike exactly like it. The custom black paint job highlighted the motorcycle's clean lines and rugged shape. Once upon a time, before he'd gotten a clue and signed up for the army, he'd dreamt of making a cross-country trip on the back of a bike, with Nicole sitting close right behind him. Open road, wind in the hair—though of course they'd both be wearing helmets—and freedom. All the things he'd never had and, since he and Nicole had begun to plan their future together, never wanted.

He wasn't even sure he wanted it now. Running wouldn't help him escape the horrible knowledge of what Nicole had been through. The images would remain in his mind, every time he closed his eyes.

But then, he thought, circling the bike thoughtfully, what did he have? A rented house with rented furniture and another man's wife. Nightmares and night sweats and the overwhelming, all-encompassing fear of something awful waiting right around every corner.

Since he'd gotten his motorcycle license at Fort Benning and he'd done his fair share of riding while stationed there, he bought the bike. A 2005 Harley-Davidson Sportster XL. Even though the price seemed reasonable, he haggled with the salesman, an older round-faced man named Scott, and got the amount down. Then he went to the bank, withdrew enough cash to cover it and the bike was his. He also purchased a helmet and a pair of riding gloves.

Once the paperwork had been completed, he talked Scott into following him home in his truck. With the engine rumbling under him, he drove his new toy slowly, carefully, getting to know the feel of the bike. Once he reached the small house, he pulled up into the driveway and parked. Climbing off, he walked around the Harley—*his* Harley—once more, amazed that he'd done something so impulsive. It felt…good.

After driving Scott back to the lot, they shook hands. When the other man thanked him for his service, surprised, Kyle asked him how he knew.

"You're kind of famous in this town," Scott said, beaming. "I feel honored that I was able to sell you that bike."

Bemused, Kyle thanked him and drove back to his little house. As he pulled up, he caught sight of the bike, gleaming in the sunlight, and smiled.

Nicole hurried outside just as he'd climbed on the bike, intending to take it for another spin.

"Oh," Nicole said, stopping at the edge of the sidewalk where it met the driveway. "I wondered where that thing came from."

"It's mine," he told her. Genuinely curious to see her reaction, he waited.

"Is it?" Her gaze flew to his face. "I remember how you always used to want one back when we were in high school. We used to talk about driving cross-country, just the two of us."

Chest aching, he nodded, not sure how to respond, what to say.

"You can still do that," she blurted. "If that's still your dream."

He refused to tell her it wouldn't be the same without her. "Maybe I will."

Inside, the baby began crying. Nicole turned, casting one more look at him over her shoulder. "Enjoy yourself. You certainly deserve it." And then she disappeared inside.

Moving slowly, he put on his helmet before he swung his leg over and started the engine. And then he took off.

The curving, tree-lined roads of East Texas were the perfect place to get familiar with a new bike. He took things easy, not ramping up the speed, not yet. He found this more soothing than he'd thought he would, and more exhilarating, too.

Maybe this bike would be the one thing that helped him find some peace.

And then a little old lady driving a huge Buick pulled out right in front of him.

Chapter 10

Reacting instinctively, Kyle laid the bike down. He knew he was damn lucky he was going the speed limit. As it was, he got some serious road rash, torn jeans and bloody scrapes, but no broken bones, at least as far as he could tell. Just wounded pride.

Limping back from where he'd fallen, he picked his bike up and inspected her. There were some scrapes on the gas tank paint, but no dents. Some touch-up paint would fix that up fine. He climbed on and restarted the motor. It started up just fine, luckily.

Meanwhile, the other driver had continued on, apparently oblivious that she'd come damn near killing him.

He thought about chasing her down and confronting her, but all the zing had gone out of him, so instead he turned the bike around and headed back home.

No longer relaxed, his normal, everyday jumpiness had returned. He braced himself at every intersection, expecting someone else to pull out or run a red light. Though no one did, by the time he pulled into his driveway, his entire body was drenched in sweat.

Nevertheless, he opened the garage and wheeled the bike inside. He placed his helmet on the seat.

As he walked into the house, Nicole caught sight of him and gasped. "What happened to you?" she asked. And then, without pausing for breath, "Are you all right?"

"I'm fine." He could feel himself sinking. Sinking into that dark place he sometimes went. He always fought that feeling, even though he never won. Today, he couldn't even summon up the strength to fight.

Careful not to make eye contact, he strode past her and headed for his bathroom. Once inside, he stripped off his ruined clothes and took stock of himself in the mirror. There were scrapes and cuts and more blood than he'd realized, but he had survived. Sometimes, he had to wonder why.

Turning the shower on as hot as he could stand it, he stepped inside. The water hitting his wounds made him clench his teeth, letting a hiss escape. Using soap, he relentlessly scrubbed himself, making sure no dirt lingered in any open sores.

Sometimes, the simple act of standing under the hot shower could restore him and bring him back from whatever dark precipice he'd strayed too close to. Not today. He knew deep down in his aching bones that tonight would be a long, rough night.

Finally, he shut the shower off and grabbed a towel to begin carefully drying off. Careful, because he didn't want some of the cuts to start bleeding again. He began putting antibacterial ointment on all the ones he could reach.

Three sharp taps on the bathroom door startled him. "Kyle?" Nicole asked. "Would you like me to take a look at those cuts for you?"

"I've got it," he shot back, his tone curt.

"I couldn't help but notice there were some spots on your side and back that are pretty torn up. I know you can't get to those."

She was right, but that didn't make this any better. In fact, he wasn't 100 percent certain he wanted her help. Only the threat of infection gave him pause.

Snugging the towel around his waist, he stalked to the door and yanked it open. "Fine," he snarled. "Come in."

Another woman might have hesitated. Another woman would have asked him what was wrong, or why he'd taken that tone with her. But Nicole knew him, or thought she did, and instead of recoiling at the simmering rage in his voice, she stepped inside and gently turned him so that his back was to the light.

"Let me see."

Without commenting, she reached for the antibacterial ointment and began smoothing it on the wounds. Her touch was gentle, and though some of them stung, he didn't make a sound. Instead, he became overly conscious of her close proximity and the fact that he wore nothing but a towel. Though he struggled not to show his growing arousal, he had to work hard to keep his breathing even.

Nicole paused. "Are you all right? Some of these

cuts look pretty raw. Maybe you should go see a doctor?"

"They'll be fine," he managed, jaw clenched. "Are you finished?"

"Just about. There are a couple smaller ones I haven't gotten to yet."

Finally, she put the ointment back on the bathroom counter and turned to go. At the doorway, she paused. "Are you going to tell me what happened?"

"Not now." He practically pushed her out. "Maybe later." And he closed the door and locked it.

Now he could breathe again. And he did, wondering how it was that she still could have this effect on him. His emotions were all tangled up, love and desire and bitterness along with the dawning realization that maybe, just maybe, Nicole wasn't the one who'd changed. He had, and not for the better.

He had no business wanting to be around a woman like her.

While Nicole wasn't entirely positive what had happened, it wasn't too terribly difficult to guess. He'd wiped out riding his new motorcycle. There must have been extraordinary circumstances, because Kyle had learned to ride dirt bikes at his foster home as a kid. Then while stationed in Georgia, he'd had access to motorcycles there. For all she knew, he might have used them while stationed in Afghanistan. He'd never told her exactly what army rangers did, and she knew a lot of it was classified.

Whatever had just happened, it couldn't have been too bad. He had cuts and scrapes and road rash, but no broken bones. And the motorcycle had appeared banged up. She watched out the front window when he'd wheeled it into the garage.

She went into the kitchen and made a glass of iced tea. As she carried it to the table, her cell phone rang. Her mother. That in itself was so unusual, but with everything that had been going on, she shouldn't have been surprised. Fran loved nothing better than to light into Nicole over her latest imagined sin. She could deal with it now or let the call go to voice mail and deal with it later. She decided to get it over with. "Hello?"

"I'm surprised you answered your phone," Fran said, skipping right over the pleasantries and making Nicole regret not letting the call go to voice mail. "I've had to avoid going into town due to the gossip about you. What on earth are you thinking, shacking up with that man?"

That man. Despite believing Kyle to be dead, despite knowing how deeply her daughter had grieved. *That man*, who happened to be the only man Nicole would ever love and who was the father of her beautiful baby boy.

"I'm not shacking up, Mother." Nicole reminded herself to breathe deeply. "Kyle was just kind enough to offer me a place to stay until my house is livable again."

"I'll just *bet* he was," Fran sneered. "And now the two of you can resume your little sordid relationship. I just don't understand why you are so determined to destroy our reputation in this town."

And that's what it all came down to with her mother. Everything was about the reputation. Clearly, Fran hadn't given a single thought to the possibility that her daughter and grandson might have been harmed in the fire or found themselves with nowhere to live.

And though she'd known she wouldn't, Nicole couldn't help but feel a twinge of hurt that her mom had even bothered to call and make sure they were safe and all right.

"First off, nothing sordid is going on. Second, I'm a widow. And finally, Kyle was kind enough to help us out. If you hear someone dragging his good name through the mud, the right thing to do would be to defend him."

"Don't you dare lecture me on the right thing to do," Fran shot back. "That boy took advantage of your innocence."

"Ooookay, I'm going to have to let you go," Nicole said. "I've got things to do."

"Wait." Fran suddenly sounded desperate rather than vindictive. "I wanted to ask…that is, I'm wondering when you plan to bring that sweet baby to see your father and me."

In shocked disbelief, at first Nicole didn't know what to say. The words coming out of her mother's mouth defied explanation. Her first reaction was actually suspicion. "What's going on?"

"What do you mean?" Fran did a lousy job feigning indignity.

"You don't sound like yourself, Mom. Are you feeling okay?"

"Of course I am," Fran huffed. "I'm not sure I like your tone. What are you implying?"

Nicole sighed. "Honestly? You've never wanted to have anything to do with Jacob."

"*Never* is a strong word," Fran protested, though weakly.

"He's three months old. You refused to come to the hospital when he was born. And you haven't come by to visit with him, not even once since then."

"Well maybe I realized the error of my ways. I'm trying to rectify that."

Now Nicole knew her mother was scheming something. Fran would rather walk on her lips over broken glass than admit to being wrong. But what? Clearly she had a reason for suddenly wanting to appear to be a doting grandmother.

"Please don't deny your son the right to know his own grandmother."

No doubt with that, Fran thought she had her. But Nicole knew without a shadow of a doubt she wanted no part of her son being around the shallow, sanctimonious and judgmental woman who'd made Nicole's childhood a living hell. She'd actually been sort of relieved when neither of her parents had shown any interest in their grandson.

Now this.

"I'll think about it," Nicole allowed. "And I'll let you know what I decide."

"I need to know by Thursday afternoon," Fran said. "We're having a Grandparents' Day celebration at church. It's a potluck and a lot of fun. Since Bill died, everyone has been asking, wanting to see our grandson. I just need him for an hour or two at the most."

Like a prop. Nicole knew she shouldn't have been surprised or disappointed, but apparently where her mother was concerned, hope sprang eternal, even when she knew better.

At least now she understood her mother's complete reversal. Shaking her head, she looked up to see Kyle standing in the doorway watching her. He'd gotten dressed in a faded T-shirt and workout shorts.

"Your mom?" he asked, pulling out a chair at the table opposite her.

"Yes." She sighed. "If anything, she's gotten more judgmental and critical with each passing year. She's never wanted much of anything to do with Jacob, and I have to say that while that hurts sometimes, most of the time I'm relieved. I don't want her imposing her narrow-minded beliefs on my son."

"She imposed them on you, and you turned out fine," he pointed out.

Startled, she had to laugh. "You know, I never thought about it that way." She told him what her mother had wanted. "It feels like she's just using him to improve her standing among her friends at church."

"True." He thought for a moment, and then shrugged. "But it's a start, right? Maybe she needs to get used to being a grandmother gradually. If her church friends make a big fuss over him—and her— it's possible she might want to spend more time with him."

She had to admit he had a point. "Thank you," she finally said. "I guess letting her have Jacob for a few hours wouldn't hurt."

His answering smile took her breath away. When he got up and headed outside, she didn't try to stop him, even though he hadn't told her what had happened to him while on his motorcycle. Truth be told, she didn't want to push too much. After all, unless he felt the need to explain, she didn't have the right to ask.

Instead, she drank a bit more of her tea and called her mother back, agreeing to let Fran take baby Jacob to church with her this coming Thursday.

To his frustration, Kyle couldn't stop thinking about Nicole. He'd never been able to, even while serving in the hellhole desert she'd always been there, in the back of his mind. But now, with her in such close proximity, he yearned for her with every cell in his body.

The simple taste of her hadn't been enough. And he suspected, would never be enough.

Once, they'd known with absolute certainty that one completed the other. Of course life, messy and difficult, had intervened. Nothing was actually certain.

Except this. His love for her. The knowledge of what Nicole had lived through nearly broke him.

She thought he pitied her, when in fact nothing could be further from the truth. Bill Mabry was lucky he was already dead.

Over the next few days, Kyle saw little of Nicole. She got up early in the morning, packed up little Jacob and left, often before Kyle had even finished showering. He knew she was dealing with her insurance company and a claim adjuster, as well as the fire department and the police. When he went to the café for breakfast, his waitress that morning turned out to be Wendy Morris, someone he'd gone to high school with. While she refilled his coffee cup, she was more than happy to fill him in on all the gossip.

People were talking, she said, about the fact that the sheriff hadn't made an arrest yet in Bill Mabry's murder. And the fire was another hot topic, coming so soon after his death. "And you, too," Wendy said, winking. "Everyone is all openmouthed at the way you got her to move in with you with Bill's body barely in the ground."

He shrugged, as if it were no consequence to him, burying his frustration deep inside. "She needed a place to stay. We're friends. And friends don't turn friends away when they need a place to stay."

"True." Wendy went to the kitchen opening, retrieved his breakfast and brought it to him. "But everyone remembers how you two were a couple for so long. That makes it hard to believe there's nothing going on now."

Aware she was pumping him for possible gossip to pass on, he dug into his scrambled eggs. After he'd washed down his first few bites with a slug of coffee, he looked up. She still stood in front of him, ignoring her other customers, clearly waiting.

"People change, Wendy," he said, returning his attention back to his meal. "What else can I say? People change."

After leaving the café, he took a stroll around town. He'd tried to force himself back onto his new bike, but like everything else inside his messed-up head, he found the idea made him shake. Actually shake, like a terrified toddler caught out in a thunderstorm. Not at all the way an army ranger should act.

This, his complete and utter lack of control over his own mind, his own reactions, was what infuriated him the most. PTSD be damned. He knew he was stronger than it was. All he had to do was get the upper hand on it.

Walking the sidewalks downtown filled him with

so many memories. In the year that he'd been away, only a few things had changed.

Main Street shops, from the shoe repair place to the ice cream store, did a steady business. There were other kinds of businesses downtown, too, law offices and dentists and doctors.

He was glad he didn't see anyone he knew since he wasn't in the mood to make small talk. The very ordinariness of this, a simple stroll in his childhood town, was exactly what he needed. Peace stole over him and he smiled.

And then a car backfired. It sounded remarkably like a gunshot.

Startled, he jumped. Heart pounding, he barely managed to keep from dropping in a "take cover" maneuver. Instead, he stumbled in a blind panic, crouching low, and as he caught himself, he tried to make the move look completely natural.

Sweating, he concentrated on his breathing. In and out, in and out, because he needed to calm the hell down.

Once he thought he had himself under control, he continued his walk, but the incident had ruined everything.

This had to stop. Now, instead of fear, anger filled him. Enough already. Hadn't he already been through enough? Whatever messed-up wiring had short-circuited in his brain needed to repair itself pronto. He'd never been the type of man afraid of his own shadow and he refused to be now.

Lost in thought, he nearly ran over an older woman coming out of the pet store with an ungainly, large black dog on a leash. He still bumped into her, but the impact turned out to be much less than it could have been if he hadn't caught himself just in time.

"I'm so sorry," he said. "Are you all right?"

Both she and the furry canine looked at him with nearly identical miserable expressions. Horrified, he realized she was crying.

"Are you hurt?" he asked, catching hold of her arm. This movement earned a surly growl from the dog, even though the beast barely raised his shaggy head.

The woman looked at him, not even bothering to wipe away her tears, and sighed. "You didn't hurt me, young man. I'm moving in with my daughter and her family in two days, and they won't let me bring Gus. I've put notices up everywhere, even online, but I haven't been able to find him a home. Doug inside the pet store thought he had a lead, but it didn't work out. I'm going to have to take him to the shelter, and I don't want to. It will be a death sentence for a dog like him."

If by "like him" she meant huge and black and furry, then he guessed she was right. Still… "Maybe he'll get adopted," he ventured, hoping to reassure her.

"It's a high-kill shelter," she replied. "And dogs that are surrendered by owner have less time than strays. He's only four years old and I've had him since he was a puppy. How can I possibly do that to him? How?"

And she started weeping in earnest, dropping to her knees and wrapping her frail arms around the large dog. Gus allowed this, even going so far as to attempt to lick away her tears.

"What kind of dog is he?" Kyle heard himself ask.

"He's a Belgian shepherd," she said, her voice garbled with sorrow. "And a good boy. A really good boy."

He couldn't say what got him more. The absolute heartbreaking love the old woman bore for her pet, or the stoic support the dog gave in return. The intelligence in the animal's eyes suggested he knew, maybe not exactly what was going to happen, but that it wasn't good.

"I've seen dogs like that before," he told her, shifting his weight awkwardly from one foot to the other. "In the military. They were trained for bomb detection."

"Yes, that's right." Pushing to her feet, she wiped away her tears. "They're a very smart breed. And Gus is smarter than any other dog I've ever owned. I've taught him to sit and lie down, to come and to roll over. He'll even give you his paw to shake."

He nodded, not quite sure what to say.

"Are you interested in giving him a home?" she asked, her voice quivering, her eyes pleading. "You'd come to love him, and he you. And you'd be saving his life."

Maybe it was the last sentence, or perhaps the force of her desperation, but he nodded. "I'll take him. But can you show me what kind of food he eats and tell me how much to feed him?"

And so twenty minutes and seventy-five dollars later, Kyle found himself the proud owner of a twenty-pound bag of dog food, bowls and a Belgian shepherd named Gus. He'd even promised to let his former owner visit him.

After an incredibly frustrating day dealing with the fire department, the sheriff's office and her insurance agent, all Nicole wanted to do was get home and put her feet up.

In reality, she couldn't go home—the fire captain had told her he hoped to soon have her house cleared for her to retrieve personal belongings, but it wouldn't be today.

So Kyle's house would have to do. She'd been lugging Jacob around so much all day that her arm and shoulder ached. When she saw his truck parked in the driveway, her heart rate kicked up.

After the day they'd had, even normally good-natured Jacob had gotten cranky. He needed to be changed and fed, in that order. She hoped once he had a full tummy, she could put him in his little play yard and he'd amuse himself with the brightly lit strand of plastic toys.

Despite everything that had happened, she got a rush just knowing she'd see Kyle again.

With Jacob in her arms, her overloaded diaper bag on her shoulder, she hurried into the house, using the key Kyle had given her.

The house was quiet, the television off. Sunlight streamed in through the big picture window. Kyle had taken a seat in the den, in the armchair facing the door, almost as if he were waiting for her. He held a book or pamphlet in his hands, like he'd been doing some reading.

She stopped short, her eyes widening as she caught sight of the shaggy giant black dog at Kyle's feet. A dog? Had she left the browser open on Kyle's computer to the article she'd read about PTSD service dogs?

"Hey," he greeted her, looking up from a pamphlet

he'd been reading. The animal looked up, regarding her with sad eyes. Immediately, her heart constricted.

"Where'd he—or she—come from?" she asked.

"He. His name is Gus." And he told her a story about meeting a crying elderly woman downtown in front of the pet store. "He's mine now," Kyle finished. She couldn't tell from his tone if this made him happy or not.

Settling Jacob into his Pack n' Play, she made her way slowly and carefully toward the huge dog. Gus raised his giant head, watching her closely. He gave three swift thumps of his plumed tail, letting her know he meant no harm.

When her fingers connected with his fur, she stroked him. "He's amazingly soft," she said.

"I gave him a bath." He studied his new pet. "I'm hoping once he gets used to being here—and me—he won't look so sad."

As she opened her mouth to agree with him, a loud crack of sound made her jump. Kyle took a dive from his chair to the floor. And Gus…in a flash the dog put himself in between the door and Kyle.

Outside, tires squealed and a vehicle gunned its engine, racing away.

At first, Nicole wasn't sure what to think. Kyle, still prone on the floor, appeared stricken. All the color had leached from his face. While she wasn't entirely sure if it would be better to attempt to comfort him or to pretend nothing untoward had happened, she made a split decision to go with the latter.

"What the heck was that?" she asked, heading for the door. The dog immediately got in front of her, blocking her way. She could have sworn the animal tried to herd her back to Kyle.

"Stay down," Kyle ordered, pushing himself up on his elbows. "Whatever you do, don't get in front of that window."

Though she obeyed, she worried. Was this part of his PTSD? While the sound could have been many things, she suspected it had been nothing more than a car backfiring. Or something equally harmless.

Except neither Kyle nor Gus appeared to think so. Now that she was no longer in danger, the black beast had returned to Kyle's side, leaning his huge, hairy body against him, as if offering a canine version of comfort.

Absently, Kyle tangled one hand in the animal's fur.

"Look." Kyle pointed, his eyes narrowed in what looked like fury. "There, the entryway wall directly across from the front door. That sure looks like a bullet."

Taking her cue from him, Nicole crawled over in the direction he'd pointed. Stunned, she realized he'd been right. "There's a bullet lodged here in the wall," she said. Turning, she checked out the front door, which was a weathered older wooden thing. "It went right through the front door. If one of us had been standing there, we could have been shot. What if I'd been holding Jacob?" Considering what could have happened, she started to shake.

"Jacob could have been hurt or killed." She could barely get the words out through clenched teeth. "Who would do such an awful thing?"

"Come here." He sat up, beckoned her over.

Though she wasn't entire sure what he meant, she complied, crawling over to sit next to him on the floor.

He hugged her again, this time just holding her, so tightly it felt as if he were both giving her strength and taking comfort from her as well.

"Someone is after you," she said. "But why?"

He gave her such a bleak look that she understood without him having to say a single word. If someone was after him, it was because of her. The shooter either truly believed Kyle had killed Bill so he could have Nicole, or their animosity toward him was because she was staying with him.

"It's all my fault that someone wants to kill you," she said softly. "We need to call the sheriff."

"Yes, we do," he agreed, his expression grave as he reached for his phone. "Because there's one other possibility you're overlooking. It's entirely possible someone wants you dead, Nicole."

Chapter 11

The sheriff himself showed up to take the report, the grim set of his mouth a hint as to his mood. "Trouble seems to follow you wherever you go, doesn't it?" he said to Nicole.

Though Kyle didn't appreciate that remark, he kept his mouth shut, waiting to see how Nicole would react. When she only smiled sadly, as if in agreement, he knew he had to intervene.

Stepping forward so he drew the portly sheriff's attention, Kyle cleared his throat. "I don't think it's fair of you to insinuate that any of this is Nicole's fault." He kept his tone even and quiet. He watched as the other man studied him.

Finally, Sheriff Cantrell nodded. "You're right. But son, that was only a joke. You see, I've known Nicole since she was knee-high. My wife and I go to church with her parents." His tone seemed to indicate that this should be the end of it.

But then Nicole stepped up to stand beside Kyle. "I do understand that, Sheriff. But this has been an awful time for me. I'm scared and I'm stressed. How about you cut me a little slack?"

At this, the older man had the grace to apologize. "I'm sorry. Now why don't you two tell me exactly what happened, so I can make my report and get out of your hair."

As he stepped into the room, Gus rose from where he'd been lying near the sofa. Huge head cocked, the dog studied the man as if performing threat assessment. Kyle had seen a few military dogs act exactly the same way, making him wonder again about his new pet's background. But now, the woman had said she'd had him as a puppy. This meant there was no way Gus could have served.

The entire time they answered the sheriff's questions, Gus watched quietly from the same spot. When the older man finally finished and turned to go, Gus pushed to his feet and followed him toward the door. The sheriff eyed the huge animal more than once, more curious than uneasy, but didn't comment or make any move to pet Gus.

Kyle stood next to Nicole with his dog at his side and watched Sheriff Cantrell drive off. Though he ached to touch her, he managed to keep his distance.

"Thank you for coming to my defense earlier," she said softly. "I appreciate it."

He shook his head. "You handled yourself pretty damn well."

Her eyes shone as she smiled at him, making his

chest ache. "Thank you," she said. "I'm learning to stand up for myself."

Damn. His entire body blazed with the need to touch her, kiss her, press his body against her and show her exactly how proud he was. But he couldn't, or he shouldn't, so he didn't. Instead, he forced his legs to move and walked away from her without another word, into the kitchen. "I'm making tacos for dinner," he announced, even though he knew she'd followed him.

When he turned, she was right there. So was Gus. The dog eyed the package of hamburger meat hopefully.

"Tacos sound great," she said. "Is there anything I can help you do?"

"No."

She didn't move.

"Did you need something?" he finally asked, carefully impersonal even though his damn heart had started up that rapid tattoo beat again. He didn't want food, he wanted her. And he had to do his damndest to keep that from showing.

Surprise and then hurt flashed across her mobile face. She shook her head and backed away so fast it was a miracle she didn't stumble and fall. At first, she left Jacob playing, but at the last moment, she picked him up, crooning to him softly as she carried him away.

Kyle almost called her back. Almost. Instead, he gritted his teeth and kept busy browning hamburger meat.

When everything was done, he called her name. She returned a moment later, all solemn and serious, which usually meant she'd want to talk. Which he definitely did not want to do. He needed to process this—all of it. His overwhelming need for her, their shared past, her recent one and the fact that someone clearly wanted to harm her.

If they were going to talk, that's what they needed to discuss. A list of potential suspects that they could give to the police.

After setting up a place near the table for Jacob to play with his rattle toy, she looked at Kyle. "With all that's going on, I'm not letting him out of my sight," she said. He agreed that was wise, still keeping his tone as impersonal as possible.

Despite this, in spite of his best attempts, electricity still swirled in the air around them, making it difficult to breathe normally. Her every movement, the rustle of her clothing, the faint scent of her body lotion, all overwhelmed his senses. He wondered if she felt it too, the über-sensitivity and the constant thrum of desire, or if this insanity belonged only to him.

She certainly appeared unaffected with her relaxed posture and easy movements.

They ate in relative silence. In addition to the taco meat, he had warmed both flour and corn tortillas, chopped fresh tomato and lettuce, shredded cheese, and gotten out some salsa. She had three tacos and declared herself stuffed, sitting back in her chair with a satisfied grin. Again, he marveled at how her smile affected him, wondering if she had any idea. Though he'd already eaten four tacos, he reached for another, which he ate as slowly as possible, mostly to avoid any chance of discussion. Discussion, hell, he wanted to pull her from that chair right on top of him, and touch and kiss her until they'd shed their clothes and he'd buried himself deep inside her.

The image not only made him burn, but his body swelled with arousal. At his feet, Gus raised his shaggy head and eyed the leftovers, despite the fact that Kyle had just filled the dog's bowl with kibble, which Gus devoured in less than three minutes.

"I'll clean up," Nicole announced, the instant he finished, clearly unaware of the way his desire for her clouded his every thought. "Thank you for a great meal." Her bright and cheerful tone made him realize she was doing the exact same thing as he—working hard to keep all interaction to the surface. Banal and friendly.

Which suited him fine. And didn't. His entire being wanted her, craved her, but his mind kept warning him against it. Maybe they should talk. Talking would be better than sitting here with detailed erotic images filling his head.

"I never did get to tell you about my day," she said, her back to him while she rinsed dishes and put them in his dishwasher.

He latched on to this quickly. "No, you didn't. What happened?"

"The police are still working all leads, the fire department has an arson investigation going on and my insurance won't pay me a dime while I'm under an arson investigation." She said the words matter-of-factly, her back straight and her posture rigid.

"In other words," she continued. "No one is going to make a move to repair my house until they make sure I wasn't the one who set it on fire."

"I'm sorry," he said, knowing the words were inadequate. "Hopefully they'll figure out something soon."

"Will they?" She put the last pan away and dried her hands on a dish towel. Turning to face him, she shook her head. "I'm beginning to feel like the entire world is against me."

He had no words for that, especially since he'd felt the exact same way since he'd returned home and learned the one woman he'd expected to always be there for him had married another man.

Sadness darkened her eyes at his lack of response. "Time for me to bathe Jacob," she said, gathering up their son. "After that, I'll probably be reading in my room. I'll see you in the morning."

He nodded, managing an impersonal smile even though relief mingled with disappointment. "I'll try to keep the TV volume down so it doesn't disturb you."

When she left the room carrying Jacob, he hoped he could finally relax. He planted himself on the couch, pulled up an action/adventure movie and tried like hell to concentrate on anything but Nicole.

The next morning, Kyle woke up early. After showering and downing two cups of strong black coffee, he headed to Walmart, where he picked up a complete security camera system. He spent the rest of the day installing it on the outside of his house.

"There," he told Nicole when he'd finished. "Now we'll have video. I think we'll all sleep better tonight."

"Between that and your big dog, I think we're well protected," she said with a wry grimace.

She seemed a bundle of nervous energy, constantly in motion, as if afraid to stop. He watched as she kept herself occupied with busywork. She'd made muffins, arranged them on a platter and had put herself to work reorganizing his pantry. Since he'd just kind of shoved stuff in there with no real method of organization, he welcomed the help, though he wasn't sure why she felt compelled to do this now.

"This afternoon is Grandparents' Day at my mother's church," she finally told him. "I'm letting her take Jacob. To be honest, I'm a little bit nervous."

"A little bit?" He raised one brow.

"Fine. I'm terrified." She swallowed hard. "My mom has never been alone with Jacob. I'm worried she won't know what to do."

"She raised you, didn't she?"

She nodded.

"And there will be a lot of other grandparents there to help her. I'm sure everything will be fine."

Though he wasn't sure if his words helped reassure her, when he ran into her as she was about to leave to drop Jacob off, she seemed much calmer.

As he watched her bundle Jacob up in the back of her car, he felt the unfamiliar urge to go out there and kiss his son goodbye. Instead, he watched until she'd driven away, and then got into his own truck and drove to the army recruiting office. Though they'd never followed through on actually calling him in to work, he'd gotten into the habit of occasionally stopping by and shooting the breeze with whoever was on duty that day. It was a pleasant way of occupying an hour or two and made him feel connected to the organization that had once represented his entire world.

When he got home ninety minutes later, he was surprised to see Nicole had not yet returned. He figured she was probably out running errands, enjoying as best she could her status as child-free for a few hours.

He made himself a tall glass of iced tea and sat down at the kitchen table with his laptop, checking his email. Several of his ranger buddies emailed to check in on him. Since they regaled him with nonclassified stories, he looked forward to reading these emails.

He'd barely gotten settled when the front door slammed open and Nicole burst through. Eyes wild, expression panicked, she skidded to a stop when she saw him. "I need your help," she said, talking too fast, the words tumbling over each other. "It's Jacob." She broke down, weeping copiously.

Jacob? A chill scuttled up his spine. Instantly, he put himself in crisis mode. Early on in his ranger training, he'd learned how to separate himself from his emotions in order to function better at the task at hand.

Instead of offering Nicole comfort, he'd find a solution instead. "What happened to Jacob?" he asked, his voice crisp. "Is he sick? Is he hurt? Where is he?"

Something in his matter-of-fact tone must have gotten through to her. She sniffled, and straightened. "Theresa Mabry has him." She took a deep breath, clearly trying not to strangle on panic. "And she's told me she's not giving him back. She says possession is nine-tenths of the law."

"She's wrong," he told her. "She can't get away with this." He pulled her close, hoping his matter-of-fact tone would slow her racing heartbeat. "Take a deep breath. I need you to be as calm and rational as possible. Tell me what happened."

To his relief, she did as he'd asked, though the way she gulped in air told him she still had a long way to go before calmness was anywhere in her radar. "I thought Jacob was with your mom," he finally prompted.

"He was. I took him over to my mother's house so she could take him to Grandparents' Day at the church. I was a little nervous, but I let her. As I told you, it was actually her first attempt at being a real grandmother." She sniffled. "I was hopeful that maybe things could change between us."

"Please tell me your mother didn't do this," he pleaded. "Tell me she didn't plan for Theresa to get ahold of our son all along."

Nicole started shaking her head before he'd even finished speaking. "She didn't. She's really upset. She let Theresa hold him while she went to use the restroom. When she came back, Theresa and Jacob were gone." Her mouth began trembling. "They don't even have an infant carrier for their car. I got back the one I loaned my mother. What if they were in an accident or something?"

"One thing at a time." He hugged her close. "Did you call Theresa or go by her house?"

"I called first. That's when she told me she wasn't giving him back." She took a deep, shaky breath. "After that, I drove over there. My mom came with me in her own car. Theresa refused to even answer the door. We knew she was home because her car was in the driveway."

"Where's your mother now?"

"I sent her home. She kept saying she didn't want people to start talking. That's what she always worries about, how she appears to others. That's my absolute last concern. Since she wasn't helping, I simply asked her to leave."

He could understand that. "What about Dan? Does he know about this?"

"I don't know." She pulled out her cell, her hands trembling so badly she nearly dropped it. "Let me call him and see."

Still holding her tucked under his arm, he waited while she called and listened.

"No answer," she finally said. "I don't know what to do."

"I do. You have no choice but to call the police."

"Let me get this straight." If anything, Sheriff Cantrell seemed unhappier than ever. "You want to file kidnapping charges against your mother-in-law?"

"Yes." Nicole stood tall, her chin lifted. "She took my son without permission from a church event. I've contacted her and she's refusing to give him back."

"Oh geez." Pinching the top of his nose, the sheriff looked down at his desk. He shuffled a few papers around before returning his gaze to meet hers. "He's her grandson," he exclaimed. "Have you been keeping her from seeing him or something?"

"What does that matter?" Nicole glared. "I fail to see how any of that has bearing on this issue. They took my son without permission. That's against the law. Since you are the one charged with keeping the law in this town, I need you to do something about it."

"Like what?" He glared right back. "What exactly do you propose?"

"Send some armed deputies over there and retrieve him. Do what you have to do—I don't care. Just get my boy back, unharmed."

Kyle, who until now had been silent, spoke up. "I

don't understand your reluctance, Sheriff. Would you care to explain?"

The older man heaved a big sigh. "This is a small town. You two know that as well as anyone. Word gets around. How is it going to look if I arrest Theresa Mabry for wanting to see her own grandson? Have you thought about that?"

"How is it going to look?" Repeating his words back to him, Nicole's volume increased with each syllable. She couldn't believe how much he sounded like her mother. "I don't care how it looks. Nor should you. The woman committed a crime." She pushed to her feet. "Get. My. Son. Back."

Finally, the sheriff appeared to understand that she meant business. Still, he hesitated. "Are you sure?"

"Absolutely positive. I want to press charges."

"I've been working here twenty-seven years," Cantrell muttered. "I might be new to this position, but I'm not new to this town. I thought I'd seen everything as a deputy. Not once in all that time have I ever dealt with anything as crazy as this." He pushed up from behind his desk, lumbering past them on his way to the door.

Before leaving, he turned and looked at Nicole and Kyle. "If you two want to come, you're welcome to ride in the back of my squad car."

She needed no second urging. Stomach churning, all she could think about was how badly she needed to see her baby and make sure he was all right.

To her surprise, Sheriff Cantrell didn't enlist any of his deputies for backup. He drove over to the Mabry's with Nicole and Kyle in the backseat. On the way there, he kept up a steady stream of chatter, most of it revolving around "domestic disputes" and how talking could often resolve family issues.

Preoccupied with worry, Nicole didn't bother to even try and keep up, never mind respond. When she sighed for the third time, Kyle took her hand and laced his fingers with hers. "It's going to be all right," he murmured. "Theresa Mabry won't hurt Jacob." She nodded, hoping with all her heart that he was right. Her former mother-in-law had clearly lost her mind. She could only pray that didn't extend to harming a defenseless infant.

When they pulled up in front of the Mabrys' house, the sheriff ordered them to wait in the car. Though doing so violated every maternal instinct inside Nicole, she complied. Vibrating with tension, she watched as he walked up to the front porch and rang the doorbell. Nothing happened. The door remained closed.

"She's not going to open it," she told Kyle.

He squeezed her hand. "Wait and see. Surely she'll see reason."

The sheriff waited another moment and rang it again, with the same nonresult. He turned and faced the squad car and shrugged. Shrugged!

"He'd better not be thinking of giving up." Nicole started to push up out of the backseat but Kyle pulled her back down.

"Wait," he said. "Give him another minute."

But instead, the sheriff returned to the squad car. "She won't answer the door. Guess I'm going to have to get a search warrant."

"Seriously?" Nicole protested. "I can't believe this."

"Maybe you could try calling her," Kyle suggested.

"She might be more amenable to listening to reason from you."

Sheriff Cantrell looked from him to Nicole and then back again. He sighed. "Damned if I know what Theresa Mabry is thinking. Must be her grief talking. She knows she can't just go around taking home other people's babies without permission, even if this one is her grandson."

"Call her," Kyle urged again.

Frowning, the sheriff finally agreed. "It's worth a shot," he said, pulling out his phone and going through his contacts. "I've got her in here somewhere."

It didn't surprise Nicole one bit that he had Theresa Mabry's number since he attended the same church. The church considered themselves all one big family.

Apparently, Theresa answered. "I've got the boy's mother in the car with me," he told her. "You need to open the door and give her back her son."

And then he listened. And listened. Though she couldn't make out all the words, Nicole could hear enough to realize Theresa had unleashed a torrent of invectives at him.

To his credit, he didn't interrupt, just waited until she apparently finished. "Nicole has informed me she will press charges," he finally said. "Since she wishes to do so, I will be getting a search warrant. If you choose not to hand the baby over peacefully, we will enter your home and remove him forcibly. And you will be arrested. Is that what you want?"

Again the sheriff listened, this time only briefly. He turned to Nicole. "If she releases Jacob to you right now without a fight, will you drop all charges?"

"Yes." Nicole didn't even have to think. "All I want is my baby back."

He relayed this information to Theresa. "Sounds good," he finally said, and ended the call. "Come on. Let's go and get your boy."

When Kyle also got out, Sheriff Cantrell stopped him with a hard look. "Son, I think it's best if you wait out here."

"No," Nicole countered immediately. "I want him with me for support."

With Kyle at her side, she followed Sheriff Cantrell back up the steps to the front door. Theresa opened the door before they reached it. She held Jacob in her arms.

"Here," she said, passing him over. "I bought some diapers and changed him, but he wouldn't take the bottle of formula I tried to give him."

Accepting her son, Nicole breathed in his precious baby scent. "He's still being breastfed," she managed, blinking back tears. "I don't understand how you could do this, Theresa. I've lost so much these past few days. Why would you want to take my son away too?"

The older woman looked at her, really looked. Her haughty, remote expression crumbled. "Jacob is all I have left of my son," she said. "Please don't take him from me too."

Nicole stared. "Theresa, ever since Bill died, you've done nothing but treat me like dirt. You've accused me of everything under the sun. Now you try to steal my child?"

Nicole shook her head. "You know what? This has been a hard time for me too. I could have used your support. You're lucky I agreed not to press charges."

With that, she turned and walked back to the patrol car. Kyle followed her. The sheriff lingered a moment or two, talking to Theresa, before he joined them.

"I think she's really sorry," he said, starting the engine. "Maybe you were a little harsh on her?"

"Or maybe not," Nicole responded. "You have no idea how awful she's been to me. And really, this is none of your business." If Theresa really wanted to mend fences, Nicole would try. But it wasn't going to be easy and it would take some time.

Once Sheriff Cantrell had dropped them off at Kyle's house and they'd gone inside, Kyle sighed. "Are you ever going to tell her Jacob isn't Bill's son?"

Stricken, she swallowed as she placed Jacob in his play yard. "I don't know," she admitted. "Not only would that be one more missile in her arsenal against me, but I kind of hate to take that last connection away from her."

"She's been awful to you."

"I know. And I hate that. Before she lost her son, she treated me okay. She wasn't ever really warm, but she was civil. Maybe the grief made her act so crazy."

Jaw tight, he studied her. "I have to say, I'm not cool with the idea of continuing to let everyone believe Jacob is Bill's son. He's mine."

Again, unwanted tears welled up in her eyes. "You're willing to publicly claim him?"

"Of course. Why wouldn't I be?"

She looked down, taking a necessary moment to get her emotions back under control. "There will be a lot of fallout, you know. My mother will be livid. The Mabrys will be shattered."

When she raised her gaze, she found him watching her. "What about you?" he asked, his voice soft. "What do you want?"

"I'm tired of lying. I want everyone to know the truth. It's what I'll tell my—our—son when he's old enough to want to know. I don't want him pining after a man who was never a father to him, biologically or emotionally." She wiped the back of her hand across her eyes.

"Thank you." The gruffness of his tone spoke to his own deep emotional reaction. "Jacob is all I have. My only blood relation, my family. I'm glad you're not willing to ask me to give that connection up."

Startled, she frowned. "I'd never ask that of you. I'm not willing to deprive my son of his father. But I would like to wait a little bit before we announce this. There's too much already going on."

"Agreed." From across the room, he met and held her gaze. "I do need to ask you though if you've given any thought to what you want to happen to Jacob in the event you're hurt or killed."

A quick flash of pain ripped through her. How easily he said those awful words. Dying before she'd raised Jacob, leaving him without a mother, would be her worst nightmare.

"Not that I plan on letting anything happen to you," Kyle continued. "I'll protect you with my own life, if need be."

Startled she eyed him. Her unspoken question must have shown in her gaze because he continued, answering it without her ever having to ask.

"Because you're the mother of my son," he said. "No one can take that away from you. Whatever happens between us, that will never change."

Though it wasn't exactly what she'd secretly hoped to hear, for now it would have to be enough.

"And no matter what the Mabrys or your parents' church will think, the fact remains that I am Jacob's father. No one can take that away from me either."

Unless she allowed it. Which she had, so far. Even now, with her entire life in such upheaval, she still hesitated to rock the boat any further.

But as she considered, she realized Kyle had a point. If she were to die right this instant, the Mabrys would gain custody of Jacob, believing him to be their own grandson. Kyle would have to go to court, force a DNA test, and more, all to try to regain custody of his own child. After all he'd been through in service of his country, he didn't deserve that.

"You're right," she admitted. "With all that's going on, I need to make sure no one could separate you and Jacob. I'll write out instructions and have them notarized immediately. Since you're listed as his father on the birth certificate, that should be enough. As for publicly…" She paused.

Expression impassive, he waited.

"This Sunday, I'll make an announcement at my parents' church. The Mabrys will be in attendance. After that, you know how fast news will spread in this town."

"While I like that idea," he said slowly, "I'm thinking the note will be enough for right now. I don't want to goad whoever set your house on fire and shot at us. Let's keep a lid on this until that person or people are caught."

And then, while she mulled this over, he crossed the room, hauled her up against him and kissed her.

Chapter 12

As his mouth covered hers, Nicole let herself melt into the kiss. She needed this—feeling, rather than thinking, desire instead of worry and fear. She needed him. She always needed him.

He tangled his hands in her hair, keeping her close.

A sound escaped her, something between a moan and a plea. He pushed his body against her, hard and muscular and fully aroused. Of course her body responded instantly.

"Kyle." Clutching at him, she tried to get him closer. But there were clothes in between them, and the best she could do was press herself into him.

And then he moved away and turned his back to her, his harsh breathing and the rigid line of his back a testament to how hard he worked to get himself under control.

Aroused and confused, she put her fist against her mouth, trying to make sense of his actions.

"I'm sorry," he finally rasped. "I promised this wouldn't happen again."

She gathered up her courage. "What if I want it to?"

Slowly, he turned the face her. The tormented look in his eyes caused her heart to break. "It won't work, Nicole."

"Why not?" she challenged him. "Sometimes, there are things worth fighting for. We can find our way back to where we were. There's even more reason to try now, with Jacob. We can be a family finally, Kyle. I know it."

"Find our way back?" he repeated, his tone incredulous. "You have no idea what happened to me, do you?"

"Of course I do. You've been through hell. You have PTSD—"

"I don't," he snarled, interrupting her. "I'm a ranger. We don't get PTSD."

His vehement denial felt like her heart had been torn in two. "Maybe not," she said. "But you can't deny you have some issues. There is help out there, if you'll just reach out for it. Let them help you, let me help you. Heck, let Gus help you. I read an article about how dogs can be trained to assist with PTSD. Maybe you could train him."

When she finished her rush of words, he simply stared at her, his expression as hard as his gaze.

"I don't need help," he insisted. "I'll find my own damn way back. Sua Sponte." And he turned and left the room. After a moment, Gus heaved himself up from his spot on the rug and followed him.

With her body still throbbing, she took a seat at the kitchen table and tried to think. Her heart ached for him, and she wished he would at least let her try to help him.

Later, she looked up the phrase and learned it meant Of Their Own Accord. The motto of the Seventy-fifth Ranger Regiment. At least she finally understood why Kyle thought he had to do everything on his own.

The next day dawned bright and beautiful, with the promise of heat later in the day. Nicole decided to drive into town and have a word with the sheriff, assuming he was working. Surprisingly, her mother had called, asking if she could babysit Jacob for a few hours that morning. "I'd really like to spend some time with my grandson," she said. "I'm really sorry for what happened."

A tiny spark of hope flared in Nicole's breast. Her mother truly sounded genuine. Add to that the fact that Fran wanted to visit with Jacob in her home rather than somewhere publicly, and Nicole allowed herself to believe.

Once she'd verified that Fran planned to stay home with him, Nicole agreed to drop him off. After that, she planned to visit both the sheriff and the fire department. She needed to get things moving so she could get back inside her own home.

Sheriff Cantrell did not look happy to see her. No, judging from the downward turn of his mouth, he'd rather be somewhere else entirely than trapped in his office with her.

"What can I do for you, Mrs. Mabry?" he asked, steepling his hands in front of him on his desk and regarding her with a weary expression.

Since he didn't offer her a chair, she continued to stand. "I came to see if you were able to find out if Bill had a mistress."

"I can't comment on an active investigation," he began.

"Really?" A spark of anger fueled her words. "My husband is killed. I find suspicious credit card statements. Someone breaks into my house, and then sets it on fire, shoots at me, and all you can say to me is that you can't comment? Do you see anything wrong with this picture?"

At least he had the grace to appear abashed. "What I can say is that you've been cleared. You're no longer a suspect."

She snorted. "As if I ever was. And I can well imagine that Theresa and Dan Mabry have been in here on a regular basis, demanding answers. I'm sure you don't try this 'can't comment on an active investigation' with them. If you did, I know there'd be hell to pay."

When he looked down, a muscle in his jaw working, she knew she had him.

"Have a seat, Ms. Mabry," he finally said. "I'll tell you what I can. It's not a whole lot, but it's something. I will need you to promise not to get hysterical when I tell you what we've learned so far."

Hysterical? Reminding herself that this man didn't know her at all, she pulled out a chair across from the desk. Once she'd taken a seat, she placed her hands demurely in her lap and waited to hear what he had to say.

"You were actually correct," he began. "Your husband did have a lady friend. Don't ask me for her name, because I'm not at liberty to say. We've also been investigating some other ties he apparently had."

"Ties?" she questioned. "The kind of ties that would make him empty our savings account?"

"Yes. We subpoenaed the bank records and saw that." He didn't look away, though his expression had softened. "He left you and his child with nothing. Even the house is heavily mortgaged, as I'm sure you're aware. I'm sorry that happened to you."

The mortgage. Something she hadn't even thought about. How on earth was she going to come up with the money to make payments?

"I'm sorry too," she murmured, filing that particular worry away for later. "But to get back on track, what exactly were these ties?"

He shook his head. "Again, I can't speculate at this time until we have proof."

"Then whatever it was is illegal?" she guessed. Though he didn't speak, he nodded.

"You cannot mention any of this to anyone, do you understand? If word gets out, it could seriously hamper our investigation."

"Of course," she murmured. She shouldn't have been surprised that Bill had extended his reach into drugs. "He also had a serious drinking problem, you know." Looking down at her hands, she forced herself to raise her chin and meet the other man's gaze. "He got mean when he drank."

Squinting at her, the sheriff finally gave a slow nod.

"We're investigating all his known associates," he continued, as if she hadn't spoken. "And we haven't entirely ruled out your boyfriend either."

He spoke this last so matter-of-factly that at first, it didn't register.

When it did, she sat up straighter. Now it was her turn to narrow her eyes. "I'm assuming you mean Kyle?"

"Yep. Unless you have another boyfriend."

She let that one slide. "First off, Kyle is not my boyfriend. Not anymore. I'm staying with him because some psycho made my house unlivable. And second, he wasn't even in town when Bill was murdered. Finally, Kyle had no motivation."

"Really, now?" Sheriff Cantrell leaned back in his chair, eyeing her as if assessing her intelligence. "How do you know that?"

"Because he told me." Realizing how that sounded, she shook her head. "I'm sure it will be pretty easy to verify his whereabouts. He drove here from Georgia and I'm sure he had to stop at least once, if not more, along the way."

"That's the thing," he drawled. "He did show us a motel receipt. But that only puts him in Mississippi two days before your husband was murdered. He had plenty of time to arrive here in town and do what he had to do."

"But…" Stunned, she could only stare. "I don't think you understand. Kyle was in a coma for months, then rehab. He had no idea I was even married, never mind to whom. At least not until he got here."

"Funny thing, that's not what your mother says. She says ole Kyle called for you from his hospital bed, shortly after he regained consciousness. She also said she passed on the news to him of your marriage then."

"She's lying." Nicole hadn't meant to speak her

thought out loud, but once she had, she couldn't exactly unsay it. "My mother has never liked Kyle. I know for a fact she wouldn't have been able to resist telling me about that call if it had really happened, if only to rub it in."

"Young lady." Sheriff Cantrell sat up straight. "You are aware of the consequences if you're covering for him. You can be named an accessory to murder and do serious jail time. You'd best ask yourself if he's worth all that."

"You can't be serious," she shot back. "Please, check out the telephone records. I'll bet when you do, you won't find any record of that call."

Gaze cool, he stood. "We're in the process of doing exactly that. While Kyle Benning isn't our only suspect, he's definitely one of the prime ones. I'd advise you to confess if you know anything."

Confess. She had no words left. "Thank you, Sheriff. Please keep me advised if you turn up any valid leads."

On the drive home, she could scarcely contain her agitation. While she had no idea who really killed Bill, damned if she was going to let Kyle be railroaded into taking the blame. Because while Kyle might have been furious to learn she'd married Bill, his anger wouldn't have been for her husband. No, Kyle had been furious with her.

And her mother. Forcing herself to stay within the speed limit, she drove to her mother's house. When she arrived, she let herself in. Fran was sitting in the rocking chair, holding Jacob. She looked up when Nicole walked in.

"He's been changed and seems sleepy, but I didn't

want to put him down for a nap, so I've been rocking him," Fran said happily. "He really is a sweet boy."

"He is," Nicole agreed. "Mom, I just left the sheriff. He claims you told him that Kyle called you from his hospital bed, right after he woke from his coma. Is that true?"

Fran's expression turned mulish. "You need to push him out of your life, Nicole. If you don't, he's going to ruin everything."

"Mother, you didn't answer my question. Did you tell Sheriff Cantrell that Kyle called you from his hospital bed and you relayed the news that I'd gotten married?"

The older woman pursed her lips but didn't speak.

"You know you're not supposed to lie," Nicole pressed. "Please, tell me the truth."

"Fine. I did say that. I really want that man arrested and away from you."

"For a crime he didn't commit?" Nicole crossed her arms. "I want you to call the sheriff and tell him the truth."

When Fran didn't respond, Nicole pushed harder. "Mother, he's already checking the phone records to see if there was any such call. You're going to get caught in a lie anyway. You might as well come clean."

Finally, Fran's shoulders sagged in defeat. "Here. Take your baby. I'll call right now and clear things up."

Jacob woke as his grandmother passed him back to his mother. He smiled up at Nicole, his eyes sleepy. As she placed him back in his car carrier, he went back to sleep.

Nicole listened as Fran spoke to Sheriff Cantrell, explaining she'd been confused. Kyle had actually come to her house as soon as he'd arrived in town, and had no idea Nicole had gotten married until she had told him. This was, as best as she could recall, shortly after Bill had been found murdered.

Imagining what Kyle must have thought made Nicole's heart ache. She could well understand how betrayed he must have felt. No wonder he'd been so furious with her.

Something of her tumultuous emotions must have shown in her face. After ending the call, Fran shook her head. "Don't look so stricken. You were married. It was the right thing to do. It'd would have been different if he'd gotten in touch with you before you married Bill."

"He was almost killed and then he was in a coma for months, Mom. And when he did try to call, my cell phone had been disconnected. Remember, Bill made me get on his plan as soon as we got engaged. Everything was under his name, so there was no way for Kyle to find me."

"That's not true," Fran argued. "He could have called the house. I don't understand why he didn't." Her lip curled. "I mean, if he was so in love with you, you'd think he would have made more of an effort."

"Your number is unlisted. Even if he used directory assistance or the internet, he wouldn't have been able to find it."

Pursing her lips, Fran finally shrugged. "I don't understand why you're still involved with him. You had a life, a very good life. Why would you want to take a step backward, into the past?"

"Mom, what do you have against Kyle? You've always disliked him."

"He was a hoodlum," Fran answered.

"Mom. He wasn't. And he joined the army after graduation. He became an Army Ranger, which isn't an easy feat. He served our country."

"True enough," Fran admitted. "But tell me honestly. What is it you see in him?"

There were several different ways Nicole could have answered that question, but every single one of them led back to the same place. Love. She'd loved Kyle from the first day she'd met him. Her love had never gone away, even when she'd mistakenly believed him dead. She wasn't going backward at all, but into the future. The future that the two of them always should have head.

But eying her mother, who stood with her arms crossed, waiting, Nicole knew Fran would never understand. She'd never been a fan of what her daughter saw in that "boy from the wrong side of the tracks."

"Never mind," Nicole responded gently. "Just promise me, Mom. No more lies."

Fran opened her mouth as if to protest, and then closed it. Finally, she nodded.

After kissing her mother on the cheek, Nicole left.

As soon as she got back to Kyle's house, she hustled herself and Jacob inside. Kyle was in the kitchen, making himself a sandwich. Gus sat right next to him, looking up with a hopeful gaze. "Hey," Kyle said, smiling. "What's up?"

"Do you mind telling me something? When did you learn I'd gotten married? Did you call my mother?"

"No." He didn't even blink. "I tried several times to call your cell phone, but kept getting a recording that it had been disconnected. I didn't remember your parents' number, and I called directory assistance, but it was unlisted. When I got to town, I drove to your parents' house. Your mother answered the door and she's the one who gleefully told me."

"Interesting." She relayed what Sheriff Cantrell had said earlier. "I stopped by my mom's house on the way home and after I got her to admit to lying, I made her call the sheriff and confess the truth."

Kyle's jaw tightened. "Thank you. But I don't understand why your mother would say such a thing. Especially to a law enforcement officer investigating a murder."

Nicole took a deep breath. "Because she has never liked you. Not when we were kids, or teens, or now that we're young adults. She'll do whatever she can to keep us apart."

"Even try to put me in jail?"

"Yes. Even that." To her annoyance, she found herself blinking back tears. She forced herself to continue. "I've never understood how a mother could not want her own daughter to be happy, but she's never wanted you and I to be together. She did whatever she could to keep us apart. Remember how I had to sneak out to see you?"

Gaze never leaving her face, he nodded. "I remember. You used to make jokes about it."

"To hide how much it hurt," she admitted. "I've never been able to figure out what I did to deserve her treating me that way, her own daughter. It wasn't only that I got pregnant out of wedlock, because she started treating me like her enemy from the time I reached puberty."

She took a deep breath. "When we received word

that you'd been killed in action, she was so happy. She tried to hide it from me, but I could tell. Even while I grieved, she was making plans to marry me off to Bill Mabry."

Without another word, he crossed the space between them and pulled her close for a hug. She let him hold her, basking in the warmth of his embrace, his touch chasing away those lingering feelings of regret.

"Okay?" he asked, pulling back enough to see into her eyes.

"Yes." She nodded. "Thank you. I still can't believe she was trying to frame you for murder."

"It'll never happen." He sounded so certain, so positive that she almost smiled. "I didn't do anything. All the lies in the word can't change the truth. Your husband's real killer is out there. If the police are focused on the facts, they'll catch him."

"Sheriff Cantrell did seem to be investigating every possible lead." She told him about Bill having a mistress, and also what the sheriff had said about possibly illegal dealings. "Of course, no one can know this. If word got out, it could hamper the investigation."

"I understand," he said. "And I won't say a word."

That night, Kyle had one of his realistic nightmares. Same as always. A flash of light, left side. Ringing in the ears. An explosion, knocking him off his feet. Even though he knew what was coming next, he couldn't seem to wake up. What was the point? Even when he finally managed to force himself to wake, he couldn't shake the feeling of terror or get the horrific images out of his head.

Heart thundering in his chest, he wanted to run.

To let his feet pound the pavement, until he could no longer breathe.

But the last time he'd done this, after lacing up his sneakers and heading out into the night, everything had gotten worse. Too many shadows and menacing figures. He'd become jumpy, for the first time ever glad he hadn't grabbed his pistol.

No, he'd stay in the house. He could better wrestle his internal demons to the ground when secure inside four walls. No other menace to deal with but himself.

Drenched in sweat, he got up and roamed the house, pacing, craving a cigarette even though he'd given up the habit almost as quickly as he'd started it while in basic training.

Gus, who'd come awake instantly, followed him from room to room, toenails clicking on the wooden floor. The dog appeared relaxed, but alert. Kyle wished he found this comforting, but he was locked too deep into the frenzy of his own inner torment.

To release some of the swirling madness inside him, he needed to hit something, so after a frantic look around the room, he began pummeling the sofa pillows.

On the floor near him, Gus whined. Distracted, Kyle's blows faltered as he glanced down at his dog. As if sensing an opening, Gus pushed his nose under Kyle's elbow. He whined again, tilting his head sideways before nudging Kyle again.

Kyle dropped to his knees, letting Gus lean into him. He buried his fingers in his pet's black fur, and Gus licked at Kyle's face, washing away tears Kyle hadn't even been aware were there.

He didn't know how long he sat there, arms

wrapped around Gus. All he knew was gradually, some of the panic and fury leaked out of him. His heartbeat slowed, his breathing evened out and he felt safe again. Almost normal. Maybe Nicole had been right. Maybe Gus could help him find a way out of this darkness. He'd check out training on the internet, though he wasn't sure Gus actually needed any. The dog appeared to be doing just fine on his own.

"Are you all right?" Nicole asked.

Kyle started, though he kept his arms wrapped around Gus. He glanced up to find her standing in the doorway, her hair tousled, her eyes still full of sleep. She wore only an oversized T-shirt, her sexy legs and bare feet telling him she'd come straight from her bed.

"How long have you been there?" he asked, his voice as rough as if he'd smoked a half pack of cigarettes.

"What?" She took a couple more steps into the room. "I just woke up. I had a feeling…" She stopped and dragged her hands through her already mussed hair. "I had a feeling something was wrong, so I came to check."

Relieved that she hadn't seen him while in his pillow-bashing frenzy, he nodded. "Everything's good. Go on back to sleep."

For a second he thought she might do exactly that, turn and make her way back to her room and the comfy mattress. Instead, she crossed the space separating them and took a seat on the other end of the couch.

"Are you sure you're…" She looked down. "I mean, it's the middle of the night and you seem a little off."

Off. Interesting way of putting it. "I just needed

to think," he said. "Gus here is helping me do exactly that."

"Is Gus okay?" she asked, her gaze going from Kyle to the dog and then back again. "I just can't shake the feeling I had. An overwhelming sense that something was wrong."

"Gus is fine. You just had a bad dream. Go on back to bed, Nicole. I really want to be alone." Which was a bold-faced lie, now. What he really wanted was to push her back against the couch cushions and find out exactly what she did or did not have on under that T-shirt. He wanted to bury himself deep inside her, and forget everything but the intoxicating feel of her body. Just the thought was enough to send all the blood rushing to one particular part of his anatomy.

To his mingled relief and disappointment, she pushed to her feet, mumbled a sleepy "Okay" and went back to her bedroom.

It took every ounce of disciplined restraint he possessed not to follow her.

He must have fallen asleep on the couch, because the next thing he knew, he opened his eyes to bright sunlight streaming in through the windows. Gus lay sleeping on the floor in front of him.

When Kyle sat up, the dog opened one eye and gave a lazy thump of his tail.

"Come on, boy," Kyle said, grinning. "Let's get you outside so you can take care of business. Then we can both have our breakfast." He felt surprisingly good, as if last night had been only a bad dream, something he should put far behind him and not think of again.

As he puttered around the kitchen, starting a pot of coffee and trying to decide what he should make for breakfast, the doorbell rang. Grateful Gus wasn't a barker, Kyle hurried to answer the door. Nicole and Jacob were apparently still sleeping.

Checking through the peephole, he was surprised to see Bret standing on the doorstep. He opened the door and welcomed his old friend inside, offering him some coffee.

"Thanks, man. I appreciate that." Bret stifled a yawn. "I've been up all night. Heather went into labor a little bit early. I have a daughter. A beautiful tiny baby girl. We named her Emma. She's on the small side, but perfectly healthy."

"Congratulations." Kyle thumped his friend on the back. "Sit. I'll get your coffee."

Bret sat. He rubbed his eyes. "I'm not going to stay long," he said. "I'm going home to try to get a couple hours of shuteye before I head back up to the hospital."

"I get it." Kyle couldn't help but grin as he teased his friend. "You look like you were out all night partying like we used to back in high school."

"I imagine." Bret grinned back. "But this was so much more awesome. I got to watch my daughter being born. It's too damn bad you weren't able to be here to do the same when Nicole had your son."

Kyle froze. He finished filling the mug with coffee and carried it over to the table, placing it in front of Bret. "What did you just say?" he asked, trying to sound neutral.

If anything, Bret's grin widened. "It's all over town, Kyle. You know how people like to talk in this town. Word is that little Jacob is your son, not Bill Mabry's. Nicole's own mother confirmed it."

Chapter 13

About to walk into the kitchen, Nicole caught the tail end of Bret's statement and gasped. Both men turned to look at her.

"Hey, Nicole." Bret's easy greeting told her he either was physically as exhausted as he looked, or really believed she already knew about the unveiling of the truth of Jacob's parentage. He probably thought her mother had called her, like most mothers would.

"Hi, Bret." She gripped the edge of the counter, trying her hardest to seem nonchalant. "I have to admit, I'm absolutely shocked at what I just heard. You say my mother—Fran Shelton, to be sure—is publicly confirming that Kyle is Jacob's father?"

"Yep." Some of the goofy pleasure faded from his face. "Are you telling me you didn't know?"

Reeling, she shook her head. "I had no idea. In fact,

I'm still thinking it has to be untrue. Why would she do that? My mother in particular wanted to keep this quiet. She was worried about how this news might change how people in town thought of me."

"Seriously?" Bret snorted, exchanging an incredulous glance with Kyle. "We're not in the fifties. Sure, it's a small town and people gossip. But everyone knew how close the two of you were—are. The surprising thing to most of us who knew you was that you got with Bill Mabry at all. No offense, Nicole." He peered apologetically at her. "But Mabry was never your type."

She didn't really have an answer for that, since he was right.

"Sit," Kyle directed. "I'll make you a cup of coffee." On the floor near him, Gus wagged his shaggy tail in greeting.

Grateful, she made her way to the table. After stopping to pet Gus, she pulled out the chair opposite Bret. Though she hadn't yet showered, she was glad she'd taken the time to dress. When she'd gotten up to check on Kyle in the middle of the night, he'd looked at her with so much intensity she'd felt as if he could see right through her sleep shirt. Her entire body had tingled, long after she'd gone back to her room. She'd despaired, wondering if this insane craving would ever go away.

Gus went to the back door and whined. Kyle let him out.

Bret shook his head. "I never pictured you having a dog," he commented. "That's a mighty-fine-looking animal you got."

"Thanks." Kyle's proud grin spoke of how highly he regarded his canine companion.

Meanwhile, Nicole still struggled to make sense of Bret's news.

"Where did you hear all this about my mother?" she asked Bret. Part of her expected to learn the story wasn't true, that someone had made it up out of boredom or spite.

"Heather and I went out with another couple for dinner yesterday, right before she went into labor. We were at The Burger Shack and ran into a couple more of our old classmates." He took a sip from his mug and gave her an apologetic grimace. "Everyone is still talking about Bill Mabry's murder and speculating who could have done such an awful thing. In the midst of all that, you and Kyle came up."

"Understandable," she allowed, accepting her own steaming mug from Kyle. "But I need to know how my mother came into all this. Forgive me for doubting, but I can't imagine her confirming to everyone in town that I got pregnant out of wedlock with Kyle's baby and then went ahead and married Bill Mabry." Even though that was exactly what she'd done.

His earnest expression kind, Bret patted the back of her hand. "It's okay, you know. No one thinks badly of you at all. We all thought Kyle was dead. Everyone saw how you almost lost your mind."

Throat clogging, Nicole managed to nod. What no one knew was how her pregnancy saved her. She hadn't wanted to live without Kyle. Only the knowledge that his child grew inside her had kept her grounded to this earth.

Kyle grunted and pulled out his own chair. Bret

shot a quick look at him before returning his attention to Nicole. "Heather's friend goes to your parents'
church. Apparently after Theresa Mabry tried to steal
Jacob, your mother decided she'd had enough of her
craziness. She confronted the Mabrys right there in
front of the entire congregation the very next day."

"Seriously? I'm having trouble believing this," Nicole said.

"I bet. Oh, Heather's friend Tildy said it was a sight
to see. Both women got loud and shrill. The pastor
had to step in between them when your mom tried to
push Theresa Mabry's head down into a big bowl of
homemade ice cream."

Kyle made a strangled sound, as if attempting to
hold back a laugh. Both Bret and Nicole ignored him.

"The two women started screaming at each other,
Tildy said," Bret continued. "The pastor tried to pull
them apart, but they weren't having it. Then Theresa
said some awful stuff about you. Your mom lost it
and told Theresa that she wasn't really a grandmother
anyway."

Closing her eyes, Nicole tried to picture this scenario. Her cold, dignified mother, always so careful to
say the right thing, constantly worried about appearances. No, this reality-show-type flamboyant person
did not sound like her mother at all.

Right then, she was leaning toward it all being a
fake story, made up just to cause trouble.

"Unbelievable," Kyle interjected. "I can't even picture it."

"Neither can I. Heather's friend actually *saw* this?"
she asked. "Or did she just hear about it?"

Her question caught Bret mid-yawn. "Tildy was

there. She watched it all go down." He took another long drink of his coffee, setting down the empty cup. "Sorry, I have to run. I've got to sleep a few hours before going back up to the hospital. But I wanted to make you both aware of what's going on so you wouldn't be caught completely by surprise. You know the entire town is already gossiping about it."

"Thank you," Nicole told him, meaning it. "I would have been blindsided."

"Yeah, me too. Thanks, bud," Kyle echoed. Bret rubbed his eyes and left.

After showing Bret out, Kyle returned to the kitchen, his expression troubled. "This has got to be a huge shock. Are you okay?"

She nodded, did not even have to think about the answer. "Actually, I am. I have to say it's kind of a relief, having the decision to reveal the truth taken completely out of my hands." She took a deep breath. "Though I have to admit, I'm now worried about Theresa. She was unbalanced before. Imagine her now. She'll be like a harpy on a mission of vengeance."

Her colorful comment made Kyle grin. "Now that is something I can more easily envision."

At the back door, Gus barked, then scratched at the screen.

"He's apparently had enough of outside." Kyle grinned. "Plus he's probably wanting his breakfast."

The affection in his tone made her smile back.

Gus came bounding into the kitchen, plumed tail wagging. Nicole braced herself for the big dog to jump on her in greeting, but someone had clearly taught him manners. He sat right next to her, tail swishing the floor, his bright gaze fixed on her intently.

When she reached down and scratched him behind his ear, she could swear Gus grinned. But as soon as Kyle poured some dog kibble in a bowl, Gus left her, raced across the room to sit and wait politely for his food.

Kyle placed the dog's bowl on the floor and watched while the dog began to eat. "Someone spent some time training him."

"He's really smart," Nicole said.

"He helped me last night." Kyle's words were nearly inaudible.

She knew better than to comment, so she only nodded.

He kept his gaze on the dog as he continued. "I'm going to look up that article you mentioned about service dogs for people with PTSD."

Though she caught her breath, she managed to keep her face expressionless. "It's an interesting article," she allowed.

Gus finished eating. Kyle picked up the bowl and carried it to the sink, where he washed it out. When he'd finished, he turned to face her. "Are you going to call your mother?"

The change of subject confused her for a second. "I probably should, shouldn't I?" she replied with no enthusiasm. "I need to hear it from her before I try to deal with Theresa Mabry."

"Why would you have to deal with her?"

"I don't know. I'm thinking she'll probably call."

As if on cue, her cell phone rang. Startled, Nicole winced. "I'm almost afraid to answer it?" But instead of her mother or Theresa, caller ID showed Caller Unknown, which 99 percent of the time meant a solicitor.

Because of this, she almost didn't answer. Almost. But because even a solicitation call felt like a reprieve, she finally did. "Hello?"

The silence on the other end of the line usually meant a recorded sales pitch would come on. But, just as she was about to end the call, a husky, feminine voice said her name. "Nicole Mabry?"

"Yes?"

"My name is Leslie Tiner. I wanted you to know that I was in love with your husband. And I think I might know who killed him."

Stunned, shocked, Nicole gulped in a deep breath before responding. She wanted her voice to be steady, despite the way her heart now hammered in her chest.

Meanwhile Kyle had come closer and watched her intently.

"Are you there?" Leslie finally asked.

"Yes. Sorry. I really don't know what to say."

"That's okay," the other woman reassured her, clearly not seeing the irony in that. "I mainly just need you to listen."

"I think you should talk to the sheriff's office," Nicole replied. "They're investigating Bill's death. And they know about you."

"About me?" Leslie sounded surprised. "How do you know this?"

Nicole explained about the credit card statement that she'd given to the police.

"Jewelry?" Leslie asked. "And lingerie? I have to say, I have no idea about any of that. Bill liked to take me dancing. Honkey-tonk'n is what we called it. When he bought me gifts, he liked to buy me clothes. Short dresses, high-heeled shoes, that sort of thing."

"Um, that's kind of a weird statement to make to Bill's wife," Nicole pointed out. "You said you had an idea who killed him. Care to elaborate on that?"

"I'm having second thoughts." Leslie's voice, previously smooth and confident, now sounded agitated. Upset even. "I'll get back to you on that." She ended the call.

After putting down her phone, Nicole raised her face to his. Her stricken expression had him crossing the room to her and pulling her into his arms. From what he'd heard of her end of the conversation, it had been an unusual phone call, to say the least.

"That was some woman claiming to be Bill's mistress."

Shocked, he grimaced. "I heard you say that she'd stated she had an idea who'd killed him."

"She did. And then she said he never bought her jewelry or lingerie. Since he didn't buy it for me either and the credit card statement clearly showed he bought it, who was the recipient?"

He had no immediate answer for that.

The doorbell rang. Loosening his grip on Nicole, he kissed her cheek. "Are you going to be all right?"

"I'm fine," she answered crossly. "I think I'm feeling angrier than anything else. This Leslie person could have saved everyone time and just gone to the police. Why she feels she could call and try to torment me, I don't understand."

The doorbell chimed again, this second round belying his visitor's impatience.

"Go." Nicole waved him away. "Answer the door. I'll be right here when you get back."

He left her in the kitchen. When he pulled open the front door and saw Nicole's mother standing on his doorstep, he almost closed the door in her face. Almost.

"The last thing she needs right now is more drama," he warned, bracing himself for the tirade of invectives sure to follow.

Instead, to his surprise, Fran simply nodded and turned away, as if to leave. Watching her, he battled an internal battle, aware he didn't have the right to dictate who Nicole wanted to see. Right when Fran reached her car, he opened his mouth to call her back. But before he could speak, she spun around and marched back up the sidewalk toward him.

Since he figured he deserved whatever chewing out she was about to deliver, he stepped aside to let her past.

Instead, she stopped. "I owe you an apology," she said, lifting her chin. "I want to let you know I'm sorry for the way I treated you all these years. I was wrong and from now on, if you'll give me a chance, I'll try to get to know you."

Dumbfounded, he could only nod.

"Now where is my daughter?" she demanded. "Since I'm in an eating-crow mood today, I've got a lot to stay to her too."

He led the way through the living room into his kitchen. Nicole looked up from her coffee, staring as her mother swept into the room.

"I'll let you two have some privacy," he murmured, backing away.

"Wait." Fran's fierce tone stopped him cold. "You sit too. You both need to hear what I have to say."

Nicole raised her eyebrows. "Mom, if you came to let us know what you told Theresa Mabry, we've already heard. Actually, thank you. I was dreading telling her, so you saved me from that."

For a moment, Fran's determined expression faltered. Then she shook her head. "I should have known. Sometimes I forget how quick gossip spreads in this town."

"Sit," Kyle gestured at a chair. "Would you like a cup of coffee?"

"Yes, thank you." Fran pulled out a chair and sank into it with a grateful sigh. "Nicole, I know you've been through a lot lately. I haven't been much help. Will you accept my apology?"

Nicole stared at her mother, her flummoxed expression revealing the depth of her shock. "Yes, of course."

"Oh, thank goodness." Then, to Kyle's consternation, Fran began to cry.

Nicole shot him a panicked look, letting him know she wasn't sure what to do. All her life, her mother hadn't even been one for casual touch, never mind hugs or embraces or even kisses. Though it seemed plain to him the older woman was sorely in need of a hug right now, he also knew Nicole had to be the one wanting to give it.

So he kept his mouth shut and busied himself making Fran a cup of coffee. Since he wasn't sure how she took it—and didn't want to interrupt her sobbing to ask—he made it the same way he made Nicole's.

When he turned back around, he saw Nicole had gone to her mother and wrapped her arms around her. "It's going to be okay," Nicole murmured. Though she appeared conflicted, when she spoke, her voice sounded confident and certain. "I promise."

He placed the coffee cup on the table in front of Fran and once again tried to beat a quick retreat. But, almost as if she had some sixth sense that warned her, Fran raised her head and pinned him with a teary-eyed glare.

"Sit," she ordered, sniffing. "I promise to pull myself together long enough to explain."

What could he do then but comply? At least he had coffee.

Once he was seated, Nicole jumped up and got her mom some tissue to wipe her face and blow her nose. They both waited while Fran composed herself. Nicole exchanged a glance with Kyle, her baffled expression revealing that she was just as perplexed as he was. He couldn't help but wonder if she'd ever seen her mother cry. In the entire time he'd known the family, Fran had always been stone-faced, cold and remote.

Finally, Fran took a sip of her coffee and looked directly at Nicole. "Your father and I are getting a divorce," she said.

To her credit, Nicole didn't react. Kyle couldn't tell if she was shocked or saddened, relieved or upset.

"But why?" Nicole finally asked, when it became clear her mother didn't plan to elaborate. "You've been married a long time. You two have always seemed so...united."

Not happy. Not in love. Not devoted. Just...united. He wondered if either woman realized how telling that was.

"We don't love each other," Fran finally confided. "But neither of us really wanted to rock the boat. Plus, you know our church frowns upon divorce, and for both of us, that opinion mattered more than it ever should have."

She swallowed, again gazing into her daughter's eyes. "Just as I let worry about what they thought ruin your chance at happiness. Your father and I forced you to marry a man you didn't love, just to save our reputation."

Nicole acknowledged the truth of this statement with a slight dip of her head. "What changed?" she asked, the slight edge to her voice telling Kyle she wasn't entirely buying all this. He couldn't really blame her either. After a lifetime of indifference and rigid inflexibility, she couldn't process this sudden about-face. He wasn't sure he could either, though he was not nearly as emotionally invested as she had to be.

"I don't blame you for not believing me," Fran said, clearly picking up on Nicole's skepticism.

"What changed?" Nicole asked again, crossing her arms. "What made you decide to see things differently?"

"Theresa Mabry abducted my grandson." The agony in Fran's quiet voice made Nicole flinch. "I didn't realize until that exact moment how much I loved that sweet baby. How much I was missing out on, just because of my stubborn pride. I wanted a do-over. But since such a thing isn't possible, I realized I had a choice. I could change the future."

While listening to Fran, Kyle kept his gaze riveted on Nicole. She'd already been through so much. Each time, she picked herself up, dusted herself off and continued to move forward. Right now, though she listened carefully to every word her mother said, her gaze seemed remote. As if she'd taken herself off somewhere far away, in order to protect herself from pain.

For that reason alone, Kyle decided to speak up. "If you hurt Nicole, I'll make sure you pay," he said, deadly calm but leaving no doubt he meant it.

To his surprise, Fran just gave a grim nod. "If I hurt her, I'll deserve whatever retribution you deal out. But I won't. I want to be on her side." She turned her attention back to Nicole. "Will you give me a second chance, Nicole? Let me get to know both you and my grandson? Please."

Kyle found himself holding his breath while waiting for Nicole to reply. But before she could speak, baby Jacob began crying, his wails signaling the fact that he was awake and hungry and needed his mother.

Nicole bolted from the room without another word, clearly grateful for the reprieve.

"That didn't go well." Fran sighed, picking at one of her perfectly manicured fingernails. She hunched over her coffee with a defeated air, acting as if she were afraid to look directly at Kyle.

For the first time in all the years he'd known Nicole's mother, he pitied her. "What can you expect?" he asked, keeping his voice gentle. "You've spent her entire life keeping her at arm's length."

"I know. And I did everything I could to split you two up." She'd been rigid and unyielding, stern and distant. When Nicole had most needed a mother, Fran had let her down.

"Not to mention forcing her to marry Bill Mabry while carrying my child," he pointed out. "Instead of supporting her, loving her, you foisted her off on a man she barely knew, never mind didn't love."

"That was her father," Fran replied, her voice weary. "When he found out she was pregnant, he became enraged. He wanted to throw her out into the street, with nothing but the clothes on her back. I argued against this, and came up with a solution I believed he'd accept."

"Marrying Mabry."

"Yes." She sighed, rubbing at her red and swollen eyes with her fists. "Bill Mabry had been after Nicole since they were little kids. He was obsessed with her. I reassured myself that at least he loved her, so much so that he was willing to marry her knowing she was still in love with you. He was a good man," Fran continued. "He was even willing to raise another man's son as his own."

This remark had Kyle clenching his teeth. He pushed to his feet, more to keep from saying anything he shouldn't than anything else. "I think you'd better ask Nicole about that," he said. 'Maybe she could tell you exactly what kind of man he was."

Though she nodded, she pursed her lips and didn't speak again.

While he really didn't want to sit in his kitchen with her, he was afraid to leave her alone. He had to hope Nicole planned to return as soon as she'd gotten Jacob taken care of. Otherwise, he'd have to be the one to send Fran Shelton packing.

Chapter 14

Taking care of her son, Nicole battled the urge to cry. She wasn't entirely sure what had just happened, but part of her couldn't help but feel like it was all a huge trick, one more horrible hit on her heart to attempt to break her. She took pride in her strength and resilience, but her mother acting so completely out of character shook her.

And there was that little matter of divorce. Fran had said she was divorcing Nicole's father. Since neither of them believed in divorce, Nicole wasn't at all sure how to take this statement.

Jacob cooed, coaxing a smile from her. One thing Fran had said resonated to Nicole's core. Her mother claimed she loved Jacob, that she desperately now wanted a relationship with her grandson. Nicole had wished for that very thing for so long that she was now afraid to trust it. If it happened, when it happened, the thought brought her the potential for so much joy. Or so much anguish, if she were to learn the possibility had been a lie.

Finally, once Jacob had been changed, fed and burped, Nicole carried him with her back to the kitchen. Fran sat across the table from Kyle in silence. Kyle jumped to his feet the instant he saw her, mumbled something about needing a shower and bolted for his room.

Fran looked up, her dejected expression disappearing when she caught sight of Jacob. In fact, she visibly softened. "There's my little man," she cooed. "Nicole, can I hold him?"

Instead, Nicole continued to hold her son while she studied her mother. "He's three months old now, Mom. Don't get me wrong—I'm thrilled that you're taking an interest in him now. But I want to know what's *really* changed?"

Another woman might have pretended ignorance. But Fran Shelton had always stood by her convictions, wrong or right. She lifted her chin and met her daughter's gaze straight on. "*I've* changed," she said. "It would be easy to give you an excuse for the way I acted before, but there really isn't any. Looking back, I realized I don't like the person I was."

Nicole nodded, but she still couldn't make herself move. Though she'd spent her entire life longing for her mother to be more...well, motherly, this change in attitude seemed to come up out of the blue. She was afraid to trust it. Because if she let herself believe, even with a tiny fraction of her being, and then Fran let her down, she knew the pain would be much, much worse. In fact, she didn't know if she could bear it.

"I understand you're skeptical," Fran continued. "But I mean it, Nicole. I'm starting over. I've quit the church, I'm leaving your father and I'd love it if you'd allow me a second chance with you and Jacob."

"This is a lot to take in, all at once." Still Nicole prevaricated. "Where are you going to live?"

"I'm keeping the house," Fran answered. "Your father has agreed to move into an apartment in town. I think he's a bit shocked, but more relieved than anything."

Nicole sank into a chair, still holding Jacob. She wasn't sure what to say.

"Please." Fran swallowed. "I'm not sure what else I can do to convince you. But you should know this. I will defend you and my grandson to anyone who dares say anything now that his true parentage is known."

"Will you?" Nicole locked gazes with her mother. "And what about Kyle? Will you defend him too?"

For once, at the mention of Kyle's name, her mother didn't look away. "Yes," she answered. "I will. If you love him, I'll learn to love him too."

Telling herself she would not cry, Nicole held out her one free arm. "Come here."

They hugged, Fran taking care not to hug too hard and smoosh Jacob. They'd just broken apart when the front door slammed open and Kyle rushed into the kitchen.

"The Mabrys just pulled up," he said. "Do you want me to send them away?"

Nicole looked at her mother, who shrugged. "Maybe you should call the police," Fran said.

"No. Mom, will you hold Jacob? I'll go out there and see what they want. I'm not letting them in the house anywhere near Jacob."

"Are you sure that's wise?" Fran frowned. "This can't be anything good."

"I'm sure." After handing Jacob over to her mom, Nicole took a deep breath, trying to quiet her pounding heart.

"I'm going with you," Kyle announced. "Because I agree with your mother. The Mabrys are most likely looking for trouble. I won't let them hurt you."

This comment gave Nicole pause. Before Theresa had tried to kidnap Jacob, Nicole never would have believed her in-laws to be capable of violence. "Good idea," she told Kyle. "Make sure you have your phone too, just in case we need to call 911."

Fran's eyes grew huge. "Okay."

Right before Nicole reached the front door, Kyle grabbed her arm. "Are you absolutely certain you want to do this?"

"No," she admitted. "I'm terrified. But I have to face them sometime. I refuse to spend the rest of my life looking over my shoulder for them and trying to hide. Except for recently, after the death of their son, I always found the Mabrys to be reasonable people. I hope once I explain, they'll understand."

His steady gaze searched her face. "I'm not counting on that."

"One can only hope," she replied.

With him right behind her, they headed out the front door.

Dan and Theresa had gotten out of their car, though they hadn't yet made it out of the driveway. Dan had Theresa's arm and appeared to be trying to argue with her. Since she had her back to the house, Dan caught sight of Nicole and Kyle first.

Before he could say anything, Theresa spun around to face them. The stark pain in her face was not what Nicole had expected. But then again, she'd had no idea what to expect.

"You…" Words apparently failing her, Theresa took a few steps toward Nicole. Her husband kept hold of her arm, probably as a precaution.

Just like Kyle stayed close to Nicole's side.

"Hello, Theresa," Nicole said quietly.

With her jawline tight, Theresa came closer. "I want to know if what your mother claimed was true. Is Jacob really that man's son?" Her gaze swept over Kyle, registering her distaste.

"Yes. I'm sorry. But I can assure you, Bill knew. I told him before I accepted his marriage proposal."

Twin spots of color bloomed in the older woman's pale cheeks. "I don't believe you." Still the cold and measured tone. This worried Nicole almost as much as if Theresa had been screaming.

"Believe me or not, it's the truth. I'm sorry you had to hear it the way you did. I'd planned to tell you eventually, but—"

"Did you?" Theresa glared. "You money-grubbing, hateful little b—"

"Enough." Dan cut his wife off before she could utter the insulting word. "Theresa, you insisted we come here so you could hear the truth from her mouth. You have. We'd best be getting home now."

But Theresa didn't move. "I want you out of my son's house. You and that bastard child of yours."

Nicole gasped. But before she could speak, Kyle stepped forward. "You need to get off my property. Now."

"Glad to." Still gripping his wife's arm, Dan tried to steer Theresa away.

"I'm not finished," she said, attempted to jerk herself free.

Gaze narrowed, Kyle shook his head. "Keep it up, Theresa. I might have to ask the fire department's arson investigator to consider you a suspect in the fire at Nicole's house. Since they were legally married when they bought the house, now that she's a widow, that house does belong to her. Community property."

Theresa's mouth worked, but no sound came out.

"Leave," Kyle reiterated. "There's absolutely no need for you to treat Nicole like this."

"No need?" Dan spoke up, a kind of calculated fury in his eyes. "All this time, she's let my wife and me believe Jacob was our grandson. I just don't understand why she—and our son—didn't tell us the truth."

"Because of this," Nicole answered softly. "Jacob is a baby. None of this is his fault. None of it. We'd agreed to wait to tell him until he was older."

"Come on, Theresa." This time, Dan's attempt to redirect his wife was successful. Without another word, the couple got into their car and drove away.

"Is that true?" Kyle asked, once they'd gone. "The reason why Bill didn't tell his parents the truth?"

"It was my truth." Nicole sighed. "Bill and I never discussed it. Honestly, I assume he didn't inform his parents because he felt it would make him look weak."

Once they'd gotten inside the front door, Kyle stopped. "I'm going to go out for a while," he said. "Will you be all right here with your mother?"

Slowly, she nodded. "Are you okay?"

"I don't know. I've got a lot to think about." With that, he walked away.

After he'd gone, Nicole took several deep breaths, trying to calm herself back down. She knew her mom would have questions, and she wanted to be able to answer them as clearly as possible.

Since from what he could hear, Nicole and her mother were getting along just fine, Kyle felt no qualms about leaving them alone together. He needed to get out and clear his head. All the time he'd been in Afghanistan, when he'd thought of his hometown, he'd thought of peace and quiet. He'd always regarded Anniversary as a sort of bucolic place, isolated and insulated, serene and restful. Not a place of murder, arson, intrigue and nonstop drama.

Since it was a small town, everyone knew everyone else, and as a result, gossip sometimes ran rampant. He'd figured boredom drove people to find something interesting to talk about and, like everyone else he knew, took the gossip in stride.

Funny how rapidly that outlook changed when talk was about someone you loved.

Instead of taking his truck, he thought he'd take his Harley for a spin and head into town. Since the accident, he'd been a bit leery of driving the bike, but he knew he had to get back on soon or he'd never ride again.

He'd barely gotten his garage open when a marked squad car pulled up and blocked the exit to his driveway.

A uniformed sheriff's deputy emerged and walked up to Kyle. Tall, thin and bald, he wore mirrored aviator sunglasses and walked with authority. Kyle didn't recognize the man, which meant he must have been hired during the time Kyle had been away.

"Kyle Benning?" the deputy asked. His name badge read Deputy Perkins.

"That's me. Can I help you?" Kyle asked. Now what?

"I need to talk to Nicole Mabry. Is she here?"

"Yes." Kyle pulled the garage closed. "Can I ask what this is about?"

"I need to speak with Ms. Mabry."

Of course. Kyle turned and headed back toward the front door. "Follow me."

When he walked into the kitchen with the deputy right on his heels, Nicole looked up, her initial smile freezing. "What's going on?" she asked quietly.

"We apprehended Dan and Theresa Mabry a block from here and they've been taken into custody," Deputy Perkins replied.

Nicole gasped. "Why?" she asked. "What did they do?"

The deputy heaved a sigh. He hadn't removed his sunglasses, despite being inside the house. Kyle found that both annoying and amusing.

"Sheriff Cantrell asked me to inform you in person, since this will be all over the evening news." Perkins pulled a sheet of paper from his pocket and began to read. "As of ten a.m. this morning, the ATF, in conjunction with local authorities, conducted a widespread sting operation. Part of this operation centered on Mabry Trucking Company." He paused for dramatic effect before continuing. "Several refrigerator semitrailers were apprehended, as well as over 500 pounds of marijuana and several million dollars of cocaine."

"What?" Nicole interrupted. "Are you kidding me?"

"Unfortunately not, ma'am. If I may continue?"

Nicole gave a jerky nod of her head.

"Dan Mabry is suspected of importing drugs, primarily cannabis and cocaine, for distribution here in Texas and points eastward. The drugs were hidden alongside legal loads when they made deliveries. Seven other individuals, including some of the truck drivers, have either been arrested or have warrants issued for their arrest."

When Nicole swayed, Kyle hurried over to her side. He slid his arm around her shoulders, offering his support.

For a moment, no one spoke. Even Fran, normally so outspoken, appeared to have been stunned into silence.

"Is there anything else?" Nicole finally asked, her voice wavering slightly.

"If there is, I wasn't instructed to pass it on," Perkins replied. "Thank you for your time. My understanding is that the press will soon be descending in swarms upon our little town. You'd better brace yourselves, because once they learn of your connection to these people, they'll be camped outside your front door."

Kyle swore, drawing the deputy's attention. "No

need to see me out," Perkins told him. "I can find my own way."

Once he'd gone, Kyle helped Nicole into a chair. Fran still held baby Jacob, who'd fallen asleep and managed to remain that way all through Perkins's discourse.

"I wonder if they timed the raid so the Mabrys were gone?" Nicole mused. "Apparently they were here when all this was going down."

"That was probably only a coincidence." Kyle kneaded her shoulder. "I have to wonder if Bill was the mastermind of all that, if his parents even knew. They may not have even been involved."

"Involved?" She gave a humorless laugh. "Bill and his mother were joined at the hip. While I think that he was probably the one that set the entire thing up, I wouldn't be surprised if his mother not only knew, but helped plan shipments. Dan's the only anomaly. Theresa may or may not have brought her husband in on the scheme."

"Drugs?" Fran finally spoke up. "Bill Mabry was moving drugs?"

"And distributing them," Kyle confirmed.

Fran looked from him to her daughter. "But he was a deacon in the church."

Nicole only shrugged. "You truly had no idea what kind of man Bill was, Mom. He was awful."

"Awful?" The disbelief in Fran's voice, even now, had Kyle clenching his jaw.

"Awful might be too gentle a word," Nicole replied. "He treated me like his possession, believing he had me cowed into not having an original thought of my own. He drank and when drunk, he used me as his very own punching bag. I'd started saving money, every penny I could out of my grocery allowance, because as soon as I had enough, I planned to take Jacob and run as far away as I could."

Stunned, Kyle swallowed hard. If Nicole's mother hadn't been there, he'd have Nicole in his arms right now and would be kissing her senseless.

Instead, he watched myriad expressions play across Fran's face. First shock, then disbelief, anger and, finally, sorrow. "I didn't know," Fran cried. "You never told me."

Nicole eyed her mother. "Seriously, Mom? Why would I? You would have refused to believe me. You and Dad made it clear to me that I was on my own once I got pregnant. You threatened to throw me and my unborn child out into the street with only the clothes on my back if I didn't marry the man you handpicked—Bill Mabry."

Again, Kyle wanted to kiss her. More than that, he wanted to cover her body with his and make love to her until he'd driven the past from her mind.

"But—" Fran began.

"No," Nicole interrupted. "Don't say another word. I'm going to try really hard to work on this new person you say you've become, but it's difficult when I remember the kind of mother you were."

Though baby Jacob still slept, Nicole extracted him from Fran's arms. "Go on home, Mom. I need some time alone to think. We'll talk again tomorrow."

Then, carrying her son, Nicole left the room without a backward glance.

Though he wanted to follow her, Kyle showed Fran out instead.

* * *

Once she'd reached the safety of her temporary bedroom, Nicole put Jacob down in the small bassinette. He hadn't woken at all, despite the shuffling from his grandmother to his mother.

She felt like a fool. Just as she had in the early days of her marriage to Bill, she'd allowed herself to hope based on words. Her mother had given her pretty words, soft words, and said things Nicole had longed to hear. But if Bill had taught Nicole anything, it was that actions were what really mattered. All the apologies and promises in the world meant absolutely nothing unless they were followed up by action. Reality rather than promises.

The truth of this sliced her open, exposing a gaping, painful wound in her psyche that she'd convinced herself had long ago healed. A hundred times she'd wanted her mother to love her, to help her, to be there with comfort and a smile and wisdom, only to understand that this matronly version of Fran did not exist. Never had, never would.

Until today. Fran had done the one thing Nicole would have sworn she'd never do. She'd announced to the entire town, including her church, especially her church, the truth about Jacob's true father. Was this enough to indicate Fran truly had experienced a major epiphany?

Nicole wasn't certain she believed it. She wasn't sure she'd survive if she allowed herself once again to hope, only to realize Fran truly hadn't changed.

Why now? She wondered, sitting down hard on the edge of her bed. What could her mother possibly have to gain by pretending she wanted to mend fences she'd torn down and destroyed years ago?

Exhausted from trying to decide, Nicole crawled up onto her bed and underneath the covers. She closed her eyes and willed herself to sleep. Maybe a nap would help her regain perspective.

Miraculously, she must have fallen asleep.

When she next opened her eyes and stretched, she felt better. And then she turned over, to find Kyle lying on the bed next to her, sound asleep. He was shirtless, wearing only a pair of shorts. The sight of his muscular body made her mouth go dry.

Damn how badly she wanted him.

Temptation had her curling her toes. She remembered, oh how well she remembered, them napping wrapped in each other's arms. The first to awake had delighted in arousing the other and every single time, they'd ended up making love.

Shaking with need, she put her hand on his chest, splaying her fingers so she could feel the steady beat of his heart.

His eyes opened, those glorious green eyes. Unclouded by sleep, blazing with a desire that matched her own.

She allowed this to embolden her. In this moment, fraught with sexual tension and the promise of fulfillment, nothing else mattered. They would lose themselves in each other, and the outside world would disappear.

He reached for her and she stilled him with a shake of her head. "Don't move," she told him. "Let me do this first. No touching until I say so."

This was something she'd always wanted to do. A

younger Kyle, less disciplined than this elite soldier he'd become, had always refused. She held her breath, waiting to hear if he'd refuse again.

To her surprise, he agreed. Lying propped up on one elbow, he watched her. It took every ounce of self-control she possessed not to pounce on him and cover his body with hers, but that would defeat her purpose. Eventually, she planned to be on top, to control their movements, but first, she thought she'd see how far she could go without letting him touch her.

"Roll over on your back," she ordered. He complied, the bulge in his front a testimony to how all this affected him.

Slowly, she stripped off his shorts. He wore no briefs underneath. A surprise. The strength and size of his already aroused body made her melt. When she reached for him, he called her name, his voice husky.

"Nicole, take off your clothes. If I can't touch, at least let me look."

At first, she thought her hands were trembling too much to accomplish this, but after she'd pulled her T-shirt off, she managed to unhook and remove her bra. Her breasts felt tight, not just her engorged nipples either. Arching her back, she removed her shorts and then her panties. Because the tension made her ache, she rubbed herself on him like a cat. His hands came up, but she hissed a warning and he lowered them back to his sides.

She took him into her mouth, slowly, savoring the unique taste and feel of him. When she moved, caressing him with her tongue, he cried out.

Again his hands came up, tangling in her hair. The instant he did this, she pulled back, putting a small distance between him and her overheated body. "No touching, remember?"

Eyes narrowed, he nodded. "I should warn you though, if you keep that up, I won't be able to control myself or what I do."

This pleased her. "Good." She smiled. "I love making you lose control."

"Do you?" he rasped. "Because Nicole, I'm about to do that right about now."

As he spoke, he grabbed her, rolling so that his body covered hers. Though she gasped, instinctively arching herself so he could enter her, she pushed at him instead. "I wasn't done. I want to be on top."

"Your wish is my command," he teased, shifting them around and reversing their positions. She pushed up on her knees, hovering over him for a second. Then, because she couldn't take any more, she lowered herself onto him, taking him deep inside her.

Though she wanted to move slowly, he bucked against her, and the two of them worked in unison. Lovemaking had always been this way with them, electrifying in its passion. Though she remained on top, he pounded into her from below, claiming her with his body. She lost her capacity for thought, for speech. Nothing else existed but this man, the only man she'd ever loved.

Kyle.

She must have cried out his name as the ecstasy built. Cried it out again as she found her release, shuddering, her body clenching around him, bringing him to his own climax.

After, they held each other, letting their perspiration-slicked bodies cool, neither speaking. She loved him and knew, even if he couldn't admit it yet to himself, that he still loved her as well.

Actions, after all, spoke louder than words.

Chapter 15

Kyle fell asleep holding her. He hadn't meant to; these days he didn't dare let down his guard. The bad dreams reliving the blast came when he slept, and he never wanted Nicole to witness what he became when in the throes of reliving what had happened to him.

And then it came.

A flash of light. Left side. Ringing in the ears. An explosion, knocking him off his feet. Pain and blood and terror. Not again. Gasping, Kyle came awake, bolting upright, battling the tangled sheets as if they were his enemies. Gus whined, crossing the room to nestle up against Kyle's leg, offering canine comfort the only way the dog knew how.

Then, a shadowy figure stirred in the bed next to him. He leapt backward, mindless in his panic, consumed by the gut-wrenching fear.

"Kyle? It's okay. I'm here. Nicole."

Nicole. He'd suddenly remembered that they'd gone to bed together. Foolish, on his part. He'd managed to convince himself that this night, because of her, his sleep would remain untroubled by his past.

"Kyle, you're here. In Texas. It's all right. I promise you, you're safe."

Something in her voice reached him, knocking the tension from his sweat-soaked body. He dragged his hand through his hair, trying to summon up a semblance of normalcy. "Bad dream," he managed to croak, squinting in her general direction. "Go back to sleep." He expected her to sigh, roll over and drift back to her dreams.

Instead, to his shock, she swung her long legs over the side of the bed and padded over to him. Without another word, she wrapped her arms around him and held him, her embrace strong and sure. Gus whined, as if to let them know he wanted in on the hug too. Kyle reached down and tangled his fingers in his dog's fur, which seemed to satisfy him. Nicole murmured something—he couldn't make out the words or whether it was directed at him or Gus, but it sounded soothing.

His pounding heartbeat gradually calmed; the quaking sense of emptiness inside him began to ebb away. Still, he held on to her as if he were drowning. He wondered if she understood that right now, in this instant, she'd become his lifeboat, helping him weather the storm.

She made another sound, low in her throat. He braced himself, knowing she'd have questions, uncertain if he'd be able to answer them. But she didn't ask, she didn't say a word, just held him. Gradually, his heartbeat slowed and his wild trembling stopped. Ashamed, he wasn't sure what to say, if anything. There wasn't much that could excuse such a thing happening to a grown man, especially an elite member of the armed forces. So much for the ranger motto—Sua Sponte. He'd begun to see that in this, the world outside the army, he couldn't handle this all on his own.

Growing uncomfortable—and unbelievably—aroused, he shifted his weight and twisted slightly to break the embrace.

"It's okay," she murmured, and let him go. While he stood eying her, his heart in his throat, aching to kiss her, she looked away. She reached down and patted Gus, who gave a doggie yawn and leaned into her, clearly enjoying the attention.

Kyle let himself drink in his fill of her, from her sexy tousled hair to the way the T-shirt clung to her supple body. Clearly, with sheets bunched up around his body, she had no clue of how strongly she affected him, and how soon after their previous bout of intense lovemaking.

Finally, when she looked at him, she yawned, covering her mouth with her hand. "Let's go back to sleep, if you can," she said. "It's two in the morning and tomorrow is going to be a busy day."

He considered, wondering if she'd be willing to go for another round. Normally after an episode like this, he'd pace for hours, unable to sleep. All the pent-up energy needed some sort of outlet. Like sex.

Except this time, he realized the tension from the nightmare flashback had left him. The only tension he felt right now was sexual, which made him both grin and wince.

Gus whined and then shook himself before lumbering back to his dog bed.

"Are you coming?" Yawning again, this time mid-sentence, Nicole plumped her pillow. "I need my rest," she continued. "You wore me out earlier." A thread of laughter ran through her sleepy voice.

"Are you sure all you want to do is sleep?" he asked, making his tone deliberately playful. He wouldn't blame her at all if she did, but it never hurt to ask.

"Mmphh," she responded, clearly already on her way back to dreamland.

He stood next to the bed for a moment or two, watching as she slipped back to slumber. Nicole. Her generosity of spirit touched him, making him wonder how he could have thought she'd changed. Nicole was Nicole, loving and giving and fiercely protective of the ones she loved. He understood finally what had driven her to do what she'd thought she had to in order to protect her unborn baby, her son. *Their* son.

And now she wanted him to come back to bed and try to sleep. As if he were an ordinary man, rather than a severely damaged one.

Oddly enough, her faith in him gave him hope. What the hell, why not? If the flashback returned, he'd know. Wariness warred with temptation. It wouldn't hurt to try. There was always a first time for everything. He got into bed next to her, carefully and quietly so as not to wake her. Once in place, he tried to get comfortable, aware he'd probably lie there awake for hours. To his surprise, lying next to Nicole, listening to her even breathing as she slipped back into slumber, he relaxed even more.

When he next stirred, he realized he must have

fallen asleep. The clock showed 7 a.m., which meant he'd slept for hours.

Exhilarated—and once again aroused—he turned to look for Nicole and found her side of the bed empty. Clearly, she'd risen before him. Maybe Jacob had awakened her. He also remembered her saying something about having a busy day ahead of her.

He found her in the kitchen, sitting at the table and nursing Jacob. She smiled sleepily at him, the beauty of that smile hitting him like a punch in the gut.

"I didn't want to wake you," she said softly. "You were sleeping so deeply and I thought you needed your rest."

"I was." He took a deep breath. "Thank you."

"For what?"

Moving toward the coffee maker, he shrugged, as if his words weren't important at all. "You helped keep the nightmares at bay."

"Oh. I'm glad." For a moment, her gaze held his. "I know I've mentioned this before, but you really might consider getting some help with all that."

Instead of arguing as he had before, this time he gave a slow nod. "I'm going to look into therapy," he said. "I want healing." Sipping his coffee, he summoned up the necessary courage to tell her the truth. "I need to get better. For you."

"No," her immediate response cut him deep. "Not for me. You have to want this for yourself." And she went back to focusing her attention on the baby.

Pain sliced at his heart, even as he silently called himself every kind of fool. There you had it. As gently as she could, she was letting him know they had no future together. What had he really expected? After everything that had happened, why had he thought she would even want to move toward the future they'd originally planned together.

The doorbell rang. Early for a visitor, but Kyle jumped at the chance to leave the room. Glad of the distraction, he yanked the door open. Deputy Frankel and Deputy Perkins, both in uniform and both wearing identical stern expressions, stood on his front porch. Kyle couldn't help but notice they wore identical sunglasses. He wondered if those were department issued.

"We need to see Nicole Mabry," Frankel said. "Could you send her out please?"

"Just a moment." Trying to remember if Nicole had been dressed, Kyle headed back to the kitchen. She'd finished nursing and now had the baby on her shoulder, burping him. She wore a pair of cotton shorts under her T-shirt and what must have been a nursing bra.

"There are two sheriff's deputies out front who want to see you," he said. "Maybe they've got some news on your husband's murder."

She gave a slow nod. Still burping Jacob, she hurried to the front door.

"Ms. Mabry," Frankel said, appearing uncomfortable for the first time as he took in the baby. "I'm going to have to ask you to come down to the sheriff's department."

"Now?" she asked, looking from one man to the other.

"Yes, ma'am. Now."

"Is she under arrest?" Kyle asked, not liking the way they were treating her.

"Not yet," Perkins spoke up, the grim set of his jaw letting Kyle know he took his job seriously.

"I don't think—" Starting to argue, Kyle stopped when Nicole place her hand on his upper arm.

"I'll go with you," she said. "Kyle, will you watch the baby?"

On the verge of insisting he go with her, Kyle remembered her earlier words, when she'd let him know clearly that he shouldn't do stuff for her. "I'll watch Jacob," he replied, for once ignoring his instinct. "But if you need me, promise me you'll call."

"I will." And she left, walking between the two deputies. Kyle watched as they helped her into the backseat, wondering what had happened now.

Nicole waited until they'd pulled away from Kyle's house before asking what was going on.

"The sheriff wants to see you," Deputy Perkins, who rode in the passenger seat, replied. He glanced back over his shoulder at her. His sunglasses made it impossible to read his expression.

She guessed she'd find out what was going on in a few minutes.

When they pulled up at the sheriff's department building downtown, the two deputies escorted her one on each side, making her feel uncomfortably like a prisoner. They flanked her all the way inside and down the hall to Sheriff Cantrell's office.

Once inside, she stopped short, stunned to see Theresa Mabry seated in one of the chairs across from the desk. The older woman glared at her, making it plain she found this entire thing distasteful. Nicole looked from her to Sheriff Cantrell, who'd stood when she'd entered.

"Sit," he said, waving her to the empty chair next to Theresa.

Stiffly, Nicole sat. Her former mother-in-law appeared to have aged ten years. She'd stopped coloring her hair, and now the brown had become liberally speckled with gray. New lines had appeared on her face as well as dark circles under both eyes. She'd always had perfectly manicured fingernails, but now they were unpainted and ragged, as if she'd been chewing on them. Nicole couldn't help but feel a twinge of pity.

Theresa caught her looking and shot her a death glare.

Sheriff Cantrell cleared his throat. "I invited you both here today because I wanted to discuss the murder investigation on Bill's death."

"She doesn't have any right to be in this room." Theresa jumped to her feet. "I don't want her here."

"Theresa," the sheriff replied, his tone calm and steady. "Nicole was Bill's wife. She has just as much right to be here as you do."

Nicole braced herself for Theresa to spew a string of insults. Instead, Theresa sat back down, her mouth a tight line, and said nothing. The rigid stiffness with which she held herself revealed her continuing protest.

"First up, I'm sorry to inform you, Theresa, that Dan has confessed to breaking into Nicole's house and setting it on fire."

"What?" Both Nicole and Theresa spoke simultaneously, with equal amounts of shock.

"But why?" Theresa asked. "Why would he do such a thing?"

"He needed to steal a key that Bill had in his desk. It was to a locker at one of those mailbox places in a strip shopping mall."

"A locker?" From the bewilderment in the older woman's voice, she had no idea what any of this meant. Nicole, however, suspected she had a pretty good idea what the sheriff was going to say next.

"Yes. It contained the cash he needed to pay for the next drug shipment. If he wasn't able to retrieve that cash, someone from the drug cartel would kill him."

Theresa gasped. "I knew you'd arrested him," she said, her voice breaking. "But I was positive he'd be cleared and released. All of this is a total shock to me. Now you're telling me my husband was working with my son and using our trucking company to make money from drugs?" Her voice rose with every word, until she was practically shouting at the end.

To his credit, Sheriff Cantrell didn't react at all. He sat back in his chair and waited for Theresa to finish. Once she'd wound down, he leaned forward. "He's given us a written confession, Theresa. I'm sorry."

"What about Bill's murder?" Nicole asked. "Have you gotten any leads on that? Have you talked to that woman who called me and claimed to be his mistress?"

"She's coming in shortly for questioning," he replied.

"Mistress?" Theresa asked, practically spitting the word at Nicole. "Now *you* of all people have the nerve to accuse my son of having a mistress? He's dead. He can't defend himself."

At first not sure how to respond, Nicole decided she'd simply tell the truth, as gently as possible. She could see the other woman was suffering a lot of pain. "Her name is Leslie. She called me once. I'm sorry, but I think there's a lot you didn't know about your son."

Facing her down, Theresa raised her hands, which she'd clenched into fists. "You have a lot of nerve," she began.

"Ladies," Sheriff Cantrell interrupted. "While I strongly suggest the two of you should settle your personal differences, this is not the time nor the place."

Nicole nodded. Theresa shook her head. "I want nothing to do with this woman."

"Fine." The sheriff shrugged. "Then you are free to leave. Go on home, Theresa. We're not arresting you, not today. You claim you didn't know anything about the drugs and right now, we have no evidence to show us otherwise." He stood, fixing her with a stern look. "Just don't leave town, you hear?"

Face flaming, Theresa managed a quick nod before she slammed out of the office and stormed down the hall toward the exit.

Heaven help her, Nicole actually felt sorry for her former mother-in-law. Theresa Mabry might have a lot of unpleasant qualities, but she'd truly loved her son.

"About this mistress…" For the first time, Sheriff Cantrell actually appeared uncomfortable. "Are you going to cause any problems if I let you two both be in the same room?"

"Problems?" After she asked, Nicole realized what he meant. Most wives would be furious and eager to confront the other woman in their husband's life. For herself, Nicole sort of wanted to thank her for taking some of Bill's attention away from her.

Since she knew she couldn't voice that sentiment out loud to the sheriff, Nicole pretended to seriously consider his question. "I think I'm more curious than anything else," she finally said. And she truly was curious to see what kind of a woman would willingly choose to be with a man like Bill Mabry.

"Nicole," the sheriff continued. "Normally, I would do everything in my power to keep you two separate. But my gut instinct is telling me something's off here. She mentioned that she'd called you. Do you think you could still recognize the voice?"

"I think so. Off how?"

"I'm not sure. She's giving her statement now. I've got two men with her. She actually volunteered to come in for questioning." He swallowed, then grimaced. "She claims to know who killed your husband."

"What?" Nicole sat forward in her chair. "I'm surprised you're telling me this. Especially since you didn't say anything to Theresa." And she knew since he went to the same church, he and his family were close to the Mabry family.

"I was afraid if I did, Theresa might come unhinged." With a self-conscious smile, he consulted a piece of paper. "Anyway, Brenda Meroni will be with us shortly."

"Brenda?" Confused, Nicole eyed him. "You must be mistaken. The woman who called me said her name was Leslie." Maybe there actually were two mistresses. That would explain why Leslie had said Bill hadn't given her any jewelry.

He frowned. "Are you sure? Because this woman's name is not Leslie. It's Brenda."

"What? That makes no sense." Nicole stared. "The only explanation I can come up with is that she gave me a fake name. I wonder why?"

"You can ask her once she's finished making her statement. The difference in names only adds to my feeling that something is definitely off."

Now she understood what he meant. In fact, it might be entirely possible that Brenda Meroni might actually be the one who'd killed Bill.

A few minutes later, a uniformed deputy came into the sheriff's office. "She's finished with her statement," he said. "Are you ready for her?"

"Yes. Bring her in."

Nicole took a deep breath, trying to calm her nerves. A moment later, a short, stout young woman with spiky dark hair entered the room. She wore a low-cut T-shirt and tight, ripped jeans. When she caught sight of Nicole, she stopped short.

"Who is this?" she asked. "Don't tell me you found the other one."

Other one? "What other one?" the sheriff asked. Right then, Nicole knew. Her suspicions had been correct.

"The other girlfriend." Impatience colored Brenda's voice. "At first, neither of us knew Bill had another one on the side."

"Not me." Nicole shook her head. She took a deep breath. "How do you know there's more than one?"

"Because she contacted me the other day. We're both masseuses at the same massage parlor, though we work different shifts. That's how we met Bill. He came in weekly for a massage."

Nicole hadn't known that. Of course, the more time that passed since Bill's death, the more she learned about her husband's other life.

"So, this other mistress, er girlfriend, called you?" Nicole asked. "How'd you find out about each other?"

"That's the good part. Apparently, Leslie had the balls to call Bill's wife. I'm not sure why. The woman's got to hate her, right? After talking with her, Leslie figured out there had to be at least two of us."

Something told Nicole that the other woman wasn't being entirely truthful, though about what, Nicole had no way of knowing. A quick glance at the sheriff revealed he, too, appeared to be studying Brenda more intently.

"That would be when she learned about Bill's credit card charges for flowers and lingerie and jewelry," Nicole supplied. "Stuff he didn't buy for her."

"Right. He bought them for me." Brenda eyed her with a kind of distant curiosity. "How do you know that? Who are you again?" she asked.

With a rueful grin, Nicole eyed her right back. "My name is Nicole. Nicole Mabry. I'm the wife."

Driving back to Kyle's house forty-five minutes later, Nicole reflected on how much like a soap opera her life had become. And now this. Her former husband, the man she'd been planning to leave as soon as possible, had actually had two mistresses. Had one of them actually killed him?

Her phone rang just as she pulled into the driveway. It was her insurance agent's office, calling to inform

her that the insurance company would be issuing a
check, made jointly to her and to the mortgage company, so she could begin repairs. Which also made
for an interesting situation, since Nicole had no idea
where she was going to get the money for the next
house payment. Since Bill had cleaned out their bank
accounts and Nicole didn't have a job, she could barely
afford to feed herself and her son.

Her mother had offered to help, so maybe she'd be
willing to loan Nicole enough to pay the mortgage.
Once the necessary repairs had been made, Nicole
realized she'd need to sell the house and purchase
something smaller and less fancy. Hopefully there'd
be enough equity to enable her to do that. Otherwise,
she had no idea how she'd survive.

Kyle opened the front door before she even reached
it. He held little Jacob in one arm, the baby's small
head resting in the crook of his elbow. Jacob grinned
and gurgled when he saw his mama, which melted
Nicole's heart.

Instinctively she reached to take her son, but Kyle
shook his head. "He's good with me," he said. "I like
that he doesn't mind me holding him."

Even though her insides turned to mush, she managed to calmly nod.

Once inside the living room, he took a seat on the
couch. Gus jumped up next to him and settled with
his head resting trustingly on Kyle's leg. Nicole took
the chair opposite them, wondering if Kyle felt the
same sense of coziness. Inhaling deeply, she told him
everything that had transpired at the sheriff's office.

He listened, his expression thoughtful while he

rocked Jacob. "It sounds like Theresa Mabry is coming unhinged."

"I actually feel bad for her," Nicole confessed. "She's an awful woman, but she's in so much pain."

"Maybe so, but she could be dangerous. I think you need to keep an eye out for her and be careful."

She promised him she would and then told him about her insurance agent's call. Because he'd been so kind and helpful, letting her stay with him and feeding her without asking for anything in return, she didn't feel right about burdening him with her money worries.

"Once your house is repaired, you'll be moving back there," he said, his face as expressionless as his tone.

"Right." Saying the words made her feel as if her heart might be breaking. "Unfortunately, I don't have a time line or anything. I need to get a few estimates, and then I'll have a better idea of how long the work will take."

He nodded and then glanced down at Jacob, who had fallen asleep. The tenderness in his face as he gazed at their son filled Nicole with so much love, she felt as if she might burst.

She cleared her throat, hoping for a steady voice. "Since he's asleep, you can put him down in his bed if you want. Just make sure he's lying on his back. That's the safest way for infants to sleep."

"Thanks, but he seems comfortable right here and I'm enjoying holding him. If you don't mind, I'd really like to continue." He leaned back, the sunlight from the window catching his hair.

If she'd have dared, she'd have liked to pull out her

cell and snap a picture. Because this moment, right here, right now, was what she'd dreamed of from the first time she'd met Kyle Benning. Being with him and their child—a family. Together.

Something she clearly would never have.

"I met Bill's mistress," she said, trying to put herself back on firmer ground. "And learned he apparently had more than one. The girl I met today was named Brenda. There's another girl named Leslie. Apparently they're now at each other's throats. The sheriff questioned Brenda and is bringing in Leslie too."

"Interesting. What's he hoping to learn from them?"

She took a deep breath. "Who actually murdered Bill. If the sheriff presses, I'm thinking that Brenda will probably accuse Leslie. And I'm willing to bet Leslie will point the finger right back at Brenda. It could have been either one of them." She thought for a moment. "Or possibly even both."

Chapter 16

Glad of the change in topic, Kyle pretended to consider Nicole's words. In reality, he cared very little about who'd actually murdered Bill Mabry, unless they meant to harm Nicole and Jacob. Since someone clearly did, the sooner the sheriff arrested that person, the better.

Kyle had survived a lot of horrible things. Losing his unit, nearly losing his life, months of rehab learning to make his brain work again. Flashbacks and nightmares that had nearly broken him. Yet they hadn't. Because he understood all too well now what he had to live for.

Yes, he recognized his own strength. He knew how to overcome just about every situation fate could throw at him. But the one thing he knew without a shadow of a doubt that he'd never make it through would be if something happened to his son, Jacob, and Nicole. This, having all of them under one roof, gave him a sense of what his life could have been like, should have been like. False hope? Maybe. Or simply a tantalizing glimpse into the possibilities of a future as a family.

If he could just get his act together, that is. He'd seen the way Nicole's expression had softened as she watched him holding their son. He also couldn't forget the fear mingled with pity in her eyes when she'd witnessed him during one of his episodes. The last thing he'd ever want to do would be to hurt her while in the grip of night-terror-induced flashbacks. She'd need to learn to stay away when those occurred. Far, far away.

Surely, with time, he could learn to manage with the help of therapy. Therapy and his loyal companion Gus, who woke when Kyle woke, remaining right by Kyle's side, letting him know he wasn't alone.

He'd never been so grateful for having a dog. Gus didn't care about reasons or logistics. Gus simply was there.

Kyle wondered how he could feel like two people sometimes. He liked who he was right this instant—Jacob's daddy, Nicole's lover, Gus's owner. Being that man filled him with a joyous sort of peace. And a tentative sort of hope for the future.

And then there was the other Kyle. The one who mostly only came out in the dead of the night. The broken soldier who'd let all his buddies die in an explosion. If the guilt and the shame weren't bad enough, he'd been cursed to continually relive the terror in nightmares, over and over again. He despised that man, and once again Kyle hoped the steps he'd taken would begin to help heal him.

"Hello?" Nicole regarded him curiously. "You were lost in thought. Is everything all right?"

"Sorry." Giving her a rueful grin, he hoped that would be enough of an apology. "I do hope they finally figure out who killed Mabry. Once the sheriff's office arrests someone for the crime, everyone can finally put this behind them and take steps to move forward in their lives."

"Agreed," she replied. "They need to make an arrest quickly, because Theresa won't find peace until they do."

He couldn't help but admire the way she continued to worry about her former mother-in-law, despite the awful way the woman treated her.

"I have a bit of news of my own," he said. "I found a therapist. I made a bunch of calls while you were gone. I lucked out because he had a cancellation and I managed to get an appointment tomorrow afternoon."

"Wow." Her gaze searched his face. "That's great."

"I sure hope so." He wasn't sure what else to say, so he settled for watching his son sleep.

"Will you let me know if I can do anything to help you?" she asked, her voice tender.

"Sure," he responded. "But I have a feeling that this is one thing I'll have to deal with on my own."

"I don't think so." The firmness in her voice had him raising his head to meet her gaze. "You need to understand one thing, Kyle Benning. I'm here for you now. You never have to deal with any problem alone from now on. You got that?"

"I got it." Her words made him ridiculously happy. He grinned at her, loving the flash of humor in her eyes when she grinned back. "And ditto," he added. "Anything I can help you with, I will."

"Well, there is something I need right now. Do you mind if I make a few phone calls of my own while you've got the baby?" Nicole asked. "I want to see if I can line up a few contractors and get some solid estimates. The sooner I can get those repairs started, the better."

He heard what she didn't say. The quicker she could get her house fixed, the quicker she could move back home, away from him. Though he'd known her leaving was inevitable, he hadn't expected it to hurt this much.

In response, he laid his head back and closed his eyes. "Go do what you have to do. Jacob and I are going to just chill."

Even though she didn't respond, he felt it when she left the room.

The next day, Kyle rose with a renewed sense of purpose. He got things done, always had, even before he'd joined the rangers. This PTSD would be no different. He'd set his mind to the task and conquer it, no matter what it took. Talking to a therapist would be the first step in the right direction.

When he walked into the kitchen, following what smelled like bacon, he found Nicole had cooked up them both an elaborate breakfast. "Hey there," she greeted him. The warmth of her smile started a fire low in his belly. "I've made scrambled eggs, bacon and English muffins. I even cut up a cantaloupe I found in the fridge. I hope you don't mind."

"Of course not. Who would mind having a beautiful woman make them breakfast?"

Though she blushed at the compliment, she grimaced. "It's all your food, so it's not much. I can't repay you with money, but I thought I could fix you a nice meal as a way of thanking you."

"You don't have to repay me," he said, meaning it. "I wasn't able to be here for you while you were pregnant or when you gave birth to our son. That food smells delicious. Let's eat."

After they'd finished, he insisted on doing the dishes while she took care of Jacob. While he washed and dried, she let him know that later in the day she planned to meet one of the contractors she'd contacted.

"I'll try to meet you there," he offered. "But I have that counseling session and I'm not a hundred percent sure if I'll be back in time."

"I'll be fine," she told him, her voice confident. "I'm only getting estimates at this stage. Once I have three, I'm hoping you can help me go over them and decide which one's the best."

Though he nodded, he really wanted to tell her she didn't need to hire anyone to work on her house—she had him. He'd worked for a custom home builder all through high school and had most of the skills necessary to make her repairs. But since she seemed so determined to take care of this herself, he decided he'd wait until after she had her estimates.

He left while Nicole was bathing Jacob. He'd have to drive all the way to Tyler, which would take about forty-five minutes. All the way there, he played the radio at full blast, smooth jazz, which he hated, but figured it would be more soothing than metal or rock. He'd hoped the long drive would help calm his jittery nerves, but it didn't.

The therapist's office was small, in a nondescript brick building on a side street. He parked his truck and sat for a moment, his stomach all twisted up in knots. He wasn't sure he could do this. Talk to a total stranger about his deepest shame—that he alone had lived while the rest of his unit had not.

Only the thought of Nicole and their son enabled him to get out of the truck and walk inside the building.

After checking in, he took a seat and waited. It took every bit of his concentration to keep himself from jiggling his leg—a nervous habit he'd vanquished in the middle of basic training. The fact that it had come back didn't surprise him. Nothing about himself shocked him much anymore.

When the door opened and a stocky man with a buzz cut stepped out to greet him, Kyle wasn't sure what to think. This guy looked exactly like one of the first sergeants he'd known back in Afghanistan.

"I'm Dr. Morrison," he said, holding out his hand.

"Kyle Benning." They shook.

Following the doctor back to his room, Kyle eyed the reclining couch and chose an armchair. He saw the doctor notice his choice.

"Why don't you tell me why you're here today." Dr. Morrison suggested.

Kyle had been expecting—and dreading this question. All during the long drive, he'd considered what he might say, rehearsing and abandoning several scenarios. Now that the time had come to actually speak, he couldn't. When he opened his mouth, no sound came out.

After a moment, the doctor took pity on him. "Let

me guess. You're having trouble sleeping. A lot of flashbacks. Night sweats. Loud noises are bad. You're lashing out at family and friends. Shall I go on?"

Kyle shook his head. "No need. You've pretty much hit the nail right on the head. Based on that, I guess what's been happening to me is pretty common?"

"Unfortunately, yes. But by seeking help, you've got a head start on conquering this. A lot of people seem to feel like they can do this on their own." Leaning back in his chair, Dr. Morrison gave a friendly smile. "You're not alone, Kyle. I'm going to help you get through this."

After his hour was up, Kyle drove home, trying to process that the doctor had said. Of course, after Kyle finally decided to open up, Dr. Morrison had done more listening than anything else. Kyle told him everything, starting with his team receiving the assignment and ending with coming home to learn he not only had a son, but that Nicole had married another man.

Nothing was resolved, no solutions were reached and the only suggestion the doctor made was to consider opening up more to Nicole. He'd said doing so would not make Kyle seem weak, as Kyle feared, but would invite Nicole to share the experience. Telling her a bit about what haunted him and why would better enable her to help him.

While Kyle wasn't sure he was one hundred percent on board with this idea, he agreed—warily—to at least give it a try. He hadn't confessed to the doctor that he was afraid of how she'd react. If she knew the truth of what was inside him, she'd learn he wasn't the man she thought he was. Kyle didn't know how he'd live with that.

One thing he'd come to understand was that civilians had a prettified idea of war. On some level, he supposed they knew there was blood and death and destruction. People blown apart, lives forever ruined, altered and often ended. But it was all in the abstract. Not gut-wrenchingly personal like it was for a soldier who'd been there.

Share with Nicole? Honestly, he wasn't sure she could handle it. He wasn't sure he wanted her to have to.

But he knew he had to try. He'd committed himself to trying to fix his problem. He couldn't do it if he went about it half-assed.

Nicole had been in her house only once since the fire and that had been to meet with the fire department and to retrieve extra bottles and supplies. The explosion and resulting fire had taken out Bill's office and most of the remaining bedrooms, since they were all in the top floor of the house. The master bedroom, which sat directly above Bill's office, had not only been partially destroyed, but half of the roof was gone. The insurance adjustor and a roofing company he worked with had put up temporary tarps, but they weren't meant to last long.

A section of the back wall had been blown out and plywood had been nailed up to seal the gap.

From the front, except for the roof tarps, the house looked normal. She'd kept the alarm service and activated the alarm, just in case someone got an idea that looting would be a good idea. Not that she had anything of great value—just the normal household electronics.

Once the house had been repaired, she planned to put it on the market. She wanted something smaller, less expensive and more manageable. Something similar to the house Kyle rented. In fact, she'd experienced more happiness, felt more joy, in that small structure than she ever had in this elaborate mini-mansion of brick, wood and stone.

Standing in the perfectly landscaped front yard, she stared at the place where she'd lived for almost all of the last year. It had never felt like home, even though Bill had purchased it two days after their wedding. She'd had no say in choosing the house they'd share and Bill had told her he didn't particularly care if she liked it or not; the house had been a good investment. Now, since she hoped to get a good price for it, she hoped he'd been right.

Now when she looked at the house, she felt unsettled. Even if she could afford to live here, she knew she'd never feel safe inside these walls again.

Shaking off her rapidly sinking mood, she carried Jacob in his infant seat and walked through the double front doors into the foyer. The upstairs had suffered the most severe damage and the fire department had blocked off the stairs with tape, warning her the floor wasn't stable enough for her to walk on.

After the fire, everything had been covered in soot and ash. Smoke had left its inky stain on upholstery and curtains, walls and ceiling and floors. The insurance adjuster had said he was including payment for some kind of super cleaning service to come in.

Walking from room to room, she realized there was

very little here that she couldn't live without. Like the house, Bill had purchased all of the furniture, with the exception of Jacob's crib and dresser. She hadn't even been allowed any say in the artwork or decorations—Bill had hired an expensive interior decorator to do all of that. The end result was she'd always felt like a guest in her own house.

Consulting her watch, she realized the contractor was late. Half an hour to be exact. She checked her phone but there were no messages. She decided to give him a few more minutes before calling to make sure he hadn't forgotten her.

Again she roamed the house, stopping outside the room that had once been Bill's office. A large abstract painting of a female nude, one of Bill's personal favorites, had been destroyed in the fire. The frame and glass had broken, and fire had consumed enough of it that if Nicole hadn't known, she'd have had no idea what the painting depicted.

How she hated that thing. And that paperweight on the desk, the one that Bill had gleefully called "vagina in a bottle." She picked it up and heaved it at the painting, taking just a tiny bit of satisfaction in the shattering of what little glass remained.

And then the painting fell to the floor. Behind it was some kind of wall safe she hadn't even been aware existed.

What the... Was this what whoever had broken in been looking for?

Gingerly using her shoes to move aside most of the glass pieces, she approached the safe. Of course it was locked. And she didn't know the combination. However, she did know Bill. He'd never had a good memory, so he tended to use the same passwords over and over. His birthday and his mother's birthday.

First she tried his date of birth. Nope. Next she tried his mom's and was rewarded with the locks clicking open. Heart pounding, she hesitated. What would she find inside? Drugs? Cash? Guns? Maybe even all three.

The sound of the front door opening made her freeze. She'd set the alarm to beep when any doors were opened, even when it wasn't armed, like now. Hurriedly, she closed the safe and rehung the picture before picking up her son and heading back to the main part of the house. She couldn't wait until her life could get back to something resembling normal.

"I'm glad you could make it," she said, as she rounded the corner into the main living room. But instead of the contractor, Theresa Mabry stood staring at her.

"Expecting someone else?" Theresa asked, her lip curling. "Because you should know, most of the construction companies in Anniversary are personal friends of mine. I've put the word out and I don't think you'll find anyone willing to work with you."

Heart pounding, Nicole worked hard to remain calm. Her former mother-in-law seemed out of it, almost as if drugged. "What are you doing here, Theresa?"

"What am *I* doing here?" Theresa repeated. "What am *I* doing in the house my son bought before you were even married to him? How dare you ask me that. I have more right to be here than you do."

Not sure how to respond to that, Nicole said nothing. Theresa's gaze drifted past, locking on Jacob. The baby was awake, waving his hands and making cute little sounds.

"There's the little bastard," Theresa commented, her gaze hard. "I can't believe I actually thought he was my grandson. He looks nothing like my Bill."

"I think you need to leave."

"Leave? Ha." Theresa snorted as she paced back and forth in small circles. Her mouth worked, as if she tried to hold back strong emotions. "Why don't you try and make me?" And then, to Nicole's alarm, she pulled a black pistol from her purse, clicked off the safety and smiled.

"What are you doing, Theresa?" Nicole's voice shook. "Put that away. I know you're grieving. You're not thinking straight."

"But I am," Theresa drawled, raising her weapon. "Right now I'm thinking clearer than I have in days. My life is over, ruined. I've lost my son, my husband, my business. All because of you. Everything that has happened to me happened because of you." Theresa's hand shook, but she continued to keep the pistol pointed at Nicole.

Horrified, Nicole tried to think of something to say. Something that would make her former mother-in-law see reason. If Theresa killed her, that would leave Jacob without a mother. "Hurting me won't bring Bill back," she said softly. "Or change anything, other than making you a murderer."

"Maybe not." Theresa shrugged. "But I'm thinking killing you and that brat of yours will make me feel a hell of a lot better."

"What?" Nicole straightened, blood roaring in her ears. "You'd hurt an innocent little baby?"

Theresa didn't respond. Instead, she tilted her head and eyed Nicole. "Why'd you have to marry my son? Why? Not only did you take my boy away from me, but you drove him to do bad things, awful things. He would never have gotten into drugs and other crazy stuff if it weren't for you."

"Take your boy away from you?" Her best bet would be to keep Theresa talking. "You mean because I married him?"

"Oh, that too." Squinting until her eyes were slits, Theresa shook her head. "But you killed him. The sheriff might not get it, but really, how dumb do you have to be? I know you killed Bill."

"Why would I do that?" Nicole was pretty sure Theresa had moved way beyond logic and reason, but figured she had to try.

"Because you found out he had other women. And I'm betting you knew about the drug trafficking and wanted a cut of the money, didn't you?"

"That'd be a bit of a contradiction, right there," Nicole pointed out. "If, as you say, I drove him to do all these awful things, why would I kill him?"

Before Theresa could respond, the alarm chimed, signaling the back door had opened. Relief flooded Nicole. Maybe the contractor had, despite what Theresa claimed, decided to make an appearance after all.

Instead, a black ball of fur streaked into the room.

"Gus," Nicole exclaimed.

As if he sensed the danger, the big dog placed himself in between Nicole and Theresa. Most important, he blocked Jacob with his body. Tears of relief welled up in Nicole's eyes. Because where Gus went, Kyle followed.

"Where did that dog come from?" Theresa demanded. "I hate dogs."

"Don't you dare hurt Gus," Nicole began.

Right then Kyle walked into the room. He took in the situation with a glance, placing himself between the weapon and Nicole. "Put the gun down, Theresa," he ordered. "You don't want to do this."

Looking from Kyle to Gus to Nicole, Theresa cursed. Now she seemed unsure of where to direct her gun. At Nicole or the dog or Kyle.

Her attention wavered for just a second and she brought the pistol up, so it was pointed at a spot above Nicole's head. Locking eyes with Nicole, Kyle barked the word *down*. At the same time, he leaped forward at Theresa, knocking her to the floor while Nicole dropped and rolled toward her son and Gus.

With a loud report, the gun went off.

Chapter 17

Kyle's forward motion knocked Theresa back. He managed to twist himself so that he fell in the opposite direction. At first, he thought he'd gotten lucky and she'd missed, but he realized he was wrong. The searing pain in his back meant he'd been shot. At damn close range too. A fleeting thought slammed him, mingled with the pain and the shock. Maybe he was finally getting what he deserved. Had the time come for him to join the rest of his unit in death?

But no. Hell no. One deep, shuddering breath and his self-preservation instinct came roaring to life. He had to live. For Jacob and Nicole and also for himself. Dying this way would change nothing, bring back no one. He pushed to his feet, working past the pain.

Dimly he realized he heard someone screaming. A high-pitched shrill sound of absolute terror. Nicole?

But no, he opened his eyes and realized it was Theresa Mabry. She'd dropped her pistol and now stood hunched over, arms wrapped around herself, keening. The vivid red of the blood splatters all over her shirt must have belonged to him. His blood.

Where was the pistol? Despite fading in and out of consciousness, he tried to reach the weapon. The last thing they needed was for Theresa to pick it up again and finish what she'd started. But he couldn't seem to locate it.

Dazed, he looked down at himself, trying to ascertain the extent of his injury. Pain radiated in his lower back and legs, and he, too, had blood spatters, but he couldn't see an injury. Maybe he'd just been grazed. Surely he couldn't have been that lucky?

Moving slowly, the pain intensified. He realized dimly that he was, in fact, bleeding. A lot. So much for the flesh wound. "I got it," Nicole said, grabbing the pistol. "Lie back. Please. You're hurt."

He must have blacked out. When he opened his eyes again, he was lying on his side and Nicole was crouched down with him. She'd found something— a towel? a shirt?—and had pressed it into his wound to staunch the bleeding. He hoped like hell it worked. The pain had intensified. She seemed to have shot him in his lower back or upper thigh. Vital organs in one, major blood vessels in the other. Nothing like facing death to make a man realize how much he truly wanted to live.

"Kyle, can you hear me?" Nicole leaned close, her expression worried, fear clouding her beautiful eyes. "I've called 911. An ambulance is on its way. You've got to hang in there."

Dazed, he nodded, looking around for Theresa. The awful noise had stopped, but she hadn't run. Instead, she'd scrunched herself into a corner, knees up, head down, clearly still locked into whatever kind of private hell her actions had caused. Shock, most likely. And maybe, just maybe, a shred of remorse.

None of that mattered now. He tried to breathe, to think past the pain as he'd been taught. If he could just reach a place where he could focus on something else...

The next time he came to, he found himself in a hospital bed. Instantly, he flashed back to before, when he'd nearly died. His heart rate skyrocketed, but when he looked around he realized it wasn't the same at all. Now Nicole sat in a chair at his side. Baby Jacob napped in a carrier on the floor next to her.

What the hell had happened? And then he remembered. Theresa Mabry had come to the house intent on harming Nicole. Instead, he'd taken her down. In the process, she'd managed to shoot him.

"There you are," she said, sounding cheerful. Laughter danced in eyes that earlier had been full of worry and fear.

He grimaced, making a face at her. "I take it I'm going to survive?"

"The doctor says you should." For whatever reason, she seemed to be struggling to maintain a straight expression. "He said if you had to pick a place to get shot other than the foot, your rear end is one of the safest. He said it's painful, but there are no major organs or blood vessels there."

"Rear end?" Pushing himself up, he ignored the

searing pain. "You're saying Theresa Mabry shot me in the…ass?"

Right then and there, she abandoned her attempt to control her mirth. The happy sound of her laughter even coaxed a reluctant smile from him. In the rangers, they'd always joked about the buttocks being the safest place to sustain a gunshot wound. He'd never actually known anyone who'd been shot there, however. Until now.

He waited until her giggles had died down. Finally, she got herself back under control, wiping at her streaming eyes with the back of her hand. "I'm sorry," she said. "But I was so scared, so worried, and then when the doctor told me that, it was such a huge relief…" She shook her head. "And then it suddenly struck me as funny. Come on, Kyle. You have to admit, it's pretty hilarious."

"Embarrassing is more like it," he allowed, refusing to see the humor in it.

Nicole immediately waved his concern away. "Pshaw. Don't take it so seriously. I for one am glad she missed vital organs." Anger flashed in her eyes. "I'd much rather be teasing you about this than agonizing over whether or not you're going to make it."

He nodded. "You have a point."

To his shock, she leaned in and kissed his cheek, her silky hair brushing his face. "Hopefully, they'll let you come home soon so I can take care of you."

Home. He liked the way that sounded when she said it. Home with her and his son and his dog.

"Where's Gus?"

She smiled. "He's safe. I put him in the laundry room of my house, along with a bowl of water and a quilt to lie on until I get back. Did you see what he did? He was intent on protecting Jacob from that crazy woman."

"I saw. He's a good dog."

"He's an *amazing* dog," she corrected. "I'm so glad you got him."

Kyle had to admit she was right. "Speaking of that crazy woman, what happened to Theresa Mabry?" he asked. "She looked like she was in bad shape. I assume she was arrested."

"They're taking her in for a psychiatric evaluation. She went into some kind of awful shock after she shot you. I think everything that's happened to her just pushed her over the edge. She lost her son, her husband, her business and her grandson, all in a short span of time."

Sweet, innocent, compassionate Nicole. He felt a rush of love as he eyed her. "You sound as if you feel sorry for her."

For a moment, she considered his words. "You know what? I actually do. I don't like her and I'm having trouble forgiving what she's done, but she's still a grieving mother. She's been through a lot."

"So have you," he pointed out. "Yet I can't imagine you doing something as crazy as what she did."

Though she only lifted one shoulder in a casual shrug, he could tell his words pleased her.

"I don't pretend to understand what went on inside her head," she said. "Before she pulled out the gun, she claimed she talked to all the contractors in town and warned them they'd better not help me repair my house," she continued. "She wanted me out of that house. She thought I stole her son. In the end, I think she blamed me for everything. All of it. She was blind to what kind of man her son really was."

"Surely contractors won't pay any attention to whatever nonsense she told them," he said. "They need to earn a living too."

"I hope that's true. I really need to get that house repaired so I can put it on the market and sell it."

Once again, she'd managed to surprise him. "Sell it?" He frowned. "Why are you going to sell it?"

She bit her lip and looked away. "Well, I could give you several reasons. I could say I need something smaller, less fancy. I could mention how I've never felt at home there, because Bill chose that house without consulting me." She sighed. "All of those things are true."

When she lifted her chin and met his gaze, worry clouded her eyes. "But the most defining factor is money. I can't afford that house. Bill drained our bank accounts, leaving me nothing. I don't have a job, though of course I'm going to have to find one. But I'm thinking if I could get enough money from selling that house, I could purchase something more modest, a place for me and Jacob to live."

"I'll help you," he said instantly.

"You're already helping me." Her sad smile made him ache to kiss her. "You've been more than generous, letting us stay in your home and feeding us. I owe you a debt I can never repay."

He waved her words away. "I mean I can help you make repairs. That way you don't have to pay a contractor. You know I've always been handy. Remember I worked for Bob's Custom Homes back in high school."

Judging by the way she looked at him, she wasn't sure how to respond. "That's really kind of you, but..."

Crossing his arms, he waited.

"But you're injured."

"So? Only my backside and my pride. I just won't sit down while on the job."

His teasing remark made her smile. "Fine. Once you're well enough, you're welcome to give me an estimate. I'm still going to get some other contractors to come out too."

"Don't bother. I'm not going to charge you for labor. Materials only. I like to keep busy, and it'll give me something to do. And you can help, if you want. It might do you good to learn a new skill."

She eyed him, her gaze searching his face. "Why are you offering to do this, Kyle? You've done more than enough, you know. You don't have to do anything else."

"I want to," he replied. "Not just for you, but for my son."

Of course. Though Nicole smiled and nodded, Kyle's words put everything in perspective. She'd been a fool to think he had begun to trust her, to love her again. He couldn't have made it clearer if he'd tried. Everything he'd done—his actions—had all been for his son. She loved him for that. But she also despaired. She wanted—needed—Kyle to love her as much as she loved him. She'd never stopped loving him. And she knew she always would, no matter what happened between them. Maybe with time, the love he'd felt for her would rekindle. She could only hope it would.

After the doctor came in to announce the happy

news that Kyle was being discharged, Nicole waited another hour while they completed paperwork. Though Kyle's clothing was in horrible shape, he refused to let her go back and get him anything else to wear. He said he just wanted to get out of the hospital and put all this behind him. They both cracked up at his choice of words. She was glad Kyle could now laugh at what had happened to him.

She helped him to her car, glad she'd chosen to follow the ambulance to the hospital. Despite his bandages and the pain medication he'd been given, it took Kyle a bit to figure out a comfortable way to seat, something she figured would be an issue until he healed.

"I hope Gus is okay," he commented. "I'm not sure how he'll react to being locked inside a room. At least since I've had him, he's used to having free reign of the house."

"I wasn't sure what to do. But no matter what, I think Gus should get an extra-large dog treat," she said. "We'll make a quick stop at the pet store so I can pick something up."

Kyle waited in the car with Jacob while she rushed inside the small pet supermarket. She chose both a large treat and a new toy and bought them, carrying her purchases back to the car and handing them to Kyle.

Kyle peeked in the bag and whistled. "He's going to love these."

"I hope so," she responded. "He deserves them."

Driving back to her old house with Jacob making happy sounds from his infant carrier in the backseat, Nicole couldn't shake the feeling that she'd forgotten something. She'd fed Jacob while at the hospital and changed him, so that wasn't it.

Her cell phone rang just as they were turning onto her street. It was the sheriff's office. "I wanted to let you know we have a confession. We now have you husband's murderer in custody."

Her breath caught. "Was it one of the mistresses?"

"Yes." He hesitated. "Well, sort of. At first, each of them blamed the other. Leslie had us convinced Brenda was the murderer, since she was the one who saw him last."

"Was she?" Nicole asked. "The one who killed him?"

"We're still trying to sort that out. With Leslie pinning everything on her, Brenda got scared and confessed that she and Leslie were both in on it. According to Brenda, the two women made a pact, determined to make sure that Bill Mabry cheated on a woman for the last time. When Bill stopped by to visit Brenda before work, she gave him coffee laced with antifreeze."

Nicole gasped. "I've heard of pets dying from getting into that. I didn't know it could hurt people."

"Yep. Unfortunately, ethylene glycol is a favorite among those who decide to poison someone. It's seductively sweet. Some people use it slowly, over time, aware it will build up and kill their victim in the end. Others—like Brenda and Leslie—put a lethal dose in whatever beverage they use."

"But that only implicates Brenda," Nicole said.

"True. But since Leslie knew about it, we can charge her with accessory to murder. We're trying to obtain proof now. What a way to go. Antifreeze in a cup of coffee."

"Wouldn't he have noticed the taste?" she asked, trying to wrap her mind around all of this.

"Maybe, maybe not. Bill also apparently had a habit of pouring a bit of bourbon in his coffee. And by a bit, I mean a lot. Both women are now in custody."

"Thank you," she said. "I'm not sure I should even ask this, but will Theresa Mabry be told?"

"Not anytime in the immediate future. She's in no condition right now." The sheriff paused. "But eventually, Theresa will be answering for her crimes."

"I understand." Mind whirling, Nicole ended the call. Dropping her phone into the cupholder, she filled in Kyle on the details. "It's over," she said. "It's really over."

They pulled into the driveway and he covered her hand with his. "I'm glad. You can finally put that chapter of your life behind you."

She sat there for a few seconds, trying to think. "I still feel like I'm forgetting something."

"It's been a rough day. I'm sure it'll come to you eventually."

He was right. It was only when they unlocked the door and went inside her house to let an overjoyed Gus outside that she remembered the hidden wall safe. She told Kyle. "Maybe that's what whoever broke in here was looking for."

"It probably was. Though we still don't know why someone shot at the house, I'm going to guess they were trying to scare you. As for the safe, if there are drugs inside, you're going to need to call the sheriff."

"Of course." They let Gus in and got him settled,

happily chewing on his bone, his new toy close by. "Come on—let's go see," she said, heading for Bill's office with Kyle following slowly behind her.

He leaned against the doorframe, watching as she once again removed the painting, exposing the safe. "Yeah, but can you figure out the combination?" he asked.

"I already have." She had to smile. "It was the second one I tried. His mother's birthday."

Kyle chuckled at that. "Good thinking."

Once she'd keyed in the combination, the lock released and she pulled open the safe door. Inside, there were several stacks of cash, rubber-banded together, along with a simple manila folder. She pulled it all out and showed it to Kyle.

He let out a low whistle. "I'll be damned."

"They're all twenties," she said. "There must be several thousand dollars here. Do I have to turn this in to the sheriff?"

"Didn't you say Bill emptied your bank accounts?"

At her nod, he continued. "I think you can assume that's where this money came from. I think all the drug money was kept at the trucking company. This must have been his emergency stash. I wonder if he had fake IDs inside that folder."

"Nothing would surprise me anymore," she said. "Let's look and see."

Setting down the folder on the desk, she slowly opened it. Inside, she found a sealed business-size envelope. "It doesn't feel thick enough for fake IDs," she commented as she slit the seal. She pulled out several folded pages, legal-size paper, and read the first page in disbelief. "It's a life insurance policy."

"Wow." Tilting his head, Kyle regarded her, his gaze steady. "Maybe he didn't leave you destitute after all."

She swallowed hard. "Honestly, I'm afraid to look. What if he made his mother his beneficiary? Or one of his mistresses? That would be something he'd do."

"You won't know unless you look," he chided.

"Okay." She began to skim over the document, stopping immediately when she found her name. "It's me," she finally said. "This is a policy for two hundred and fifty thousand dollars. And I'm the sole beneficiary."

It was too much. Heaven help her. She covered her face with her hands and started to cry.

Kyle came over and pulled her into his arms. He didn't speak, just held her, while she struggled to make sense of what she'd just found.

"It had to be his way of making amends," she finally whispered. "I can't think of why else he'd do such a thing. He certainly didn't love me."

"Are you sure?" Kyle asked, stroking her hair. "I mean doesn't it seem like he did, maybe a little?"

"No. He loved the *idea* of me. I was nothing more than a possession to him." She shook her head. "A man doesn't treat a woman he loves the way he treated me."

Kyle didn't respond, not at first. Instead, he took her face in his large hands, so she had to look at him. His eyes were full of warmth, the emotion blazing from them unmistakable. "I love you," he said.

She blinked. "What?"

"I love you. With all my heart and my soul, with everything that I am or will ever be."

Somehow, she dragged her eyes away, aware how

easy it was to get lost in his gaze. "Why now, Kyle? Ever since you returned, I've been trying to get you to let me love you, hoping you felt something, anything in return. Instead, you said we were friends, nothing more. You told me everything you did was for our son."

"Of course, it was. I'd do anything for our boy." Expression earnest, he searched her face. "What kind of father would I be if I didn't? But Nicole, I did stuff for you too." He kissed her then, the press of his mouth gentle, inviting her to respond. With a sigh, she gave in. Where Kyle was concerned, she'd always want him. Always.

But this time, she summoned the strength to pull away. Fighting tears, she even took a step back from him, needing to put some distance between them so she could keep her mind clear. Though her throat had clogged with emotions, she pushed the words past. "You didn't answer my question. Why now? Why tell me you love me now?"

He dragged his hand across his face. "I'd hoped I showed you."

Actions, not words. Any time she'd needed help, Kyle had been there immediately, no questions asked, even if what she needed didn't involve Jacob. He'd let her move in with him, even after he'd believed she'd betrayed him. And he'd begun therapy, starting the road to helping himself recover from the demons that haunted him. He'd been steadfast and strong, gentle and kind. A perfect father. An amazing lover. The only man she'd ever truly loved.

Still, letting herself hope for more terrified her.

"I'm not sure what to say," she began.

"Shh." He shook his head. "Nicole, I love you. I love you so much it hurts. I was afraid, afraid I'd accidentally hurt you when I had one of my flashbacks, afraid I'd never be able to get back to the man I was before, the man you loved."

He took a deep shuddering breath. "But I have hope. I've started therapy. I have a dog. I know I can be a good father—no, a *great* father. I was hoping you could see that, figuring I could wait. But this," he waved a hand. "All of this has made me realize life's too short. And I've never been a patient man."

That was true. Kyle had always been headstrong, impulsive. She'd figured the army had curbed some of that out of him.

"Don't think I only want Jacob, because I want more. I want everything, the entire package, my family—our family. I want *you*. So now I'm telling you, hoping my actions back up my words," he continued. "I love you, Nicole. And, if you'll give me a shot, give *us* a chance, I think we have an entire future of happiness ahead of us." He swallowed hard, his voice raw. "The future we should have had."

Her pulse skittered as a warm glow filled her. About to respond, she opened her mouth. But before she could speak, Jacob let out a cry of annoyance. Looking down, she saw he'd dropped his pacifier. Before she could go to him, Kyle retrieved it from the edge of his carrier and handed it to him. "Here you go, son."

That simple action made her realize she wanted a hundred moments like that. Breathtakingly simple, yet exactly what she'd envisioned.

Once Kyle straightened again, she went to him and

wrapped her arms around him, careful to avoid his bandaged injury. She held on to her man as if her life depended on it. In fact, she suspected it did.

When he gazed down at her, she reached up and pulled him to her for a kiss. The kind of kiss that curled her toes. When they finally came up for air, she smiled at him, putting all her love and joy into that smile.

He smiled back, though she thought she saw a hint of worry in his eyes. "Well?" he finally asked. "Aren't you going to say anything back?"

She thought about teasing him, because she knew deep down, he was aware of how she felt. "I'm surprised you really need to hear me say it," she told him, unable to resist.

"I…"

"Actions speak louder than words," she managed, before she had to laugh. "Kyle, you know I love you. I've never stopped loving you, nor will I ever."

"Whew," he said, though he'd started grinning like a fool. "That means we can make plans and start being real family."

"Kyle?" She kissed him again, lingering over his mouth. "We already are."

* * * * *

"Why did you leave your service revolver on my bathroom
counter?" Armstrong asked as they stood at the bus stop, waiting
for her return ride.

"I can't risk keeping it strapped on me and I was afraid one of
the girls might go through my bag and find it. I knew it was safe
with you."

"I don't like you not having your gun."

"I'll be fine. I have a black belt in karate and jujitsu. I know how
to take care of myself!"

Armstrong nodded. "So you keep telling me. It doesn't mean
I'm not going to worry about you, though."

Danni rocked back and forth on her heels. Deep down she was
grateful that a man did care. For longer than she wanted to admit,
there hadn't been a man who did.

Armstrong interrupted her thoughts. "There's a protective detail
already in front of the coffee shop and another that will follow you
and your bus. There will be someone on you at all times. If you get
into any trouble, you know what to do."

Danni nodded. "I'll contact you as soon as it's feasible. And
please, if there is any change in Alissa's condition, find a way to

let me know."

"I will. I promise."

Danni's attention shifted to the bus that had turned the corner and was making its way toward them. A wave of sadness suddenly rippled through her stomach.

"You good?" Armstrong asked, sensing the change in her mood.

She nodded, biting back the rise of emotion. "I'll be fine," she answered.

As the bus pulled up to the stop, he drew her hand into his and pulled it to his mouth, kissing the backs of her fingers.

Danni gave him one last smile as she fell into line with the others boarding the bus. She tossed a look over her shoulder as he stood staring after her. The woman in front of her was pushing an infant in a stroller. A boy about eight years old and a little girl about five clung to each side of the carriage. The little girl looked back at Danni and smiled before hiding her face in her mother's skirt. The line stopped, an elderly woman closer to the front struggling with a multitude of bags to get inside.

She suddenly spun around, the man behind her eyeing her warily. "Excuse me," she said as she pushed past him and stepped aside. She called after Armstrong as she hurried back to where he stood.

"What's wrong?" he said as she came to a stop in front of him

"Nothing," Danni said as she pressed both palms against his broad chest. "Nothing at all." She lifted herself up on her toes as her gaze locked with his. Her hands slid up his chest to the sides of his face. She gently cupped her palms against his cheeks and then she pressed her lips to his.

Don't miss
SEDUCED BY THE BADGE by Deborah Fletcher Mello,
available June 2018 wherever
Harlequin® Romantic Suspense books and ebooks are sold.

www.Harlequin.com

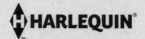

LOVE
Harlequin
romance?

Join our Harlequin community to share your
thoughts and connect with other
romance readers!

Be the first to find out about promotions,
news, and exclusive content!

Sign up for the Harlequin e-newsletter and
download a free book from any series at
www.TryHarlequin.com

CONNECT WITH US AT:

Harlequin.com/Community

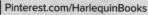 Facebook.com/HarlequinBooks

Twitter.com/HarlequinBooks

Instagram.com/HarlequinBooks

Pinterest.com/HarlequinBooks

ReaderService.com

 HARLEQUIN®

**ROMANCE WHEN
YOU NEED IT**

Earn points from all your Harlequin book purchases from wherever you shop.

Turn your points into *FREE BOOKS* of your choice
OR
EXCLUSIVE GIFTS from your favorite authors or series.

Join for FREE today at
www.HarlequinMyRewards.com.

Harlequin My Rewards is a free program (no fees) without any commitments or obligations.